THE LIE OF THE LAND

THE LIE OF THE LAND

*Migrant Workers
and the California Landscape*

Don Mitchell

 University of Minnesota Press
Minneapolis
London

Portions of this text appeared earlier in *Antipode* 25 (1993): 91-113, Blackwell Publishers, in *Environment and Planning D: Society and Space* 12 (1994): 7-30, Pion Limited, London, and in *Historical Geography* 23 (1993): 44-61.

Published by the University of Minnesota Press
111 Third Avenue South, Suite 290, Minneapolis, MN 55401-2520
Printed in the United States of America on acid-free paper

Library of Congress Cataloging-in-Publication Data

Mitchell, Don, 1961–
    The lie of the land : migrant workers and the California landscape / Don Mitchell.
      p.   cm.
    Includes bibliographical references and index.
    ISBN 0-8166-2692-8. — ISBN 0-8166-2693-6 (pbk.)
    1. Migrant agricultural laborers—California—History—20th century.
2. Migrant agricultural laborers—California—Social conditions.   3. Labor disputes—California—History—20th century.   4. Human geography—California.   5. Landscape—California.
HD1527.C2M58   1996
334.5′44′09794—dc20   95-30081

For Susan

Contents

Acknowledgments

Even, as these days, when expressed in the national imagination as a suite of dystopian images, the look of the land in California has remained a fertile ground for both popular and scholarly exploration. Rarely, however, do these explorations explicitly connect the shape of the California landscape to the processes of work that made it. That is my goal in this book. It has meant attempting to wed a literature on landscape with that on labor history. To the degree that I have come to any understanding of the interplay between labor struggles and landscape, it has only been by gratefully amassing large intellectual debts. As will be clear through my citations, I particularly owe a great deal to those who have written about California agricultural labor before me. The histories of Varden Fuller, Ellen Liebman, Stuart Jamieson, and especially Cletus Daniel have been invaluable resources both for understanding the general historical development of California agricultural labor and for helping me assess archival or other primary information.

In many ways, my model and inspiration in this study has been the writing of Carey McWilliams. McWilliams's work remains the most accessible, and perhaps important, analysis of agricultural labor during the period I examine—and it is one of the few that attempts to link labor explicitly to landscape. As an activist lawyer, chief of the Division of Immigration and Housing from 1939 to 1942, editor of *The Nation*, and, not least, an author of great power and insight, McWilliams repeatedly publicized the relationship between the reality and the image of California agriculture. I have drawn freely on McWilliams's work to help find my way through the intricacies of labor and landscape. For as a model of an activist-scholar, I can think of none better than Carey McWilliams.

As will also be evident throughout the text, I owe a debt of a different kind to the work of John Steinbeck. His fiction and his reportorial work provided both a touchstone of and a means for refueling my own argument. Steinbeck's imagery of the California agricultural landscape during the Depression was exact, and provides a wonderful means for thinking through one of the main questions of this book: how is it that ordinary workers negotiate the chasm between image and reality in the California landscape?

More immediate debts have also piled up rapidly. I couldn't ask for better help than I received from the staff of Bancroft Library as I struggled through nearly a hundred cartons of California Commission (also called Division) of Immigration and Housing records (and a great deal of other material, too). That they so ably performed this work at a very trying time of budget cutbacks in the California university system in general and in the libraries in particular makes me all the more grateful. I thank them also for granting permission to quote from their archives. Portions of this book have appeared (in different form) in articles published in *Historical Geography, Antipode,* and *Society and Space,* and I thank the editors, Carville Earle and Ann Mosher, Dick Walker, and Geraldine Pratt, along with their reviewers, for helping me sharpen my arguments. I appreciate their permission to use that material again here.

Deryck Holdsworth has been a friend and mentor since I first went to graduate school. His advice, and his example as a historical geographer, has been invaluable. I thank him also for reading an earlier version of the manuscript in its entirety. Bob Lake likewise read a complete draft of the manuscript, and from a very early date urged me to tighten my arguments concerning the role of the state in landscape production. At various times Bria Holcomb has provided a room, friendship, and dinners, and she too offered important and helpful comments on an earlier draft. A remarkable group of fellow students at Rutgers University, where I originally wrote *The Lie of the Land* as a dissertation—among them, Andy Herod, Julie Tuason, John Tiefenbacher, Tamar Rothenberg, Mohammed Razahvi, Laura Reid, Tanya Steinberg, Alan Frei, Sanjay Kharod, Brian Brodeur, Leyla Vural, and Andy Stewart—made for excellent companionship and an atmosphere of intellectual excitement. The Center for the Critical Analysis of Contemporary Culture at Rutgers gave me financial support and introduced me to a group of stimulating colleagues during a year of writing.

Cindi Katz has provided moral and intellectual support as needed. I owe a special word of thanks to Joe Foweraker, who convinced me to keep trying, and provided some key contacts, at a quite frustrating moment in my search for a publisher. Denis Valdés, Peter Rachleff, and an unknown geographer provided supportive and critical comments as I was revising this book for publication, and I thank them for prodding me to strengthen my argument. I know I haven't satisfied them on all points, but I hope they like the final result anyway. Janaki Bakhle at the University of Minnesota Press has been supportive even at times when it may not have seemed wise, and I appreciate that. Likewise, Jeff Moen has kept me from panicking, and copy editor Kristine Vesley helped clean up the prose. I thank both of them.

The Department of Geography at the University of Colorado has become a wonderful home for research, writing, and teaching. While all my colleagues have provided support and friendship, I especially appreciate the critical and supportive comradeship of Lynn Staeheli, Brian Page, Colin Flint, Courtney Flint, and Caroline Nagel. The Friday-afternoon discussion group has provided continual insight, and has ensured that none of us takes ourself too seriously. Scott Kirsch and Dana Triplett, in addition to offering numerous helpful ideas and suggestions, did me the huge favor of quickly reading and criticizing some or all of the manuscript as I was rushing to meet deadlines. I look forward to returning the favor.

My greatest professional and intellectual debt, and the one I relish the most, goes to Neil Smith, a "friend, colleague, comrade." Neil combined needed criticism with dinner, drinks, money, and more support than any student should expect of an adviser. He is a model now not just for my writing and research, but for my teaching and work with graduate students. I hope I can repay him by being as good to my own students as he was and continues to be to me.

My parents, Jim and Bunny Mitchell, along with Susan Millar's parents, Bob and Ann, have provided wonderful homes for research and writing on the west coasts of the United States and Scotland. But most, they provided warmth and support even when they knew they would probably not agree with my politics, and hence with much of my research. My debt to them is one I will never be able to repay, but it makes it all the more meaningful knowing they probably wouldn't really want me to.

Finally, Susan has suffered through all my work and frustrations, and shared my excitement when things have gone well, even though she herself has been struggling with the frustrating process of writing a dissertation, while also adjusting to the liminal, and not particularly satisfying, status of "not in residence" student, extension teacher, and "faculty spouse." It is not enough, but for her selflessness and love, I dedicate this book to her.

Introduction / Migratory Workers and the California Landscape, 1913–1942

"Discovering California," Carey McWilliams begins *California: The Great Exception,* "has been an ongoing, somewhat erratic exercise of the imagination." It has also been a great deal of work, for California has not so much been discovered as *made*—and not only in the imagination. The construction of the California landscape has been the work of steelworkers, pavers, chip assemblers, dam builders, drywall nailers, textile workers, and, quite importantly, army upon army of migratory workers planting crops, repairing railroads and highways, chopping down trees, mixing cement, and harvesting cantaloupes. While writers, newscasters, filmmakers and songwriters have discovered a rather fascinating California of the imagination, ordinary, and often very poor, working people have assembled the material constituents of the state out of which the erratic imagination can do *its* work. They have made its infrastructure of roads, bridges, and canals, its unsurpassed industrialized farms, its bungalows, skyscrapers, mountain retreats, and seaside resorts, and they have made the homes, squatter settlements, hobo jungles, and camps in which workers live. As McWilliams's lifetime of work showed, the exercise of imagination that conjured up all manner of fascinating, heavily freighted representations of California as an Edenic, or hypermodern, or Jeffersonian landscape were intimately connected to the ongoing work of landscape production "on the ground." This book explores, in the context of struggles over the form that the reproduction of labor power in industrialized agriculture would take, the connection between the material production of landscape and the production of landscape representations, between work and the "exercise of the imagination"

1

that makes work and its products knowable. Together, these are the "making" of the California landscape.[1]

In a set of "Theses on Landscape," the art historian W. J. T. Mitchell claims, "Landscape is a natural scene mediated by culture. It is both represented and presented space, both a signifier and a signified, both a frame and what a frame contains, both a real place and its simulacrum, both a package and the commodity in the package." Or in Kenneth Olwig's terms, *landscape* is one of those words (he also mentions *nature, nation,* and *culture*) that is so freighted with unsaid meaning it becomes "integral to an ongoing 'hidden' discourse, underwriting the legitimacy of those who exercise power in society." Landscape is at once patently obvious and terrifically mystified. To the degree that words like landscape "tend to be used as if their meaning were unambiguous and God-given," Olwig notes, they "'naturalis[e]' the particular conception which remains hidden behind a given usage." The more the word landscape is used, the greater its ambiguity. And the greater its ambiguity, the better it functions to naturalize power.

This relationship between ambiguity and power is critical. The multifarious meanings of the term—a picture representing a view, the art of depicting that view, the (human and natural) landforms of a region, a "way of seeing," or the area that can be comprehended in a single view—in fact make the idea of landscape quite important to understanding the labor history of a place. As a material "thing" and a representation (no matter how abstracted) of that thing, landscape structures relations of labor. It is, as Cosgrove and Daniels have stressed, a powerful visual ideology; but it is also a structured portion of the earth within which people work and live and sleep, eat, make love, and struggle over the conditions of their existence. To me, the key questions facing students of landscape are: What is the link between the morphology of landscape and landscape representations? What role does that link play in structuring the lived relations of places? How is it obscured or operationalized in social practice? Similarly, for a historical geography of labor, how does the link between landscape and representation structure the conditions under which people work and reproduce their labor power? And what is the role of labor(ers) in constructing, maintaining, and contesting the link between landscape and representation?[2]

In what follows I narrate a labor history that explains why the landscape looks as it does in California. At the same time I provide an analysis of landscape that explains why labor relations in agricultural California have taken the shape that they have. These are two (inseparable) sides of the questions listed above, and developing answers has meant finding a way to wed three intellectual traditions. The first is best represented by art-historical approaches to landscape, which seek to understand the meaning and functioning of representations, and in the best of this work, seek to show how representations are essential not just for depicting but also for structuring social relations in particular places. The second tradition is located in cultural and historical geography that is concerned with explaining the morphology of landscape. Similar to the art-historical tradition, the best of this work seeks to show how the historical form of a place structures the social relations of that place. The third tradition is that of labor history, which seeks to tell the history of a place from the perspective of working people. Even more, it asserts that it is impossible to understand the making of places without attending to the history of working people. And again the best of this work centers on an understanding of the recursive structure of social relations within places. The similarities in all three discourses, then, are quite obvious. Oddly, though, there has been little work that examines the fertile ground created when these traditions are put into contact with each other.

Landscape and the "Reassertion of Space in Critical Social Theory"

There is good reason to make connections between these discourses, not the least of which is that they allow us to write a better, and more politically charged, regional history. It is better because it is explicitly *spatial*. More and more scholars are coming to the realization that attention to the spatiality of society is central to their intellectual and political projects, that all manner of spaces—material and metaphorical—underlie the functioning of society. In Edward Soja's phrase, "the reassertion of space in critical social theory" has led to a reinvigoration of discourses that seek to understand the contours of what Gramsci called the "social integration" of society. The work of analysts as diverse as Henri Lefebvre, Michel Foucault, Bruno Latour, Edward Said, Mike Davis, and Fredric Jameson (and geographers such as David Harvey, Doreen Massey, and Neil Smith) have shown that the constitution and continuation of capitalism or colonialism—and the reproduction of labor power that makes these possible—requires the creation of very specific (if still universal) *geographies*. In a like manner, scholars and critics concerned, for example, with the constitution of the body, or with the making of "race," understand, as perhaps never before, that these too have geographies, that they are impossible without them. The work of society is geographical. Bringing the critical project of "reasserting space" from the more general notion of "space" to a more specific one of "landscape" (which itself is a certain, lived, and perceived *kind* of space) allows us to glimpse how, in Lefebvre's terms "representations of space" (ordered, planned, abstract space) always and everywhere articulate with "representational spaces" (the lived spaces of everyday life). Given both the complexity and the banality of the idea (and fact) of landscapes, understanding the making of landscapes is a vital aspect of both spatiality and social integration, even as it is a most contested business.[3]

For a time in the 1980s it looked as if geographers might embark on a project that would bring a new, critical spatial sensibility right to the heart of landscape studies, that they might indeed develop the tools to bring geography, art history, and labor discourses into fruitful contact with each other (and thus continue the project Carey McWilliams started with his insightful studies of the imagery and reality of the California labor landscape). Denis Cosgrove's thorough reconsideration of the landscape tradition in geography, for example, seemed to be leading in that direction. Cosgrove was concerned to show how one of the most basic conceptual tools used by geographers—the landscape— carried with it an unacknowledged ideological history, a history that tended to erase the politics and actuality of work from the view. Moreover, the history of the idea of landscape, Cosgrove showed, was inseparable from the construction of capitalist geographies based on the full commodification of the land (and thereby the "freeing" of labor) and the subsequent need to represent ownership (or nonownership) as a natural order of society. Morphological approaches to landscape, like those geographers specialized in, were not just incomplete, but were theoretically and politically suspect as long as the ideological biases built into the landscape concept were not squarely faced. But if they were squarely faced, a more thorough, more accurate, and more critical account of landscape could be provided; and it would be an account, unlike much traditional cultural geography, that was quite politically relevant. As I suggest in Chapter 1, however, landscape geographers have turned in other directions, preferring to explore a politics of representation that is seemingly quite disconnected from issues of labor.[4]

More than from labor, much cultural geography is disconnecting itself from a concern with material spaces, sometimes arguing that since "brute reality" is unknowable, cultural geographers should concern themselves with how landscapes are *only* representations, *only* ideology. I think this is a misguided project, and prefer instead to center my examinations of landscape on Henri Lefebvre's reminder:

> What is an ideology without a space to which it refers, a space which it describes, whose vocabulary and links it makes use of, and whose code it embodies? What would remain of religious ideology . . . if it were not based on places and their names: church, confessional, alter, sanctuary, tabernacle? What would remain of

the Church if there were no churches? The Christian ideology . . . has created the spaces which guarantee that it endures.[5]

Lefebvre's point is quite simply that it is impossible to talk about ideology (as the "new cultural geographers" certainly want to do) without examining and explaining the spaces that give that ideology currency and serve as its referent. By abandoning the traditional concerns of geographers with material form, the "new cultural geography" runs the risk of allowing its analysis of ideology to spiral off into an untenable idealism. If we want to write spatial histories that have both intellectual and political import (and I do), then we cannot simply abandon the material field as if it does not exist—especially since capital does not, and cannot, make a similar abandonment. On the contrary: the relationship between material form and ideological representation must be the center of our examinations.

On the part of more art-historical approaches to landscape, there is a growing concern as to how, in the words of W. J. T. Mitchell, landscape *works*. But here again the concern is largely with pictures of landscape rather than with the relationship between those pictures and the places they are meant to represent. The essays in Mitchell's collection, for example, remain very much art histories, rather than social histories, of landscape, exploring Dutch landscape painting, Turner's pictures, territorial photography, and so forth. While in these topics there is plenty of room to explore the relationship between the signifier and the signified, the frame and what is in the frame, with scant few exceptions, the lens is turned rather exclusively on the pictures themselves. Even so, when Elizabeth Helsinger, in the best essay of the collection, turns to the early work of Cosgrove to examine the relationship between landscape ideologies and the needs of rural capitalism in Turner's England, the value of combining a more morphological approach with a close examination of the politics of landscape representation becomes obvious. Helsinger's discussion of mobility by the rural poor, and the transformation of the countryside "which accelerated the transformation of rural labor into wage labor" hints at an important course of study. While Helsinger's analysis is of the complex politics represented in Turner's pictures, one is left wondering about the structure of the lives represented and aestheticized in oil and watercolor. To explore that requires a much closer attention to the historical geography of the times than art-historical scholarship typically provides.[6]

And so we return to the issue of labor and labor history. In essence, the question lurking behind, but remaining unanswered in, the work by geographers and art historians alike is precisely: Why does the landscape look like it does (because it has a clear function in its present form), and who *made* it look that way?

The Ontology of Labor

This is not at all an easy question. But we can start with some relatively simple postulates: First, to the degree anything is made (including a landscape, however defined), it is a process of labor, of work. Second, in human society, if there is work, there is social organization. Finally, the organization of work is (has been, will be) fraught with relations of power and conflict; the cooperative effort necessary to make anything—much less anything as complex as a landscape—is not at all natural but is socially constructed.

That much seems obvious, but the implications of these simple postulates are quite large. In the first place a landscape is a "work"—a work of art, *and* worked land. But, as Raymond Williams, like Cosgrove, was at pains to point out, one of the purposes of landscape is to make a scene appear unworked, to make it appear fully natural. So landscape is both a work and an erasure of work. It is therefore a social relation of labor, even as it is something that is labored over. To ignore the work that makes landscape, it seems to me, is thus to ignore a lot of what landscape *is*. In this manner, the production of landscape is quite similar to the production of nature that Neil Smith describes: it is a hugely mystified, ideological project that seeks to erase the very facts of its (quite social) production.[7]

But there is another rationale for attempting to meld landscape studies with labor history. For all the importance of ideological, representational aspects of the idea of landscape, we need also to remember the geographical sense of landscape: the morphology of a place is in its own right a space that makes social relations. It is a produced space. In the most general terms, it is part of the "human condition" that we continually produce and transform landscapes. Likewise, as Marx wrote, labor "is a necessary condition, independent of all forms of society, for the existence of the human race; it is an external, nature-imposed necessity, without which there can be no material exchanges between man and Nature, and therefore no life." Hence, when Carl Sauer, an early proponent of landscape studies in geography, wants to speak of the joining of "land and life" (as the collection of essays in which his important "Morphology of Landscape" appears is entitled), he needs also to speak of labor, of the work that people do of necessity. Marx refers to the socially organized labor of people as a "metabolism" between humans and nature, and the metaphor is exact: the work of people (re)produces a (socialized) nature—and, perforce, it produces landscapes, it transforms the land.[8]

Now, of course, it is not enough simply to assert that work makes landscapes. The process is more complex than that, and is necessarily imbued with all manner of ideology. The "space" opened for ideology in the labor process is perhaps also part of the "human condition":

> [Man] opposes himself to Nature as one of her own forces, setting in motion arms, and legs, head and hands, the natural forces of his own body, in order to appropriate Nature's production in a form adapted to his own wants. By thus acting on the external world and changing it, he at the same time changes his own nature. He develops his slumbering powers and compels them to act in obedience to his sway. We are not now dealing with those primitive instinctive forms of labour that remind us of the mere animal. An immeasurable interval of time separates the state of things in which a man brings his labour-power to market for sale as a commodity, from that state in which human labor was still in its first instinctive stage. We pre-suppose labour in a form that stamps it as exclusively human. A spider conducts operations that resemble those of a weaver, and a bee puts to shame many an architect in the construction of her cells. But what distinguishes the worst architect from the best of bees is this, that the architect raises his structure in imagination before he erects it in reality. At the end of every labour-process, we get a result that already existed in the imagination of the labourer at its commencement.[9]

The weight of Marx's analysis, of course, is directed toward showing how, despite the natural necessity of laboring, humans have historically erected not just cells like bees, but elaborate social structures that have the effect of alienating workers from their labor. It is one of my goals here to show that maintaining this alienation is itself a lot of work, and it is an arena of struggle in which the landscape plays a large role. When an "architect" imagines a project, he or she doesn't imagine just its shape and structure, but also how that project will be achieved (who will do the work and under what conditions), what that project will mean, and how it will benefit particular parts of society.

To the degree, then, that labor and its products are social, we need to inquire about how labor is organized and reproduced. Answers to these questions require that we examine both the facts of production and its representations (and the contestations that are part of these). We need to delve into the complex labor history of a region to be better able to describe and analyze its geography. And, as I think the pages that follow show, by examining the labor geography of a place—how it is that labor is spatially and socially organized (through struggle) and how it quite literally makes places—we can better describe and analyze the labor history. The bulk of *The Lie of the Land* is given over to exploring just these issues. I provide a fine-grained analysis of the spatial practices that made portions of the California landscape, and, in turn, I show that the morphological and represented landscape—its very shape *and* its function as ideology—was integral to shaping those spatial practices. My claim is that we simply cannot understand the form (or the meanings) of the landscape without attending closely to the relations of labor that were indispensable to its making. To ignore labor, as so many other histories and analyses of the California landscape do, may provide insight into how representations circulate, and indeed, how these representations of California may induce all manner of social activity. But such studies remain incapable of theorizing and describing the links between the representations and the actual form of the land. One cannot understand a landscape, Daniels and Cosgrove remind us, independent of how it has been represented. Absolutely. But neither can one understand a landscape independent of its material form on the ground (and thus independent of how it was made). This book is an attempt to understand the interplay between production and representation of landscapes, while at the same time restoring an ontology of labor to the center of landscape geography and history.[10]

Representing the California Landscape

California, as McWilliams indicated, has long been an arena of the imagination. "Early myth makers were writing about 'California'—and locating it on maps—before they were quite sure it existed." Biblical imagery has been particularly important to the structures of meaning in the state. Consider, for example, John Steinbeck's use of the coastal mountains and valleys of California for his retelling of the Cain and Abel story (or, for that matter, the retelling of the exodus in *The Grapes of Wrath*), literary critic David Wyatt's discussion of the relationship between landscape and literature in California, *The Fall into Eden,* or Joan Didion's reminiscence of her schooling in Sacramento, where she was taught to picture California as a "promised land." And "picture" is an apt term. Perhaps more than elsewhere, the stories we use to understand and explain California to ourselves are intimately connected to the lie of the land. The evidence of California's rise, and perhaps these days its fall, is written right there in its very spaces. The landscape is clear proof of California's epic place in our society. Quite literally, we *see* California *as*—as palm trees, golden hills, extensive orchards, suburban sprawl, apartments scaling hillsides in San Francisco, towering redwoods, the valleys of Yosemite and Imperial. These all come to represent, in the way their look conjures up (with the help of now two centuries of European writing on California), much more than just the land itself. Like tales in the Bible, they are metonymic representations of huge stories, the trajectories of which become morality plays for America (and perhaps the rest of the world) as a whole.[11]

The imagery with which we talk and think about California is both immensely important and vastly overdetermined. The representation of the state, and particularly of the state's landscapes, takes on a life of its own, seemingly quite disconnected from the realities of both the material landscape from which it arises and from the everyday life and work of the people of the place. Allowed to float free, untethered to any material world, representations of landscape become pure ideology, able to be reshaped by all manner of powerful interests, and available to be put to use to structure and control not just meaning, but also the lives of those who live in the landscape. But images of California are quite clearly, if exceedingly complexly, linked to physical, material spaces. And so, if they do become untethered from materiality, it is only because they are (socially) *allowed* to.

I begin my account of the making of the California landscape with one particularly apt set of images: the view of California as Eden that John Steinbeck's Joads saw when they crested Tehachapi Pass and first spied the resplendent agricultural landscape of California. Steinbeck's use of a rather hackneyed set of representations is subversive. His goal is to show the radical difference between what California advertises itself as and what it is—and how that chasm is negotiated, how connections between image and reality are made by ordinary workers. My goal in Chapter 1 is the same. This first chapter therefore elaborates the questions outlined above; namely, what is the relationship between the produced form and the representation of the California landscape, and what is the role of labor in establishing that relationship? In the course of developing these questions, I create what in shorthand could be called a "labor theory of landscape," which I believe is not just applicable to the case at hand—the development of the industrialized California agricultural landscape between 1913 and 1942—but can apply equally well to all manner of capitalist landscapes and their representations.

Chapter 2 begins the historical analysis per se of the making of the California landscape, and it and each of the following chapters combines both historical narrative and continuing elaboration of the theory developed in Chapter 1. My narrative works on two levels. First, it is a telling of an important historical story. Second, it is an empirical and theoretical exegesis of the complexity of "landscape." The tension between these two goals, I think, allows for a much more nuanced understanding of the links between labor, landscape-as-morphology, and landscape-as-representation. The Wheatland riot, with which I open Chapter 2, was epoch-making in California agricultural labor history. From it developed the Progressive, interventionist California Commission of Immigration and Housing (CCIH), a state agency charged with assuring both that migratory labor camps were safe and sanitary and that violent outbursts like Wheatland were never to be repeated.[12] CCIH's methodology, under the leadership of Simon Lubin and its chief theorist Carleton Parker, was spatial in the first instance: it sought to transform the landscapes of agricultural California such that revolt would be both impossible and unnecessary. This project led to all manner of environmentalist theorizing, bolstered, perhaps contradictorily, by a program of labor espionage designed to neutralize radical migratory workers. The workings of these spatial and espionage programs, workers' resistance, and their incorporation into the landscape (and landscape images) of the state are examined in Chapters 2 and 3. As will be seen in these chapters, the system of agriculture in California called up a need for an exceptionally mobile labor force. This need served both to pauperize workers and to provide opportunities for subversion. Chapter 3 examines how this subversive mobility (along with capital's and CCIH's response to it) was integral to shaping the landscape around the time of World War I. As will also be seen, the mobilization of labor also called up a set of interlinked representations of the existing California landscape by agribusiness and by state agencies like CCIH that were designed to explain the very naturalness of the labor relations of the state.

Labor in the abstract never made anything. Labor power is embodied. And in California those bodies have been marked by ideologies of race and gender, or more generally of inferiority. The sense that migratory laborers were seen to be naturally inferior was evident right from the start in Carleton Parker's theorizing, but as a general ideology it was useful to growers both for legitimizing their appalling labor conditions (to themselves) and for arguing for a need for highly racialized labor supplies, supplies they hoped they could control utterly. Chapter 4 explores the intersection of ideologies of race, inferiority, and landscape as they structured labor relations during the 1920s, while Chapter 5 examines the restructuring of the agricultural industry that makes the logic of constant brutalization of workers more understandable. While this logic may be understandable, it did not go uncontested, and by the end of the 1920s workers, particularly Hispanic workers who themselves were apprehended by growers with a mix of paternalistic and more brutal racism, were reexpressing the radical impulses that have long marked California migratory workers. The necessary empirical detail involved in explicating the relationship between social relations and landscape seems to sometimes overwhelm the importance of landscape representations in structuring both the landscapes and the relations that are part of them. Chapters 4 and 5 both end with a reminder that social relations—such as ideologies of race and gender—are not just reflected in landscapes but are actively incorporated in them.

As that is the case, struggle against the structure of social relations in California agriculture is also necessarily a struggle against landscape. I mean this in two ways. First, it is a struggle against the very spaces in which workers are expected to produce and reproduce themselves and their labor power. Second, landscape serves to objectify those "in the view," to strip them of their subjectivity and invest it instead in the viewer. As workers become radicalized, they reclaim their subjectivity, shattering the landscape that enframes them. The Depression was a time of unprecedented radicalism among migratory workers in California, and through this radicalism workers sought to create new spaces in which to maneuver, spaces set in opposition to the landscape that had been developing during the 1920s. Chapter 6 analyzes the spatial strategies employed by workers as they sought not only to fight for better wages and living conditions, but also to destroy the landscape so that it could be remade in a more just image. In a series of battles—Alameda and Corcoran most notably—migratory agricultural workers invented new *spatial* forms of power with which to engage their struggle against agricultural capital and the state.

By this time CCIH had been all but eliminated as an effective voice in the structure of migratory labor relations, and new state forms had to be invented to both control worker radicalism and protect the profitability of agribusiness. Chapters 7 and 8 explore the state's role in reasserting control over the spaces of agricultural labor reproduction. Actually, the new forms of intervention in labor relations were almost the same as those pioneered by CCIH: the development of better labor camps and other sites of labor reproduction such that revolt would be unnecessary, and a stepped-up program of surveillance and espionage. Likewise, the goal of the state by the middle of the 1930s was also just the same as CCIH's, to remake the spaces of California agriculture after an image of worker contentment such that worker revolt would never happen again. The purpose, quite clearly, even for those politically and morally opposed to the power of agribusiness in the state, was to find a means for reproducing profitable agriculture.

And here we return to landscape in its most general sense. How is it that the landscape looks as it does? The ongoing struggle on the part of capital to find a way for labor power to be properly reproduced and the ongoing struggle on the part of workers to resist their constant objectification and marginalization are what made and structured the land. That struggle gives lie to the land—in both senses of the term. The ever-partial resolution of these struggles has allowed for the ossification of labor (or more generally, social) relations at any given moment. In turn, this resolution allows the landscape to materialize as a view. And, clearly, this resolution, this landscape, is a very bloody business. "Whatever theoretical considerations may be entertained concerning the use of violence in labor disputes," Carey McWilliams maintained at the end of the bloodiest decade in the history of California agriculture, "it is evident that, from the historical point of view, migratory labor has made gains in California when it has been militant." It is also evident, from the historical point of view, that any violence on the part of workers has been met with a much greater violence on the part of California growers fearful of losing their (actually rather tenuous) stake in the California landscape.[13]

All this violence, the following narrative makes clear, has been structured around one major question, a question written plainly in the fields, ditch-bank settlements, shantytowns, government-run labor camps, strikers' encampments, and growers' labor camps: "How does the geographical configuration of the landscape contribute to the survival of capitalism?" This is not just a question of theory, but is the very question that has shaped the struggle—both for those wishing to see capitalism's survival and for those seeking to transform it—over the look of the California landscape.[14]

1 / California: The Beautiful and the Damned

After abandoning their farm in Oklahoma and joining the exodus across the desert to California, after seeing their family torn apart by the forced mobility of modernity, the Joads reach the top of Tehachapi Pass and gaze out over California's San Joaquin Valley. All of a sudden, the power and promise of the California landscape reveal themselves in a startling vista of color and pattern, instantly erasing the disillusionment that had accompanied the family all along their journey. In *The Grapes of Wrath,* John Steinbeck reduces this view to a list of characteristics, as if describing a painting: "The vineyard, the orchards, the great flat valley green and beautiful, the trees set in rows, and the farm houses." The Joads have at last reached the American apotheosis. "Pa sighed, 'I never knowed they was anything like her.' The peach trees and walnut groves, the dark green patches of oranges. And red roofs among the trees, and barns—rich barns . . ." The beauty and the wonder of the scene before them overwhelm the Joads: "And then they stood, silent and awestruck, embarrassed before the great valley. The distance was thinned with the haze, and the land grew softer in the distance. A windmill flashed in the sun, and its turning blades were like heliograph, far away. Ruthie and Winfield looked at it, and Ruthie whispered, 'It's California.'"[1]

This is a complex scene in which all the standard characteristics of landscape painting are present—a constructed, formal beauty, perspective represented by the thinning haze, a sense of proprietorship in the embarrassed gaze, a near complete absence of visible labor. It serves to represent California as dream, as spectacle, as a view to behold and perhaps to own. It shows California as a cul-

Figure 1. California agriculture seen as landscape. The hazy hills in the background and the fields converging on the farmhouse (providing perspective) give a sense of pastoral beauty and calm. Scenes like these comprise the California landscape image that drove the Joads and many like them to come to California. Significantly, a sense of visible work is nearly completely absent in this view. Photo circa 1900. (Courtesy, Bancroft Library.)

mination of the American Dream—perhaps not a shining city of a hill, but a prosperous, rural, Jeffersonian, yeoman, countryside ideal (Figure 1). But Steinbeck is a wise writer, and he knows that to show this landscape as America, one must truly show it as an image, as a dream. All that has led the Joads to the top of this hill tells us that the perspective from there hides something, that the beauty of the place can only be an image constructed by hiding what makes it. The California Dream, the American Apotheosis that is California, can only be seen from afar. The dream itself is impossible without a certain haze that closes off perspective, that hides the struggle that goes into making landscape. Steinbeck thus has the Joads come down off the mountain, and he thereby opens up the view to show how it is constructed.[2]

Hidden in the bushes along the creeks and irrigation ditches is the other side of the California Dream, a side that has been there all along, but that is easy to overlook from atop the hill: the invisible army of migrant workers who *make* the landscape of beauty and abundance that awed the Joads. Supposedly quiet,

Figure 2. The other side of the landscape. This photograph, from the 1920s, was typical of conditions found by the California Commission of Immigration in 1913 and by migrants like the Joads in 1939. Without interiors like these, exteriors like that shown in Figure 1 are impossible. (Photo: California Commission of Immigration and Housing.)

pliable, unorganized, they exist and reproduce themselves in landscapes of the most appalling deprivation. "There was no order in the camp; little grey tents, shacks, cars were scattered about at random." The first house the Joads see in the camp they stumble upon is not the craftsman bungalow that historian Kevin Starr has argued represents a pinnacle of rural civility only possible in California, but is simply "nondescript."[3] Another shelter is simply "a huge tent, ragged, torn in strips." Without camps such as these (Figure 2), however, the view from the top of Tehachapi Pass would be impossible. The pattern and color of the California landscape are mortgaged on the backs of an endless stream of workers:

> The young man squatted on his heels. "I'll tell ya," he said quietly. "They's a big-son-of-a-bitch peach orchard I worked in. Takes nine men all the year roun'. . . . Takes three thousan' men for two weeks when them peaches is ripe. Got to have 'em or the peaches'll rot. So what do they do? They send out handbills all over hell. They need three thousan' and they get six thousan'. They get men for what they wanta pay. If ya don't wanta take what they pay, goddamn it they's a thousan'

men waitin' for your job. So ya pick an' ya pick, an' then she's done. . . . When ya get 'em picked, ever' goddamn one is picked. There ain't another damn thing in that part a the country to do. An' them owners don't want you there no more. Three thousan' of you. The work's done. You might steal, you might get drunk, you might jus' raise hell. An' besides, you don' look nice, livin' in ol' tents; an' it's pretty country, but you stink it up. They don' want you aroun'. So they kick you out, they move you along. That's how it is."[4]

Both indispensable as a class and completely expendable as individuals, it is quite clear that it is farmworkers who actively make what is visible as a land-scape. The two landscapes—the broad, perspectival, aesthetic view from atop the hill, and the ugly, violent, dirty landscape of workers' everyday lives—are intimately linked.

Steinbeck's enduring value, as George Henderson has shown, was his ability to juxtapose these two aspects of landscape in such a way that their interdependence becomes obvious. In so doing Steinbeck was able to illustrate clearly the costs of capitalist agricultural development both in terms of the violence done to workers' lives and the violence done to cherished American ideals of yeomanry and the good life.[5] In this book, I suggest that such violence has in fact been *necessary*, not just to the construction of American Dreams, but to the workings of the economic system itself. Moreover, such violence has been me-diated through the landscape itself: in all its complexity the landscape, as both more general view and more local, constructed environment, is an important player in the drama of capitalist development in California. Steinbeck had it right in two essential aspects. First, landscape must be understood as an inter-connected relationship between view and production, between the aesthetic pleasure the Joads find on Tehachapi Pass and the reality of hobo jungles, Hoovervilles, labor camps, and skid rows they find down below. Second, in some very fundamental senses, it is the workers themselves who, in their struggle to make lives for themselves within and against a ruthless political economy, make the landscape—and it is they who are the glue that binds its two aspects.

For making these connections, for exposing the underbelly of the California Dream, Steinbeck saw his book banned and burned in Bakersfield (where the Joads buried Granma after they came down off the hill), and he was roundly denounced by agribusiness and industrial concerns throughout the state as un-American. But these are precisely the connections that need to be explored if we are to understand both how the agricultural economy is continually re-produced despite its obvious unjustness and why the landscape looks the way it does. As we will see in the pages that follow, these are hardly separate questions.

The look of the land plays a key role in determining the shape that a political economy takes.[6]

Imagining the American Apotheosis

Members of the radical Industrial Workers of the World (IWW or Wobblies) in the first decades of the twentieth century liked to talk of "California, the Beautiful—and the Damned" precisely because they were continually forced to make the sorts of connections between landscape imagery and landscape reality that Steinbeck has the Joads make. Their phrase catches precisely the bloody irony of the California landscape. It is beautiful *because* it is damned. As Agnes Benedict wrote in *Survey* in 1927,

> To see country life as it really is means blotting out of the picture many of the cherished associations of beauty and glamour which we have put there as visitors going to the country on a vacation or as grown-ups looking back at our childhood on the "dear old farm" of another and simpler time. It will mean substituting for the rosy picture a less colorful one—a picture that includes the grayness as well as the sunshine of country life.[7]

Most commentators on the California landscape, however, have been little interested in showing the connection between both sides of the landscape, and how these sides are dependent on each other. To be sure, there is a significant strain of dystopianism in California literature that seeks to counteract the typically rosy hype of most landscape accounts, but even now it remains a minority tradition, confined as often as not to fictionalized accounts. Until recently, ignoring the blood and turmoil, the split heads and ruined lives, that allow the landscape to look as it does is an honored tradition in social-scientific, historical, and literary discourse on the California landscape. This discourse seems to imply, in the words of geographer James Parsons, that the landscape "is morally neutral." As neutral, both people and landscape may be transformed in their mutual encounters, but the moral content of the landscape remains fixed and imperturbable. It just is. The landscape is thus often understood in two interrelated ways: it is a relict rather than an ongoing construction; and it is organic, natural, and aesthetic. In the first case, the landscape is understood to be immutable at least in terms of the normal human life span. Rather than being molded directly by people, the landscape's immutability allows it to shape humans. In the second case, the landscape is something to be passed through and admired along the way.[8]

Parsons typifies these ways of understanding the California landscape. His strategy is one of description: "Even in the barrios of Mexican and Filipino farm workers, a transient population whose economic status and system of values are reflected in the untidy but honest and lived in appearance of the houses and yards, the spirit of the place is somehow evoked." The paternalism implicit in seeing space as landscape here becomes explicit, and the lives Parsons seeks to describe become mere representations of the "honest" diversity of the place. Mexican and Filipino workers become curiosities to be gawked at, simply an adjunct of "the visual, aesthetic dimensions of the built environment or cultural landscape and the magnificent diversity of crops yielding the bumper harvests of food and fiber that make California agriculture one of the wonders of the world." Missing in Parson's account is precisely the connection between what he calls "the valley . . . as a symbol of capitalism gone rampant," and the aesthetic view he so highly values. Rather, he suggests that "the valley is [not] any less interesting, or its color and geometry any less worthy of attention, because some of its harvests enrich soulless corporations, [and] its landscapes are the creations of the producers of nonunion table grapes or boycotted wines." The landscape is purely a place of aesthetic wonder. How it got that way is of little concern.[9]

Workers lose even their symbolic status as a cipher for the uninhibited capitalist exploitation of the agricultural valleys of California in William Preston's account of landscape evolution in the Tulare Basin area of the San Joaquin Valley. Even as late as the Depression, while the Joads were making their way over the pass and into the Central Valley, Preston claims that migratory workers, though "vital to the success of intensive farming," had "participated only marginally in the growth and development of basin communities." Two of the key moments in the construction of the California agricultural landscape of which Tulare Basin is a part—the Mussel Slough incident memorialized in Frank Norris's *The Octopus,* and the 1933 Corcoran cotton strike (see Chapter 6)— are dismissed in a few sentences. If Preston's goal is to explore "land and life in the Tulare Basin," it is hard to see how this dismissal can hold. Labor historians and geographers concerned with patterns of landholding (and thus with the material context of life) argue that these incidents are absolutely central to understanding the construction of California landscape patterns. The connection that workers lives and their labor make between landscape-as-view and landscape-as-form, between the land and life Preston wants to examine, fades in his account so that he can focus instead on the making of Visalia, Porterville, Tulare, and Hanford as towns of middle-class respectability, as pinnacles of American rural culture.[10]

Kevin Starr, the chronicler of the "California Dream" from statehood to the end of the Depression, shares this concern with uncovering California as an

Eden of middle-class respectability (and to a lesser extent, showing where that Edenic goal has fallen short or been corrupted).[11] "In the beginning and always, was the land," he writes. The land itself "was the first and last premise of the California experience." The early years of Anglo-American farming, the time when land monopolies were created at a ruthless pace, represent to Starr an aberration rather than an apotheosis of the American political economy. They were an accident of the gold economy run amok. Land and landscape merely became resources waiting to be exploited by rapacious wheat barons intent on mining the fields as the hills had been mined. But the bust of bonanza wheat farming ushered in an age of bourgeois California enlightenment in the guise of what Starr calls "fruit culture." Fruits and vegetables became, by the 1890s, their own advertisements of the California Dream as reality:

> In the color of a plum or an apricot, in the luxuriance of a bowl of grapes set out in ritual display, in a bottle of wine, the soil and sunshine of California reached millions of Americans for whom the distant place would henceforth be envisioned as a sun graced land resplendent with the goodness of the fruitful earth.

Harking back to ancient Greek and Roman civilizations and seeing in fruit cultivation a certain biblical respectability, Starr claims for California a lineage of agricultural integrity and promise reached perhaps nowhere else in America:

> Fruit culture nurtured the values of responsible land use, prudent capitalization, cooperation among growers in the matter of packing, shipping and marketing. Above all else, fruit culture encouraged a rural civility in the care of homes, the founding of schools, churches and libraries, the nurturing of social and recreational amenities which stood in complete contrast to the Wild West attitude of wheat.

Starr's analysis makes invisible the material conditions—the army of pauperized, temporary laborers that picked and canned the fruit, the monopoly conditions (rather than simple cooperation) that packing and marketing cooperatives reinforced, the dismissal of workers when the season ended—that make possible this "fruit culture," this flowering of rural civility.[12]

The beauty of pastoralism California-style blinds Starr to the damned lives that workers in the fruit industry led. An undercover agent for the California Commission of Immigration and Housing spent part of the 1914 packing season lugging crates of oranges in the Tulare Basin town of Lindsay. Responding to calls broadcast around the state for more than five hundred men to work in the Lindsay packing houses, Frederick Mills found that far fewer were needed; many of the "men had been brought to town to lie idle around the tracks." Mills himself found occasional work in a small packing house that employed "about 24 packers, women and girls. About one-half are local people, farmer's wives [*sic*] and daughters, country type. Rest come up from the South for the orange crop." For "rustlers" like Mills, the work was grueling, and not particularly well paid:

> Friday night I was about as tired as one could be. . . . I had arisen at 5:15 after sleeping some six hours by the road. Walked seven and one half miles along a R.R. track before breakfast. Started work as a "rustler" at 8:30; "Rustling" is admittedly the hardest job in a packing house. This place—Drakes—has been unable to keep any "rustler" more than 3-4 days. There are 2 rustlers here, each attending to about a dozen packers; When a packer wishes a box, she yells sharply, "box." The rustler punches her card and carries the box to a bench from twenty to thirty yards away, where a top is put on. Each box weighs 70 lbs. From 500 to 700 are carried in a day. I worked at this till 9 P.M. Friday night with two hours off for meals. By the time I was finished, my feet were blistered, my hands were torn, my arms almost numb, my back aching, and each of my thighs with a red hot sear across it where the edges of the box rubbed. I no longer wonder why there are so many I.W.W.s. Why are there not more anarchists?

When he finished, Mills was able to find lodging on a ditch bank next to the orange groves. After working an even longer shift on Saturday, Mills asked the owner "for some money due me. . . . Instead of money I am given a meal ticket— 'Good for five dollars in meals' at one George's Place."[13]

Kevin Starr presents the packing scene differently. It is the fulfillment of the pastoral promise (Figure 3):

> Today, a half century since citrus culture passed its peak, surviving evidence—old photographs especially—come forward to justify that . . . pastoralism: the groves themselves . . . extending from seashore to mountain range, and the great packing sheds adjacent to them, sweeping, open structures, forcefully aesthetic in their utility, banked by stands of eucalyptus trees which channelled breezes to an advantageous angle . . . and within these sheds, the work of sorting, washing, wrapping each fruit . . . tasks performed in the main by young women who regard us today from the pages of old magazines, their hands folded atop white aprons in a moment's repose as the photographer asked them to cease work so that he may record the scene.[14]

Similar images have been repeatedly called up to valorize and celebrate the "way of life" that California agriculture had become by the turn of the century. *Only* by erasing—or completely aestheticizing—the workers who made that way of life is its celebration possible. *Only* by seeing California purely as a landscape view can we see beauty without understanding the lives of the damned who are an integral part of that beauty. And that move, erasing the traces of work and struggle, is precisely what landscape imagery is all about.[15]

Such a reckless erasure of the lives of ordinary people in order to celebrate

Figure 3. A turn-of-the-century fruit-packing house in Santa Clara, California, similar to the packing houses Frederick Mills investigated in the San Joaquin orange district. The scale and the intensity of the work that Mills noted are only hinted at in the sense of pastoral calm the photograph achieves. (Courtesy, Bancroft Library.)

California as visual spectacle reaches something of a climax in Jean Baudrillard's postmodern tour of the state during the 1980s. Celebrating the hypermobile, decentered character of California "culture," Baudrillard can only see the working classes when they mimic the mobility of the dominant classes. Baudrillard spends a night at Porterville, just up the road from Lindsay, and in the heart of the interior orange district,

> a driveway lined by fifty palm trees, all the same height and absolutely symmetrical, leads up to a planter's house that is minuscule by comparison. It could be a colonial scene. . . . The road down to the town that is not really a town is as straight as the rows of orange trees and is peopled by Mexican slaves who have bought up their masters' old 1950s Chevrolets. . . . All the cars drive up and down the main thoroughfare in slow or animated procession, a collective parade. . . . It is the same ceremony, on a smaller scale, as the slow nocturnal cruising on the Strip in Las Vegas, or the procession of cars on the Los Angeles freeways simply transformed into a Saturday night provincial extravaganza. The only element of culture, the only mobile element: the car.

This mobility is the defining experience for the California landscape, according to Baudrillard. "Speed creates pure objects. It is itself a pure object, since it cancels out the ground and territorial reference points, since it runs ahead of time to annul time itself. . . . Driving like this produces a kind of invisibility, transparency, or transversality in things simply by emptying them out." Hypermobility, by emptying all objects of content, creates an ahistorical society, one that is pure image. "History and Marxism are like fine wines and haute cuisine," Baudrillard asserts (in an analogy telling for its exclusive focus in the desires of the francophile bourgeoisie). "They do not really cross the ocean in spite of the many impressive attempts that have been made to adapt them to new surroundings." There is no point in struggling to critique and understand capitalism, he goes on to say, because "it always stays a length ahead" of those who would fight against it. Without history, and with an ever-changing capital calling the shots, "things fade into the distance faster and faster in the rear-view mirror of memory." Hypermobility and the speed of time make the lives of the people who make Baudrillard's images—his pure objects, his simulacrum— quite invisible in the landscape, if not entirely irrelevent to it.[16]

Baudrillard's emphasis on hypermobility ignores the rather different mobility of the army of California migratory farmworkers whose lives are grounded not in an empty immense space, but in a ruthless, severe landscape that Baudrillard is incapable of understanding. At times, as many as 200,000 workers have tramped up and down the state in search of agricultural work, passing through, and making possible Parson's "color and geometry," Starr's "pastoralism," and Baudrillard's orange groves "laid out neatly on wild hillsides that are carpeted with undulating grasses like animal fur and resemble the hills of Tuscany." Their movement makes it impossible to accept such bourgeois fantasies of a purely aesthetic California. The mobility that attracts Baudrillard and Parsons and Starr thus becomes a lot like the image of the landscape they carry in their heads: California is represented purely as a playground of beauty in which the damned remain quite invisible. For historian Starr, the Pan-Pacific expositions in San Francisco and San Diego in 1915 represent the apotheosis of this ideal of aesthetic mobility. California writers, artists, bohemians, and politicians succeeded at these expositions in placing before the eyes of the nation a California at once solid and ethereal. In both expositions mobility was celebrated as a metaphor for the California experience. But it was a mobility not of labor working the fields and orchards, mines and forests of the state, but one that rather spoke of the unity of culture and nature that Californians had somehow managed to construct. John Muir's lonely treks in the Sierras and the peripatetic wanderings of literary bohemians were both celebrated at the fairs. For such mobility to be emblematic of the California experience, space itself had to be made into landscape—it had to be seen as immutable, as the contentless vast desert that Baudrillard celebrates, devoid of all affective life, existing only as a symbol of human desire.[17]

Literary critic David Wyatt has sought to explicate how the immutability and desirability of landscape has structured California literature. For him, landscape is something we live in, pass through, and respond to, and in this way the landscape defines us. Wyatt illustrates this point by examining Frank Norris's *The Octopus,* the story of the Mussel Slough incident in which the Southern Pacific Railroad forced squatting small farmers off the land. Norris's character Presely exemplifies the California landscape experience, according to Wyatt: "Presely moves through a space distinctive in its very vacancy. . . . It is a space at once vulnerable and immune to impress." Wyatt's analysis of space as absolute and immutable is complex, and he shows that as the weight of white European history gathers on the land, individual experiences of landscape become inextricable from the scene that produces them. Writers in California do not merely stand upon the hill and gaze, but actively experience the scene that is before them. Nature (for Wyatt, landscape is natural) is complexly intertwined with history. But for Wyatt, this is a history of decline: as history advances, the California landscape works not to create heroic individuals, but rather to wear them down.[18]

Wyatt sees two central eras of California writing that define for the rest of the world the nature and meaning of the California landscape. In both eras, the landscape stands as separate and autonomous, as a view to behold, as an externalized shaper of human emotion and action:

> The early naturalists see landscape as validating human behavior, the later novelists see landscape as controlling or restraining it. John Muir, Mary Austin and Clarence King each celebrate the spiritual liberation conferred by a particular California region. Norris, Steinbeck and Chandler map the advance of human hopes against the steady encroachments of space.

Despite the long history of human habitation in and transformation of California, despite the ugly anti-Chinese riots, the vigilante movements, the ruthless consolidation of land monopolies, the steady army of migratory workers, and the already sprawling cities of the early twentieth century, Wyatt posits the purely "natural" landscape as the true meaning of the California experience. "California acts as a site for such discoveries [of self] because her landscapes are beautiful, looming and austere, a dominant fact in the experience of her culture." Even more, "California intensifies the natural myth that America has been set apart from the beginning by its freedom to test itself against the unmediated." Nature, and the view, is everything. And it is determinate.[19]

In Kevin Starr's hands, this narrative of decline begins with a detailed rendering of landscape and social evolution in California—an evolution wrought through the enslavement of Indians, and the proletarianization of Mexicans, Chinese, Japanese, Filipinos, and Asian Indians. As white European influence deepens in the land, however, his focus shifts from the interplay of capital and labor with the land to a series of personality sketches aimed at showing the ultimate depravity of both the artistic community and the political elite in California. Starr shows this depravity to be entirely *personal*, borne of Californians' inability to come to terms with the natural abundance around them. The social relations of production that make that abundance possible fade quickly from Starr's view.[20]

By the end of his analysis, Wyatt (unlike Starr) begins to have misgivings, worrying that history inscribed on the land does seem to matter, that nature is not all. To explore these misgivings, Wyatt turns to the geographer Carl Sauer for guidance, but finds there that "the facts of geography emerge as fiction—a momentary stay against confusion—dependent for its stability on a suspension of historical perspective." The making of this fiction puts Sauer right in the thick of modernism, according to Wyatt: "'Modernism' can in fact be read as the triumph of the fiction of space: Certainly its major adepts strive for a form that denies or ignores the pressures of an ongoing and irrepressible time." Space—which for Wyatt is the same as landscape—is held steady so that the movement of people can be seen against it, so that we can see how people, not landscape, are formed in the encounter. Wyatt gives Sauer the credit for this way of seeing:

> Place (the "morphology of landscape") is the stopped frame in the continuous film of change. In his scholarly and unassuming way, California's most eminent geographer joins the company of imagineers who brood on the dimensions in which we live.[21]

Representing Landscape

Carl Sauer published "The Morphology of Landscape" in 1925 both as an epitaph for the environmental determinism that had ruled American geography for the preceding generation and as a programmatic statement of an emerging geography closely aligned with morphological sciences. The landscape for Sauer was the sum of its morphological components—the totality of buildings, infrastructure, population (density and mobility), production, communication, and so forth. It was an entity that could be mapped to show "the impress of the works of man upon an area." The landscape was thus a material, physical form that wedded Nature to Culture, and which could then be read to divine the values, needs, desires, and levels of development of a people. Therefore, landscape study had to be an exercise in historical reconstruction that sought to show how a particular culture, working on and through the natural landscape, created a cultural landscape.[22]

Geographers, according to Sauer, should engage in a search for the genesis of landscape form, and trace the ways in which this form becomes the basis for alteration as subsequent culture groups move into an area. The focus, therefore, was not on individuals, but on larger cultures as they reworked natural or preexisting landscapes: "Human geography . . . unlike psychology and history, is a science that has nothing to do with individuals but only with human institutions or cultures." To uncover the significance of a particular culture (or a trait of that culture), the geographer turned to the morphology of the cultural-natural landscape complex. "Area or landscape is the field of geography because it is a naïvely given, important section of reality, not a sophisticated thesis." The landscape was thus unproblematic: it was the visual data upon which historical reconstruction of past cultures was built. Sauer's concern was with the examination of culture as it was worked out "on the ground" in particular places. The goal of Sauerian landscape studies, however, was (and is) not purely ideographic. Rather, such studies seek through morphological analysis to detect the *generic* traits of landscape types. Their goal is to take a unique assemblage of material items and to represent them as a *typical* landscape that expresses the nature of a culture—and in this their goal closely parallels the goal of representing landscape as an artistic type and an ideological form.[23]

Sauer's programmatic statements on landscape have proved enormously influential, spawning both elaborate studies of local landscapes and heated debates about the usefulness of these studies. James Duncan has asserted that Sauer and his students have "exerted such influence over how cultural geographers have thought about landscapes that they have shaped a corpus of scholarship that has shown remarkably little variation over the years." There is good reason for this. A focus on the processes by which landscapes come to be made, and what they thereby represent, is of great importance for what it tells us about how societies function, and because, in our everyday lives, we engage continually in precisely this exercise of reading landscapes for their meaning, in hopes that they will guide us in our actions. But as Duncan and a growing chorus of others have pointed out, Sauerian landscape studies are deeply flawed by their inability (or unwillingness) to theorize and problematize any of their key terms: *nature, culture, landscape*. Everything is always obvious. "Culture" is largely superorganic, a whole greater than the sum of its parts. Nature is clearly what is not "culture." And landscape is purely visible, always open and naked to the eye that chooses to look.[24]

Partially in response to these shortcomings, geographers in recent years have turned to exploring the landscape not so much as morphological evidence, but as "ideology." In these studies, as Stephen Daniels and Denis Cosgrove note, "landscape is a cultural *image,* a pictorial way of representing, structuring or symbolizing surroundings" (emphasis added). The focus is thus shifted from the determinants of form and toward the way that ideology-laden landscape images are constructed. For geographers such as Cosgrove and Daniels, two who pioneered much of this shift in focus, landscape study has meant a study of the making of landscape representations—paintings, parklands, gardens, photographs—and their role in systems of meaning. Cosgrove, for example, has shown that the very idea of landscape as a "way of seeing," as a particular kind of view rendered through a rationalization and mathematical ordering of perspective, has a history that is inextricably bound to the hypercommodification of land that came with the capitalist transformation in Europe. The development of perspectival views, in gardens and parklands and on canvases and maps, allowed ownership to become explicit and abstract; and it rendered peasants and other workers invisible or relegated them to part of the "natural" scene. Landscape represented as perspectival view, as Raymond Williams and John Barrell have explained, lends the countryside the appearance of being *unworked,* a part of the order of nature, precisely at a time when the *social* relationships of human labor and life were remade in the image of an incipient capitalism. This erasure of work and workers is no less evident in traditional geographical studies of landscape. The assumption that landscape is "simply" a product of culture has the effect of erasing the work that makes landscape. Landscapes appear not so much as the solidification of the work of people in society, but more as an unconscious outcome of a "culture" that is larger than any individuals. As Peirce Lewis has put it, landscape "is our unwitting autobiography."[25]

"Landscape," analysts such as Cosgrove and Daniels tell us, signals a certain kind of representation of place and social life that seeks to order social relations by making all that is uncomfortable or unaesthetic to the owners of property (or more generally to the bourgeoisie) invisible or "natural," especially at times of great social change. As Cosgrove suggests, landed classes in Renaissance Europe learned to possess, or at least deepen possession of, the land *by* ordering it and viewing it as a landscape. Similarly, in contemporary American geographical accounts, such as that by Lewis, the unspecified "we" of American culture can better possess the landscape to the degree that "we" learn to look at it as a landscape: as unwitting, unconscious, naturalized. In both these senses, landscape-as-ownership and landscape-as-unwitting-autobiography of a "culture," representations of landscape "dissolve and conceal" tangible relations of power; they are duplicitous.[26]

Much of the work in geography on landscape-as-ideology and -representation has developed as a reaction, and thus in partial opposition, to the older landscape-as-morphology school. If a clear fault with the older landscape school in geography was its inability and unwillingness to adequately theorize its objects of study, to take them too much for granted, the primary fault of the newer landscape-as-ideology school has been to move too far away from the study of morphological production. Cosgrove's work in the mid-1980s explored in great detail the relationship between representation and material form, but his more recent work, like much of what gets called the "new cultural geography," has moved rather to a nearly exclusive study of (seemingly) disconnected images. And the most extreme forms of the "new cultural geography" have abandoned all interest in the world outside language and symbolic structure, outside representation. This has led to some theoretical positions that are hardly supportable. For example, Cosgrove has correctly shown that landscape as an object of knowledge is always an "outsider's" way of knowing. That is, while the term connotes at one level a shaping of the land, to see and understand a place *as* a landscape requires distance both from the place and from the labor that makes it. Landscape is thus not just ideology, it is *visual* ideology. "Landscape" is not so much experienced as *seen*. If landscape is thus a way of seeing, Peter Jackson has therefore concluded, "then there are potentially as many ways of seeing as there are eyes to see." Potentially, perhaps. But this ignores the fact that "landscape" is a relation of power, an *ideological* rendering of spatial relations. Landscapes transform the facts of place into a *controlled* representation, an imposition of order in which one (or perhaps a few) dominant ways of seeing are substituted for all ways of seeing and experiencing. "Landscape" developed from a "bourgeois, rationalist conception of the world," as Cosgrove has argued, and thus certainly does not and *cannot*, "reflect a plurality of cultures." That would defeat its ideological function.[27]

Trevor Barnes and James Duncan, the editors of a recent collection of papers on the politics of landscape representation, even go so far as to deny the existence of any prediscursive material world. While their larger point—that we must attend to how landscapes materialize in discourse—is well taken, the abandonment of the material world as an object of study in order to focus exclusively on the politics of reading, language, and iconography represents a dangerous politics. As we will see in great detail in the pages that follow,

the workings of an unjust political economy in no way make a similar abandonment. Connections between representations of landscape and "brute reality" (to use Barnes and Duncan's term) are continually made in social practice, as Frederick Mills showed, and as Steinbeck made the Joads eventually
understand.[28]

Cosgrove has argued that Sauer's methodology was inadequate, because

> despite the genetic treatment of individual forms . . . the process of development
> and change in the whole are arrested at [a] particular historical moment so that
> the areal synthesis can be established and a timeless unity of form composed. Under
> the morphological method landscape becomes a static determinant of scientific
> enquiry.[29]

What has been less recognized in newer studies of landscape-as-representation
is that this is precisely how landscape *functions*. Wyatt in this instance was correct: Sauer was reflecting the move made in all representations of landscape.
The constant motion of social relations and social struggle is suspended both in
a picture of landscape and in the material landscape itself. Newer landscape
geographies have not yet adequately theorized how this process works, how it is
that, on the ground, landscapes solidify social relations, making them seem
natural and enduring. Rather than seeking to improve on the insights of Sauer
and his students, which seemed to take this process of solidification as given,
newer theorists of landscape have sought to examine the intricacies of pictures.
This is an important endeavor, but it is only half the landscape story.[30]

Despite the shortcomings of both "new" and "old" cultural geographies,
geographers should be able to build on the tools of both traditions to begin to
explicate the nature of the connections between representations and materiality. "Landscapes" are produced in two ways. On one hand, there is labor—the
work of shaping the land. This labor, of course, is organized not just locally but
within a spatial division that cuts across myriad scales. On the other hand, the
re-presentation of the products of labor *as* a landscape represents an attempt to
naturalize and harmonize the appropriation of that labor and to impose a system of domination, consent, control, and order within the view. Contestatory
readings of landscapes are certainly possible, and they are ongoing (this book is
certainly one), and these contestatory readings work to reshape both the morphology and the view that is landscape. Landscape is thus a unity of materiality and representation, constructed out of the contest between various social
groups possessing varying amounts of social, economic, and political power.
Meanings are both posited in and developed out of the landscape's morphology. There is, as "new cultural geographers" insist, an iconography of land-

scape, but that iconography must be constructed within the context of the form that landscape takes. Moreover, the morphological landscape is usually not produced in order to be read; rather it develops as both a product of and a means for guiding the social and spatial practices of production and reproduction in an area. In Henri Lefebvre's words, landscapes are made not "in order to be read and grasped, but rather to be *lived* by people with bodies and lives in their own particular . . . context."[31] Yet landscapes *are* read and grasped; that is part of the process of transforming spatiality into landscape. Landscapes, and landscape representations, are therefore very much a product of social struggle, whether engaged over form or over how to grasp and read that form. And these struggles, of course, are fully recursive.

John Steinbeck knew that to understand the lives and political economy of places, to understand the landscape, to understand how and why it is made as it is and why it functions in social relations as it does, to understand why it looks as it does, one must explore not just landscape morphology or landscape representation, but the interdependence of the two. Local morphological productions—landscape in the first sense outlined above—are *generalized* in landscape views—landscape-as-ideology—even as ideological ways of seeing social relations *as* landscape structure the social relations that produce landscape morphology. The passive voice here is convenient but misleading. The questions that always arise when such grand statements are made are: *Who* generalizes? Who else is involved? Under what conditions do these people interact? What processes govern their ideas and productions? At what scale do people and processes operate to create landscapes? How can we theorize the connections between production and representation that Steinbeck hinted at?

Producing Landscape

For Steinbeck, the answers to the above questions start with the work of common people, and they proceed with an evaluation of how that work is organized (as the "interchapters" of *The Grapes of Wrath* show with their evocation of great, nearly immutable systems of finance, mechanized production, and mobile armies of the dispossessed). The connection between local morphology and the representations through which those morphologies are ordered and sent into circulation is, simply, labor. This is neither far-fetched nor over-reductionist. In a fascinating essay Kenneth Olwig reminds us that the "various uses of the term landscape . . . suggest that the landscape is an area carved out by axe and plough, which belongs to the people who have carved it out. It carries suggestion of being an area of cultural identity based, however loosely, on tribal and/or blood ties." Under capitalism, however, the fruits of labor are alienated from those who make them. The shape of the land is the product of people, but it is not necessarily owned or controlled by them. While the appropriation process that structures landscape is certainly one of legal ownership of the land, it is also one of advancing and appropriating meanings in a way that tries to make the alienation of labor from the landscape seem at once natural and incontestable.[32]

Landscape is thus quite a complex concept. A theory that seeks to explore the connections between landscape production and representation, it seems to me, must fulfill three basic requirements (which, while analytically separable, are so highly connected that their separate exposition is always artificial). First, a theory of landscape representation and production must tell us what landscape *is* (how we understand "landscape" and what its relations are to the material world). Second, it must explain how "landscape" is *produced* as part of socially organized systems of production and reproduction (for landscapes in no way exist external to the functioning of society). Finally, landscape theory must specify the processes by which material landscapes and their representations *function* in society (which is a different question than the second).

What Landscape Is

We have already spent a good deal of time discussing what landscape is, at least as far as geographers of differing perspectives have understood it. We can now go a step further. "Landscape may first be seen," in the words of Sharon Zukin, as a "contentious compromised product of society," shaped by "power, coercion and collective resistance." Social struggle makes the landscape, and the landscape is always in a state of becoming: it is never *entirely* stable. Yet landscape is also a totality. That is, powerful social actors, as we have already suggested, are continually trying to represent the landscape as a fixed, total, and naturalized entity—as a unitary thing. Landscape is thus best understood as a kind of produced, lived, and represented space constructed out of the struggles, compromises, and temporarily settled relations of competing and cooperating social actors: it is both a thing (or suite of things), as Sauer would have it, and a social process, at once solidly material and ever changing. As a produced object, landscape is like a commodity in which evident, temporarily stable, form masks the facts of its production, and its status as a social relation. As both form and symbol, landscape is expected by those who attempt to define its meanings to speak unambiguously for itself.[33]

In this sense, landscape "is an instrument of cultural power, perhaps even an agent of power that is (or frequently represents itself as) independent of human intentions. Landscape thus has a double role with respect to something like ideology." In W. J. T. Mitchell's terms, "It naturalizes a cultural and social construction, representing an artificial world as if it were simply given and inevitable, and it also makes that representation operational by interpellating its beholder in some more or less determinate relation to its givenness as sight and site." As Zukin has put it, the landscape "represents the architecture of social class, gender and race relations imposed by powerful social institutions." And to a degree it does, but, as Zukin's earlier words indicate, the landscape is no simple reflection of the needs and desires of the domineering classes. Rather, it represents an important social contradiction within a unity of form: the reproduction of inequality and supposed powerlessness that is codified and naturalized in the landscape carries with it the seeds of revolt. Subordinate social actors can and do develop contestatory readings of landscape and can and do continually seek to impose a different, perhaps more equitable, suite of spaces and landscape forms in the place of the imposed architecture of social class. Yet if *productive* landscapes are to be maintained under the conditions of inequality that make capitalism possible, then revolt must be minimized, and threatening social groups must be neutralized. Powerful social actors thus seek to build elements of landscape as a means of mediation, as a means of insuring neutralization—either by subverting subversion itself through cooptational blandishments (substituting better housing for the unjust social and economic conditions that make bad housing "acceptable," for example), or by seeking to reinforce the landscape as a representation of what is "natural."[34]

The very *form* of the landscape incorporates the give-and-take of this process, now becoming solidified one way, now another, depending on the array of power at any given moment. The landscape itself, as a compromised unity, is therefore even more of a contradiction, held in an uneasy truce as ongoing and everyday social struggle forms and reforms it. In the midst of (as well as before and after) these struggles, social actors of all types continually seek to represent the landscape to themselves and to others in order to make sense of the struggles in which they are engaged. Landscape is thus a fragmentation of space *and* a totalization of it. People make sense of their fractured world by seeing it as a whole, by seeking to impose meanings and connections. But since social struggle is strategic, compromises often gain the appearance of stability: landscapes become naturalized; they become quite unremarkable.[35]

How Landscape Is Produced

Landscape, as a material object mediated through all manner of representations, is a social production. But how can we systematically understand and describe the social processes that go into its making? Recent work in the sociology of science provides a useful analogy for seeing landscape as a compromised incorporation of social struggle. Bruno Latour has shown that many of the "things" we take for granted—protein and morphine are two of his examples—were in the past no more than unstable lists of activities and processes; they were not yet *formed*. They had "*no other shape than this list*" (all emphases in this paragraph are in the original). Not until the struggles over these processes had been settled, not until a settled shape had been given to the list—the list had been stabilized—through a process of contest against opponents who would represent the list in other ways, did the activities and processes come to be embodied as a thing or a definable object with a set morphology, "with limits or edges." At this point, according to Latour, the set of processes "is literally *reified*." In science, laboratories and other institutions have developed and been accorded the social power to determine these morphologies; largely, they are "powerful enough to define *reality*." And "reality, as the Latin word *res* indicates, is what resists. What does it resist? *Trials of strength*. If, in a given situation, no dissenter is able to modify the shape of the new object, then that's it, it *is* reality." Hence, reality is a product of struggle; morphology arises out of social contest. "The minute contest stops, the minute I write the word 'true,' a new formidable ally appears in the winner's camp, an ally invisible until then, but behaving now as if it has been there all along: Nature." Nature is socially produced.[36]

An embodied set of processes that gains shape through struggle and contest (and is represented as self-evidently true), the landscape is akin to Latour's scientific objects: it is a social product that becomes naturalized through the very struggles engaged over its form and meaning. It is *enacted* in the process of struggle. And as with morphine or protein, the shape of the landscape gives rise to new (social) realities. New battles are begun as soon as one shape is settled. The look of the land becomes at least partially determinate in the struggles that are to follow.

Latour's more recent archaeology of the morphology of technical artifacts allows us to extend this analogy even further. Concerned with the "symmetrical" relationship between social actors and the things they produce (that is, treating objects as agents), Latour suggests that technological artifacts develop out of a continual process of negotiation between competing social interests *and the objects themselves*. Latour develops the example of a new high-tech public transit system in France, and shows how the form of the system developed out of attempts to compromise the competing interests of the local mayor, a trade union worried about job loss, a carriage manufacturer concerned with profitable production, the transit company, and commuters who might use the system. But so too was the shape of the system a player. Engineers began by both developing and departing radically from the form of existing systems. Each competing interest reviewed the engineers' proposal, and in the next round the system was recreated—*reformed*—to account for and settle disputes between parties, while retaining the need to make sure the system would function. Thus the form of the second prototype did not just reflect but actively incorporated: (1) previous form; (2) alterations to ensure jobs for train operators; (3) prestige for the mayor; (4) profit for the manufacturer. Again the plans were reviewed, and again struggle ensued that was incorporated in the artifact's morphology. The very look of the artifact, and also the meanings associated with that look, was created through these processes of negotiation and social struggle. Form and meaning were settled out of—created by—social struggle.[37]

Latour contends that the historical development of an artifact is *dependent* upon these struggles, that the production of artifacts is impossible without them. This is the process of an artifact's production: morphology guiding conflict, conflict reforming morphology. He calls the resulting artifacts *quasi-objects* to suggest that they are not only material reality, but also an embodiment of the relations that went into building them. Similarly, a landscape may be seen as a *quasi-object,* embodying all the multifarious relations, struggles, arguments, representations, and conclusions that went into its making—even if it often appears as only an inert, or "natural," thing. As a *quasi-object,* and like a commodity, landscape structures social reality; it represents to us our relationships to the land and to social formations. But it does so in an obfuscatory way. Apart from knowing the struggles that went into its making (along with the struggles to which it gives rise), one cannot know a landscape except at some ideal level, which has the effect of reproducing, rather than analyzing or challenging, the relations of power that work to mask its function.[38]

How Landscape Functions

Landscapes are produced and represented within specific historical conditions. While the development of a generalized theory of landscape production has been necessary, it is just as necessary to recall that agricultural California developed as (and remains) a part of an expanding capitalist economy. The promise of Eden that the Joads saw from Tehachapi Pass, and the reality of the Hoovervilles and unemployment that awaited them down below, were both part of a general process of capitalist development and of the local conditions within which that development occurred. Hence it is necessary to understand both how landscapes in general and the particular landscapes of rural California function within capitalism. We need now to examine the role that landscape plays in reproducing capitalist agriculture, and the social relations that allow the agricultural system to work. As will be developed in the following chapters, by defining reified "natural" or rational relations of place through struggle over morphology and meaning, the production of landscape materially affects the equation for the extraction of surplus value within a region. To the degree that labor unrest, demands, or moves toward self-development and autonomy (Latour's trials of strength) within a region can be stilled by the imposition of naturalized forms of reproduction (when labor or other social groups give up the battle, when trials of strength are abandoned), surplus value can be expanded; reproduction is not threatened. Landscape production, therefore, is a moment in overall processes of uneven development. The "seesaw" motion of capital, restlessly searching out new opportunities for the production of surplus value, seeks differentials not just in land rent or locational advantage, but also in the "natural"—reified—needs and tendencies of labor. Both labor quality and labor quantity can be locally or regionally conditioned by the efforts of capitalist and state institutions (which may or may not have similar goals or values).[39]

David Harvey has argued that "labor qualities, once acquired, do not, unlike many other forms of investment, necessarily run down over time. The productivity of labor (like that of the soil to use an analogy that Marx invokes to great effect) can build up over time, provided proper care is taken." But given "proper care," just the opposite can also be the case. Labor qualities can be devalued or labor surpluses created (so that quantity substitutes for quality). The real wages of laborers can be driven down by lessening social needs, provided, of course, that labor is in no condition to press demands for its own improvement. The production of landscape, by objectifying, rationalizing, and naturalizing the social, has often had just this effect. If, as Harvey has also argued, the landscape of capitalism is often a barrier to further accumulation and has to be creatively destroyed or otherwise overcome, then it is just as true that the landscape is often a great facilitator to capital (by helping to determine the "nature" of labor in a particular place). As this happens, workers must overcome not just conditions of inequality and the oppressive work of power, but the stabilized landscape itself. They must destabilize not just the relations of place, but the very ground upon and within which those relations are situated and structured.[40]

Landscape is thus an uneasy truce between the needs and desires of the people who live in it, and the desire of powerful social actors to represent the world as they assume it should be. Landscape is always both a material form that results from and structures social interaction, and an ideological representation dripping with power. In both ways, landscapes are acts of contested discipline, channeling spatial practices into certain patterns and presenting to the world images of how the world (presumably) works and who it works for.

It helps, therefore, to understand "landscape" as a complex moment in a system of social reproduction. In this book, my focus on social reproduction will revolve around the reproduction of labor power on the industrialized farms of California, but the theory I develop should by no means be limited to that realm, especially since, as feminist scholarship has so clearly shown, the separation of production from reproduction is untenable. My concerns with California labor relations, with the kinds of lives represented by the Joads, are many, not least that I would like to show the importance of "landscape" to the economic development of the state. And in this goal, a focus on *re*production is essential. For as Marx wrote in the first volume of *Capital,* the "maintenance and reproduction of the working class is, and ever must be, a necessary condition of the reproduction of capital." The reproduction of labor power (and thus of society) proceeds in historically specific ways; it (like landscape) is the site of constant struggle. Marx was surely wrong, however, when he argued that the social reproduction of labor power could be left "safely to the labourer's instinct for self-preservation." Rather, his point earlier in *Capital* is closer to the mark: reproduction (specifically in its relationship to the production of surplus value) possesses a "historical and moral element," which may often *appear* as a set of "natural" or "necessary wants," but which, of course, has been socially constructed.[41]

Landscape production and representation play an important role, materially and ideologically, in the development of Marx's historical and moral element, and it is the goal of the pages that follow to spell out in empirical detail the processes by which this occurred in California during the period between the Wheatland riot of 1913 and the Bracero Program of 1942. These pages will show that no matter how beautiful, no matter how seemingly immutable, no matter how much it appears as a simulacrum, landscape is certainly not neutral. Nor are aesthetics ever free of the blood that goes into their making. In California, at least, there can be no beauty without a simultaneous damning.

2 / Labor and Landscape: The Wheatland Riot and Progressive State Intervention

The Wheatland Riot

Both the form of the California agricultural landscape and the form of the struggles over that landscape in the first half of the twentieth century can be traced to the summer of 1913. Early that summer, the Durst Brothers Hops Ranch of Wheatland, California, distributed notices throughout California, southern Oregon, and Nevada, proclaiming that "all white pickers who make application before August 1st will be given work" picking hops. The flier promised that "the going price" would be paid for "clean picking." Moreover, a bonus of ten cents per hundred pounds harvested would be paid to those pickers who worked until the end of the season (perhaps a month). The Dursts also promised that "model" camping facilities would be provided. Nearly 2,800 workers, comprising some twenty-seven nationalities, arrived at the ranch by the beginning of the season. The call for white workers reflected a resurgent nativist sentiment that gripped the state at this time of economic depression, but the Dursts hired Hispanic, Black, or Asian workers whenever they could. Nonwhite workers, growers throughout the state surmised, were "naturally" better suited to agricultural tasks (see Chapter 4). They also knew that the racist climate of the state made it possible to pay nonwhite workers a lower wage than white workers. Some of the workers comprised what a later investigation euphemistically termed "the better middle class [who were] in the habit of using the hop and fruit season as their 'country vacation'"—that is, they were working families that supplemented their income by harvesting crops during the summer when the children were out of school. Women and children constituted nearly 50 percent of the workforce at the ranch. The rest were full-time migratory workers who followed well-established migratory routes as crops matured up and down the state.[1]

Instead of work for all, good camp conditions, and "the going rate," workers arriving in Wheatland found that the Dursts were paying ten cents less than the going wage—the difference became the "bonus" paid at the end of the season. The "model" camp, according to an official report,

> comprised a motley collection of tents, timber stockades called "bullpens," gunny sacks stretched over fences, and camp wagons. . . . A great number [of workers and families] had no blankets and slept on piles of straw thrown onto the tent floors. These tents were rented from D[urst] at 75 cents a week, though some of the old tents were donated by him free of charge. Before these and other accommodations were ready, men slept in the fields. One group of 45 men, women, and children slept packed together on a single pile of straw.[2] [See Figure 4.]

Nor was there work for all who applied: at best 1,500 pickers were needed, but even this number precluded the ability of workers' making enough money to stake them over until their next job. There were only five wells, and these were far removed from the picking fields (and temperatures approached 110 degrees in the shade during the first week in August). Most wells ran dry early each morning, and those that did not were quickly polluted with human and animal waste. Dysentery and typhoid epidemics ravaged the camp. The Dursts had dug only eight to eleven pit toilets for all their workers, and most of these were filthy or in disrepair even before workers started to arrive. Carleton Parker, the official investigator of conditions at the ranch for both California and the federal government, scolded the workers (particularly foreign workers) for having "as a rule, unclean personal and camp habits, expos[ing] themselves at the pumps while washing, and [being] indecently careless in the presence of women and children," but it is hard to see how they could have been otherwise. There were no other bathing or showering facilities available.[3]

Pay was by pounds of hops picked, and since Ralph Durst hired too few weight checkers, waiting in line at weigh stations often lasted three to four hours; frequently workers found that at the end of their wait, they would have to re-sort their harvest because Durst "required an unusual standard of cleanliness for his hops." The daily wage at the beginning of the season for individuals working a twelve-hour day varied between seventy-eight cents and one dollar. Since the picking day lasted well into the evening, there was no time to go to town for food, so most workers were forced to spend their day's pay for

Figures 4A and B. Housing at the Durst Brothers Hops Ranch, Wheatland, California, at the time of the August 1913 riot. (Photo: California Commission of Immigration and Housing.)

overpriced food at the camp store (which was, of course, owned by the Dursts). During picking hours, Ralph Durst refused to allow water wagons into the fields, claiming that there were hop vines planted in the roads. These vines, however, stopped neither a stew nor a "lemonade" wagon (both operated by a cousin of the Durst brothers) from working the fields, providing lunch and drinks to workers for a charge. If workers bought stew, they could get a glass of water also; if they bought lemonade, they were given a cup of citric acid diluted with water—a concoction prepared by the pharmacist in town. When later asked how it was that concession wagons could move through the field when a water wagon could not, Ralph Durst no longer claimed that vines blocked the roads, but rather that a third wagon would have "cluttered up the field."[4]

The Durst brothers knew what they were doing. Similar advertising strategies and camp and work conditions had in the past ensured that very few workers stayed through the season, and the Dursts were able to pocket the so-called bonus. They also assumed that sixty years of agricultural development in California, coupled with an economic depression that was throwing ever more workers into the migratory life, had made farmworkers powerless to protest these conditions. Resistance to what were in fact rather typical working and living conditions in California had not materialized in the past—unless one counts quitting and moving on as resistance—and they were sure it would not materialize this year.

On this second point the Dursts were quite wrong. By August 2, led by "a small number who were familiar with the teachings of the IWW [Industrial Workers of the World]," hops pickers had organized and presented a list of demands for better living conditions and fair wages to the ranch management. This petition, which had "the overwhelming support of the workers," according to historian Cletus Daniel, was met with an acquiescence to a few of the minor demands but a flat rejection of the major ones. Durst argued later that the workers' demands were unreasonable because the conditions on his ranch were neither unusual nor anything less than what migratory workers deserved. Indeed, without the agitation of the IWW, Durst claimed, the workers would have been quite content. The workers voted to strike.[5]

The next day, as workers met near a dance pavilion in the camp, Ralph Durst and a local constable attempted to arrest one of the strike organizers, former IWW Richard "Blackie" Ford. The crowd forced the constable to back off when he could not produce a warrant. Durst then phoned the Yuba County sheriff to report, rather hyperbolically, that there was a riot in progress on his ranch. The sheriff, several deputies, an armed posse of farmers and townspeople, and the district attorney responded to the call. Some of the deputies arrived at the ranch in Ralph Durst's automobile, leading the impression among strikers that they were "Durst's police." To their evident disappointment, the posse did not find a rioting mob, but rather a peaceful gathering of about 2,000 workers singing songs from the IWW songbook. Ford had just finished a speech, declaring as he held a sick baby above his head, "It is for the life of the kids that we do this." In response to the singing and speech making, one of the deputies waded into the crowd and fired a shot into their air "to sober the crowd."[6]

The effect was just the opposite. A Puerto Rican worker wrestled the gun from the deputy and killed both the deputy and the district attorney (who was also the Dursts's personal lawyer). The Puerto Rican and an anonymous "English boy" were killed in the shoot-out that ensued. Scores of others were injured. When the dust settled, the posse fled back to nearby Marysville (the Yuba County seat), and workers departed the ranch by any means available. Governor Hiram Johnson sent the state militia to Wheatland, but when they arrived the next morning, the troops found the camp mostly empty and the area calm. Mostly to soothe the nerves of the local residents, the militia stayed in Wheatland for the week.[7]

In the annals of United States labor history, the Wheatland riot is hardly remarkable. It was brief and violent, but so were so many other labor battles of the era.[8] The importance of the riot lies less in the events themselves than in the conditions that led up to it, and in the chain of events that it touched off. As importantly, the Wheatland riot served as a fulcrum for leveraging a simultaneously progressive and repressive transformation of the California agricultural landscape. The Wheatland riot can be seen as an important moment in the production and eventual solidification of the twentieth-century rural California landscape, even if that moment itself developed out of already well-established patterns of migrancy, labor relations, spatial practices, and, not least, representations of the landscape within which it occurred. This riot changed the shape of the California landscape—and it changed how that landscape would henceforth be seen.

Seeing Discord

Carey McWilliams called the Wheatland riot California's first labor "cause célèbre." For Progressives like Carleton Parker, the riot was nothing if not a startling introduction to just how "unnatural" and chaotic California agricultural labor relations had become:

> This new labor status in the state is menacing in its potentiality for spasmodic waves of unrest and sudden perplexing strikes of unorganized workers. "Passive

resistance," the new method in labor warfare, not at all the product of the ortho-dox labor movement, becomes paralysis because the method, being new, finds no effective legal doctrine or procedure to combat it.

The seeming spontaneity of the riot, as well as its implications for changing power relations in the fields and orchards of the state, threatened many of the cherished myths upon which the state's economic development had been mort-gaged. "Difficult though organization may be," Parker argued, "a coincidence of favoring conditions may place an opportunity in the hands of a super leader. If this comes, one can be sure that California would be both very astonished and very misused"—astonished, perhaps, because it was just this type of radical dissaffection and industrial turmoil that the image of California-as-yeoman-Eden tried to mask.[9]

The most immediate response to the riot by state and local officials and in-censed growers was to begin a campaign of "wild and irresponsible persecution" of any radical worker that could even remotely be connected to Wheatland. The Burns Detective Agency was deputized on behalf of Yuba County, and its agents spread throughout the west searching for Wheatland "conspirators." Herman Suhr (an early organizer at the ranch who had left Wheatland before the riot) was arrested in Arizona and returned to Marysville to be tried for murder. Blackie Ford was likewise later arrested and made to stand trial on charges of murder, even though he never fired a shot. Other workers were rounded up from around the state and held for months without charges. Alfred Nelson, for example, was arrested by a Burns detective in Guerneyville (north-west of Santa Rosa), and in the weeks that followed was shunted from Santa Rosa to Sacramento, San Francisco, and finally Martinez in Contra Costa County. He was never formally charged, nor was he allowed to seek counsel. At Martinez he was held for a few hours in the county jail and then taken to a saloon, winding up eventually in a hotel room, where he was beaten repeatedly by Burns detectives and urged to confess that he had seen Ford shoot the Yuba County district attorney.[10]

The riot and the subsequent dragnet was enthusiastically covered by the state's press, lending to the whole event a sense less of being a cause célèbre and more of an atmosphere of gross spectacle. Public attention in California was riveted as it never had been before on the conditions under which the impres-sive agricultural abundance of the state was produced—and on the landscape within which these events occurred. For as Carleton Parker influentially argued at the time: "As a class, the migratory laborers are nothing more nor less than the finished products of their environment. They should therefore never be

studied as isolated revolutionaries, but rather as, on the whole, tragic symptoms of a sick social order." The question before California, Parker suggested,
was twofold: how did such a sick social environment develop, and what could
be done about it?[11]

The Wheatland riot threw a normally invisible worker discontent into
shocking visibility, exposing as it did so the iniquitous nature of the California
landscape in a way it had rarely been exposed before. To be sure, there had long
been arguments over the course that the development of California agriculture
should take, and there had been concern that a system based on such vast
armies of migratory, pauperized labor was neither healthy nor desirable. But
now these issues gained a certain urgency by dint of labor's new visibility.[12]

The Wheatland riot may have been shocking in its suddenness, especially to
the urban middle classes. But it should not have been. By 1913, "the pattern"
of California agricultural relations—land monopolies, highly capitalized agribusiness, and a constant, necessary, highly mobile oversupply of labor that assured
both profitability and pauperization—had been well set, whether or not the
urban bourgeoisie chose to notice them. As early as 1880 this pattern was attracting attention around the world. "I should be very much pleased," Karl
Marx wrote to Friedrich Sorge that year, "if you could find me something good
(meaty) on economic conditions in California. California is very important to
me because nowhere else has the upheaval most shamelessly caused by capitalist centralization taken place with such speed." The capitalist centralization—
especially in agriculture—to which Marx referred was in the first place premised
on a ruthless round of land monopolization—and the concomitant "freeing"
of labor—during the second half of the nineteenth century. "Latifundia," Lord
Bryce once remarked, "perdunt California." The monopolization and industrialization process, in turn, required an abundant and highly fluid labor force,
one capable of materializing almost instantly in order to harvest crops before
they perished and just as quickly disappearing from sight when the work was
done. In this sense, California was not so much different from other agricultural regions in the United States as it was, in Carey McWilliams's words, "more
so." There is an abundant literature on land-owning patterns and the industrialization of California agriculture. Rather than repeat it here, I turn instead to
how the patterns of agriculture in the state were apprehended and transformed
in the wake of Wheatland.[13]

Benevolent Repression after Wheatland: Remaking the Landscape

Carleton Parker's interest in the nature of migratory labor was a direct result of
the events at Wheatland. The hundreds of thousands of agricultural workers

necessary to the economic survival of the agricultural system, he discovered in his researches, lived, to a large degree, in a series of private labor camps maintained by private growers as a means of assuring the return of labor power to their fields every day it was needed during the harvest season—and for assuring that workers did not stay on in the area after their labor was no longer needed. The riot at Wheatland fundamentally threatened this system of labor reproduction.[14]

Cultural geographers have long argued that material items in the landscape reflected the "culture" of a place and people, and to a large degree Parker would have agreed with them (though his analysis is at times quite complex, and he would have also argued in the opposite direction: that landscape could quite possibly determine the culture of a people). The camp at the Durst Brothers Hops Ranch suggested in its very spatial arrangements (bull pens, corrals, rag tents, dilapidated toilets, polluted water, and reliance on vast oversupplies of destitute mobile labor to toil in the sun-scorched fields) an entrenched and commonplace set of relationships between different factions of society and the space itself. For Parker, they represented "a relic of early California days when our people were good-naturedly willing to put up with almost any housing conditions." Hence, "the improvement of living conditions in the labor camps will have the immediate effect of making the recurrence of impassioned, violent strikes and riots not only improbable, but impossible." The form of the landscape was thus an important input to the reproduction of the labor system as it was developing in California. If the efficient extraction of surplus value out of the soil of California was to be maintained, the form of the landscape itself would have to be altered. "The employers must be shown," Parker announced,

> that it is essential that living conditions among their employees be improved, not only in fulfillment of their obligations to society in general, but also in order to protect and promote their own welfare and interests. . . . They must learn that unbearable living conditions inoculate the minds of the otherwise peaceful workers with germs of bitterness and violence, as was so well exemplified at the Wheatland riot, giving the agitators a fruitful field wherein to sow the seeds of revolt and preach the doctrine of sabotage.
>
> On the other hand, the migratory laborers must be shown that revolts accompanied by force in scattered and isolated localities not only involve serious breaches of the law and lead to crime, but they accomplish no lasting constructive results in advancing their cause.[15]

To teach both lessons, and to better rationalize labor relations in the rural areas of the state, the legislature charged the newly created California Commission of Immigration and Housing (CCIH) with investigating the Wheatland riot and with working with state farmers to improve the "normal" labor, housing, and sanitary conditions that had developed in the state along with the growth of industrialized agriculture (and other rural industries that used "casual" labor, such as mining and lumbering).

The California Commission of Immigration and Housing

CCIH was largely a product of the energy and political skill of Simon Lubin, a prominent Progressive and the executive officer of the Sacramento department store Weinstock, Lubin and Company. The original impetus to the creation of CCIH (which was formed some six weeks before the Wheatland riot) was concern, in 1912, about the imminent completion of the Panama Canal and the wave of immigration to the state that likely would result. With the assistance of Dr. David Blaustein, who had been his professor at the Columbia School of Philanthropy, Lubin presented to Progressive California governor Hiram Johnson a plan for the creation of a state immigration board, which would "coordinate municipal, private and social efforts" in assimilating new immigrants to the state. The governor appointed a special committee, chaired by Lubin, to study immigration issues and to recommend legislation to "prevent the dreadful conditions of poverty [like those] that prevail in the great cities" of the eastern United States.[16]

The study commission proposed establishing a state-level, permanent California Commission of Immigration and Housing that would investigate immigrant and housing matters. Lubin originally opposed the addition of "Housing" to the commission title, arguing that it would dilute the commission's focus. Other committee members, however, countered that housing was the first point of significant contact for immigrants with American institutions, and thus should be a special concern of any new commission. Moreover, housing was not at this time the specific concern of any other state agency, and preliminary work by the study commission had shown that tenement conditions in California cities were beginning to rival those of New York and Boston. Lubin was swayed, and the commission made concern with the built environment an explicit part of its mission. With the addition of an amendment sponsored by the California State Federation of Labor barring the commission from inducing or encouraging immigration to California, the California Commission of Immigration and Housing was established by legislative act exactly as Lubin and his committee envisioned it.[17]

The scope of CCIH was quite wide. It was charged with making inquiries into the "condition, welfare, and industrial opportunities of all immigrants arriving and being within the state." Such inquiries were to include agricultural land surveys to assess the possibility for settling immigrants in rural districts, and studies of labor supply and labor need for both agriculture and industry. CCIH was also authorized to act as a semiofficial employment agency by cooperating with public, private, and philanthropic employment agencies in an effort to "aid in the distribution and employment of immigrants." A further task for CCIH was to survey the education of immigrants, compile lists of immigrant children to be given to school districts, and to establish "Americanization" programs to aid immigrants in assimilating into their new communities and jobs. And CCIH was empowered to "refer to proper public officials all violation of laws regulating the payment of wages, child labor, employment of women, factory inspection," and so forth. Finally, the Commission was given the power to hold hearings and subpoena witnesses, though it rarely used that power until Carey McWilliams became its chief in 1939.[18]

The activity with which CCIH was most closely associated, however, was not originally part of its charter. Under section 7 of its authorizing act, CCIH received authority to inspect all labor camps "with the object in view of rendering the immigrant that protection to which he is entitled," but the Commission had no right to enforce any of the recommendations it made. Concurrent with the passage of legislation creating CCIH, the California Legislature passed a Labor Camp Sanitation Act and gave the state Board of Health responsibility for its enforcement. The legislature appropriated no money for this task. With the uprising at Wheatland, however, the legislature gave CCIH both authority and funds to inspect and improve labor camp conditions.[19]

Lubin was named the chair of CCIH, and one of his first acts was to hire Carleton Parker, a labor economist at the University of California, as its executive secretary. In Parker, Lubin had found a like-minded reformer anxious to put into practice experimental Progressive reform programs. Even before CCIH opened its first office, it was charged by the governor with investigating the Wheatland riot, and it was soon similarly empowered by the United States Commission on Industrial Relations to make investigations on behalf of the federal government. Through his role as primary investigator of the riot, Parker became the most prominent analyst of the newly visible phenomenon of the migratory worker. For Parker (as for Lubin and for Parker's successor, George Bell), migratory workers, especially those aligned with or influenced by the IWW, were psychological aberrants, human expressions of an environmentally induced inferiority. And this construction of the problem points directly at the form that CCIH's interventions in the rural California landscape would take.[20]

Diagnosing Environmental Psychosis: Progressive Science and Carleton Parker's Theory of Landscape

The goals of CCIH as it investigated Wheatland were twofold: to determine the cause of the riot so that such events would not happen again, and to block attempts by radical organizations like IWW from organizing migrant and immigrant workers. During its first decade, CCIH worked tirelessly to ensure that social advancement for casual laborers was the responsibility of the Progressive movement rather than the province of self-organizing workers, whom Progressives viewed as a competing social class.[21] Parker put the goals of the Commission (and of the state) this way in his report on Wheatland:

> The concrete problem in California is; What must be done to IN FACT remedy the evils of the existing industrial relations between casual seasonal workers, and their employers, so as to forestall or prevent the insidious violent work of the agitator who is not interested in improving living and wage conditions, but who rejoices in bad conditions which afford opportunities for stirring up discontent to fan the flames of the "Revolution" of his dreams? [Original emphasis]

The "remedy of necessity means the institution of a third party," according to Parker, which, of course, was CCIH.[22]

The IWW and CCIH thus agreed on one point: bad wages and bad camp conditions were central factors in the growth of unrest in the California fields. One IWW member told Lubin that the IWW "would tie up the whole hop industry unless better housing provisions and higher wages were offered." And in his report to the U.S. Industrial Relations Commission, Parker wrote, "The shrewdest IWW leader I found said, 'We can't agitate in the country unless things are rotten enough to bring the crowd along.'" The mechanisms of causality, the means by which the state had been brought to this point, however, were not so clear to CCIH. Rather, that was one of the first things CCIH sought to discover.[23]

To this end, Parker hired several of his students from the University of California to work as undercover "hobos" and charged them with the dual mission of gathering basic data on the lives, mores, and customs of migratory laborers, and of keeping tabs on the militant activities of the IWW. Parker's first statewide investigations of camp conditions, carried out by his newly hired agents during the spring of 1914, found "a fairly universal condition of unsanitary conditions and camp neglect," not unlike the conditions at Wheatland the previous year. Of 308 camps inspected, 137 were rated bad, "which, measured by the standardization adopted by the Commission means camps imminently dangerous to both the health and the decency of their working communities." The "bad" camps housed roughly 50 percent of the workers covered by the survey. Only forty-two camps were "up to the modest requirements of the Commission." The remaining 131 camps were rated fair, which meant that they were in violation of the Labor Camp Sanitation Act in at least one instance.[24]

Just as importantly, CCIH agents and camp inspectors provided information that, when coupled with hundreds of interviews conducted with migratory workers and others at the Wheatland murder trials, allowed Parker to develop a scientific profile upon which he could theorize the relationship between landscape—or "environment"[25]—and the behavior of migratory labor. At the time of his investigation of Wheatland, a colleague at the University of California lent Parker two books by Sigmund Freud. In these Parker felt he had "found a scientific approach which might lead to the discovery of important fundamentals for a study of unrest and violence," an approach that provided a theoretical framework for the mass of data his agents were beginning to report. In turn, Freud's work led Parker to

> general psychology, physiology and anthropology, eugenics, all the special material I could find on Mendelism, works on mental hygiene, feeblemindedness, insanity, evolution of moral character, and [I] finally found a resting place in a field which seems best designated as Abnormal and Behavioralistic Psychology. My quest throughout this experience seemed to be pretty steadily a search for those irreducible fundamentals which I could use in getting a technically decent opinion of that riot.[26]

Rather than finding causes in the structure of the political economy of the state, in the historical development of an agricultural system that demanded an oversupply of labor, Parker followed his Progressive instincts to find the locus of protest in the psychology and biology of the individual worker. Casual laborers were inferior, Parker argued, and their riots were a product of that inferiority. If agribusiness concerns were at all culpable, then it was only because they unwittingly helped reinforce, rather than ameliorate, that inferiority.[27]

In his search of psychological, biological, and environmental causes of labor inferiority, Parker traveled in good company. Like Robert Yerkes, H. H. Goddard, and other prominent researchers into the biological construction of "natural" difference in humans, Parker placed his faith in the ineluctability of innate biological and environmentally induced differences between "men." But unlike the rigid biological determinacy that spawned early intelligence testing (and a whole history of falsified data created to validate determinist scientific theology), and unlike the rigid environmental determinacy that marked much academic geography of the same era, Parker's diagnosis of inferiority was derived from a complex interaction of these two, largely immutable properties. He came to believe that personality, especially irrational personality, was multiply determined: differences among humans resulted from encounters between innate biology and "thwarting" environments.[28]

Parker argued that science had shown "it is impossible to view an I.W.W. as a mobile and independent agent, exercising free will and moral discretion." Even so, as "products of their environment," they could be refined, but only by transforming a "thwarting" environment into one that channeled the biological determinants of personality in a productive direction. All humans, Parker theorized, possessed "innate and insuppressible tendencies," including sexual and familial ones, ability to think, gregariousness, mobility, desire for "the hunt" (including "the sex chase"), leadership, willingness to follow a leader, and need for open space (because humans "feel revulsion at confinement"). These tendencies were the building blocks of what made humans truly human. But, according to Parker, not all humans were gifted with these tendencies in equal proportion. Parker found that the quality of being human was refined by the progressive development of the individual away from more coarse biological tendencies (such as simple grasping and hoarding) and toward more refined ones (such as leadership and workmanship). He found support for this idea in a variety of sources, but most particularly in the work of the eminent experimentalist John Watson, who had shown that Black babies ("with a more recent and virile biological memory," in Parker's words) possessed a far greater affinity for the most basic instincts, and a less developed sense of the more refined ones.[29]

To explain this process of refinement, and its obverse, Parker theorized that the environment worked in opposition to these innate tendencies—not as a *direct* creator of them. Working against their environment, humans refined or frustrated their biological tendencies. Human development was thus a two-part process:

> First, . . . these [biological] tendencies are far less warped by the environment than we believe, . . . they as motives in their various normal and perverted habit form can at times dominate singly the entire behavior and act as if they were a clear character dominant.
>
> Secondly, . . . if the environment through any of the conventional instruments of repression such as religious orthodoxy, university mental discipline, economic inferiority, imprisonment, physical disfigurement, such as short stature, hare lips, etc., repress the full psychological expression in the field of these tendencies, a slipping into abnormal mental functioning takes place, and society accuses the revolutionist of being either willfully inefficient, alcoholic, syndicalist, super sensitive, agnostic, or insane.[30]

Taken as a whole, the environment has a final say in determining behavior and action: it creates inferiority (and other dysfunctional states such as rebellion and agnosticism) through its ability to thwart instinct. Nature produces, and *then* the environment stifles. "As the Harvard biologist words it," Parker wrote, "nurture has triumphed over nature, the environment has produced its type." Importantly, in Parker's complex formula, there is little or no room for under- standing structural determinants (like the political economy of California agriculture) in the social production and reproduction of the "inferiority" that expresses itself in migratory labor. There is little or no room for a critique of economic systems that *demand* migratory labor as essential to their very functioning. This is important, of course, because in the end, as much as Parker wanted to assign culpability to growers who provided appalling con- ditions, he actually removes blame from them and places it at the intersection of some nebulous "environment" and the "innate" qualities of the workers themselves.[31]

Sciences, Donna Haraway has written, "are woven of social relations throughout their tissues," but for Carleton Parker, the social world apparently was not; it was woven of the multiple determinacies—biological and environ- mental—that only Progressive science and Progressive social engineering were equipped to remake. The need for Progressive scientific and technical reform was pressing, Parker argued. Workers, especially the "casual" migratory laborers of the west, were forced to exist in an environment that was

> suggested in the phrases monotonous work, dirty work, simplified work, mecha- nized work, the servile place of labor, insecure tenure on the job, hire and fire, winter unemployment, the ever found union of the poor district with the crime district, and the restricted district with prostitution, the open shop and labor turnover, poverty, the breadlines, the scrap heap, destitution.[32]

These environmental factors ultimately determined the life of the laborer: "A slum produces a mind which has only slum incidents with which to work." Against these environments, the laborer struggled to fulfill all her or his innate tendencies. "In just what kind of perverted compensations," Parker asked, "must the laborer indulge to make endurable his existence?"[33]

In answer to his query, Parker found that the reaction of the western casual laborer to his balking environment was a pure distillation of wanderlust. But this wanderlust brought its own inhibitions to instinctual fulfillment—"mo- notony, indignity, dirt and sexual apologies"—which invariably found their compensation in one of two ways. The worker either "weakens, becomes inef- ficient, drifts away, . . . drinks, deserts his family," or indulges in a true type-inferiority compensation and in order to dignify himself, to eliminate for himself his inferiority in his own eyes, he strikes or brings on a strike, he commits violence or he stays on the job and injures machinery, or mutilates the materials; he is fit food for dynamite conspiracies. He is ready to make sabotage a regular part of his habit scheme. His condition is one of mental stress and unfocused psychic unrest, and in all accuracy could be called a definite industrial psychosis. He is neither willful nor responsible, he is suffering from a stereotyped mental disease.

The whole of the environment conspires against the worker, creating nothing less than a naturalized inferiority that can only be compensated for in violent, psychotic behavior. And this, for Parker, is precisely what explained Wheatland. The riot was not merely a reaction to the appalling conditions workers found there, but rather an expression of disease and inferiority that the environment triggered. Parker had created the perfect diagnosis for the paternalistic idealism of Progressivism: Progressive involvement in the landscape would therefore be geared toward making environments that would produce, in Parker's words, a "new man" who was now content to perform the work desired of him.[34]

Certainly Parker did not shy from damning modern industrial capitalism for its role in creating thwarting environments, but he laid the full brunt of his scorn not at the feet of industrialists, but rather on the heads of the supposedly ill workers whom he saw as his (and CCIH's) patients. Under the guise of removing blame from the worker for such events as Wheatland by explaining radicalism as mental disease, Parker removed any sense of agency from the workers themselves and invested it with a "militant minority" of social workers, mental health workers, industrial and sanitary engineers, theorists such as himself, and Progressive agencies such as CCIH, which together would remake the world after an image of instinctual fulfillment wherein biological potential (which was not evenly distributed across the population) matched environmental amenity—where nurture worked with, rather than against, nature. The material landscape in places like the Durst Brothers Hops Ranch—an important component of Parker's "environment"—would be restructured through the good offices of CCIH so that workers could be healed and made content.[35]

In the meantime, however, militancy was growing not among Parker's minority, but among the workers themselves. Migratory workers, organized in part by the IWW, seemed to engage in an epidemic of strikes, sabotage, and union organizing throughout California (see Chapter 3), all of which signified to Parker the great depth of industrial psychosis infecting labor relations in the state:

The most notable inferiority compensation in industrial life is the strike. The strike has two prerequisites,—a satisfactory obsession in the labor mind, and a sufficient decay in the eyes of labor of the prestige of social norms, to allow the laborer to make those breaches of the law and conventional mores. . . . [As shown by Veblen and Totter], our strikes tend to reflect without serious modification both the psychic ill-health generated by the worker's existence, and the rapid decay of the respect and popularity of the law, the courts, property, and the rich man.[36]

Such was Dr. Parker's diagnosis of the ills that produced the Wheatland strike, and such were the conditions that CCIH set out to correct.

Progressive Engineering: From Science to the Technology of Liberatory Repression

Following Parker's diagnosis, CCIH implemented a program of environmental alteration designed to replace the spaces of production (and the reproduction of labor power) which balked instinct (and thus produced psychosis, strikes, and riots) with a landscape that would produce a psychic liberation and fulfillment, and which therefore protected the needs of industrialized farmers in California. Soon after completing its investigation of Wheatland, CCIH published its *Advisory Pamphlet on Camp Sanitation,* which consisted of a series of blueprints and budgets for the various components of "model" labor camps. The pamphlet was well received and republished numerous times. The Commission was explicit in its reasons for intervening in the production of labor camps. The widespread construction of proper labor camps would promote "an increase in the willingness and efficiency of labor." Bad camp conditions in the past have caused "petty strikes and a labor force continually quitting." By attending to the manner in which labor power was reproduced in the fields, CCIH proclaimed, farmers' profits could be safeguarded. The standardized labor camp plans developed by sanitary engineer J. J. Rosenthal, with the advice of a board of prominent public health authorities, stressed not only the public health component of proper and scientific camp management and construction, but also the economics of healthful camps. Good camps, properly constructed and maintained, eliminated the "'soldiering' of discontented workers." The construction of model camps was therefore a means of disciplining workers, replacing their tendency to rebel with a sense of satisfaction within the system as it existed.[37]

The plans for model migratory labor camps were quite precise. Camps were to be located on dry, well-drained ground, and tents or portable homes were to be "arranged in rows so that the area can be kept clean easily." Kitchens and other community service buildings were to be separated from living areas, as were stables, sheep pens, and manure piles. The Commission recommended that drinking water be "wholesome" and "absolutely free from organic contamination." Wells should thus be located away (and uphill) from cesspools and privy vaults. CCIH also specified the minimum cubic feet of space required for each person in a tent and window requirements for bunkhouses; and it suggested flooring tents whenever possible. Some of these recommendations were codified in the newly enacted Labor Camp Sanitation Act, but CCIH preferred to employ "friendly co-operation" and education rather than arresting recalcitrant farmers to achieve the goals of its labor camp program. In fact, CCIH made only one arrest for violation of the camp act out of all the camps it found that were "imminently dangerous to both the health and the decency of their working communities" before World War I. The manager of a camp owned by the Pacific Casualty Company in Colusa County was fined five dollars for operating an insanitary camp.[38]

The education program of CCIH consisted of frequent inspection tours, dissemination of standardized plans, development of model demonstration camps at state construction projects, assistance in labor camp construction, promotion of community camps in areas of small farms, and scale models of sanitary camp buildings constructed from CCIH blueprints. These last were designed to help farmers and other labor camp operators "further visualize the practicality of this work" of camp improvement. CCIH engineers and inspectors fanned out across the state, making public presentations and cajoling farmers to improve their camps, and the labor camp program quickly became the most important part of CCIH—and remained so until after 1919, when postwar conditions, a resurgent nativism, and the seeming quiescence of labor activism led to a gradual dismantling and bureaucratization of CCIH's functions.[39]

In 1914 and again in 1915, the IWW, incensed over the murder trials of Blackie Ford, Herman Suhr, and two others, and not at all convinced that the work of CCIH was attacking the root problems of the disturbance, threatened complete boycotts of the hops harvests. Both CCIH and its allied growers were clearly worried. Numerous hops growers in the Wheatland district signed up with CCIH to improve their camps in anticipation of the 1914 season, and through this interest, CCIH refined its technological interventions into the built environment of migratory labor. Of particular pride to CCIH were its technical advances in sanitary engineering. It pioneered, for example, new sanitary toilets, built to the specifications of the latest advances in environmental health, but still affordable to hops growers who operated camps only a few weeks each year.[40]

The hops growers (with the notable exception of the Dursts) and other rural industrial concerns responded enthusiastically. E. Clemmens Horst, owner of the largest hops company in the state (and a private petitioner to Governor Johnson requesting the total elimination of IWW "agitators" in the fields of California) wrote to CCIH about his experiences after creating a model camp on his property:

> There is no doubt in our minds but that the efficiency, health, and good spirit of ranch employees is considerably increased by the maintenance of model camps. From our experience we are convinced that it is a good investment on the part of the employer to maintain proper living conditions for the ranch laborers.[41]

This sentiment was echoed in the lumber districts (where many harvest workers also labored at various times of the year). A manager of the McCloud River Lumber Company wrote to the Commission that because of improved camp conditions, "we are able to maintain a steadier and higher grade type of men than where the camps are not sanitary." Improved camps seemed to be having just the effect that Parker thought they would: they were creating a more content, more psychically satisfied worker. Improvements in camp conditions seemed to minimize the need for more brutal forms of worker control.[42]

Revolutionizing the Landscape

So effective did CCIH view its experiment in environmental renovation that it declared in 1919 that it had "revolutionized" labor conditions in the state, and that in the five seasons since Wheatland "no serious labor disturbances have taken place in California." Publicly, CCIH claimed that this had been a quiet revolution, always receiving the fullest cooperation of industrialists throughout the state. Commission inspectors, CCIH claimed, "found little, if any, antagonism, some procrastination, and a great deal of good feeling and hearty cooperation" in their efforts to remake the migratory landscape. The records of the Commission, however, tell another story. Grower cooperation was only secured through an intensive campaign by CCIH and other Progressive organizations to rein in (and in fact to take over) the overwhelming power historically possessed by landowners in the face of relentless organizing and threats of rebellion by the IWW.[43]

Simon Lubin began the campaign by pressuring Horst, a man influential in the Progressive wing of the Republican Party, to cooperate with the inspectors and engineers of CCIH. Lubin explained to Horst that the goal of CCIH was to appeal to the consciences of individual growers throughout the state rather than take "legal action of any kind." When Horst agreed to allow his camp in Wheatland to be transformed from a typical filthy labor camp into a model for all hops growers, Lubin was elated. "Regardless of the sincerity of [Horst],

I take it that this experience alone is enough to justify the creation of our Commission." Moreover, Lubin felt that Horst's cooperation was precisely what was needed to "whip" the Hops Growers Association, an organization "which has the power to clean up the disreputable housing situation in this State, as far as that industry is concerned."[44]

Horst's cooperation, however, was not enough to placate labor relations in the field. Angered by Ford and Suhr's conviction by a Marysville jury in 1914, the IWW called for a statewide boycott of the hops industry. The IWW understood (in a way that, at least publicly, CCIH did not) that the Wheatland riot was not only about sanitation and housing conditions, but was rather the entry point to a wide-ranging struggle over the very economic and political conditions that both made the Durst ranch possible *and* sent Ford and Suhr to jail. The IWW thus linked its propaganda campaign against appalling work conditions to the support those conditions received in the California justice system. "The Politicians and the Kept Press," read one IWW flier distributed throughout California's agricultural districts during the 1914 harvest,

> are working overtime to make you believe that the Hop fields will be Heaven this year. *You Know Better.* They are trying to get you to SCAB on the Hop Pickers who refuse to pick until FORD and SUHR are free. . . . Carleton Parker's Commissioners are helping him to make Model Hops Picking Camps. Unless Ford and Suhr are free by August, let Carleton Parker and his commission pick the hops. [Original emphases][45]

Throughout the hops districts, stickers appeared listing the IWW demands for the 1914 season. Topping the list, of course, was the demand that Ford and Suhr be freed. The remaining demands resembled closely the very recommendations made by CCIH in its reports on Wheatland and in its *Advisory Pamphlet*: increased wages, no bonus system, free tents, plentiful clean water, and one toilet for every fifty workers.[46]

Many growers remained reluctant to face the new power relations that IWW militancy implied. Their camps were as good as any worker deserved, they reasoned, and agitation could be quelled by other, more direct, means. Representative of the recalcitrant growers was Ralph Durst. Upon publication of CCIH's investigation of the Wheatland affair, Durst organized a second riot investigation conducted by outraged growers and citizens of Yuba County. From the beginning CCIH was hostile to this investigation, feeling that it would only serve to invigorate the IWW, and redound against the growers themselves. Durst, in fact, "considered the conviction and sentencing of [Ford and Suhr] as a vindication of himself" and steadfastly denied that conditions on his ranch were a root cause of the riot.[47]

But with the IWW boycott threatening his harvest, Durst was persuaded by CCIH and other growers that it was in his economic interest to improve his camp, and indeed to ensure that his was the camp with the best conditions during the 1914 season. Reluctantly, Durst allowed CCIH engineers to transform the camp on his Wheatland property. Throughout this process, Ralph Durst proved to be a rather difficult grower to work with, and sent a steady stream of letters chastising Simon Lubin both for the work of the Commission and for Lubin's political views. Threats by the IWW were serious enough, however, that Ralph Durst allowed the improvements on his ranch to be completed by the opening of the 1914 hops season. Only a year after the fateful riot, the Durst ranch was transformed into the most outstanding of model camps (Figure 5)— an achievement CCIH pointed to repeatedly in propaganda aimed at a skeptical legislature as the Progressive star waned in the years after World War I.[48]

Progressive Repression: The Meaning of the Produced Landscape

The goal for CCIH in transforming the Durst ranch was the same as it was for their overall program of intervention in the landscape of extractive industries in the state. It sought to create what Foucault would have called "social enclosures": the closing off of certain forms of activity and behavior. CCIH's sponsorship of labor camp improvement had as its central goal the (re)establishment of "normalcy" in the fields of California, a normalcy that the Commission feared had been fully displaced by the deviant outburst at Wheatland. The sort of work that CCIH was engaged in was designed precisely to eliminate any cause of disorder exogenous to the individual worker. In Parker's view, by transforming the environment, a "new man" could be made, one no longer prone to violence, sabotage, striking, or other means of expressing his "inferiority." This is not to say, as we have seen, that Parker theorized a simple environmental determinism. Rather, one of the ideological roles of a landscape (understood both as place and as a way of seeing) is the "naturalization" of inequality, constraint, and appropriate behavior. In other words, representations of landscapes and the people who occupy them—such as those advanced by CCIH—are often meant, as Stephen Daniels claims, to reflect what is "natural" about the social world. Create landscapes that both reflect the natural social relations of a place *and* guide workers and others away from "deviant" behavior—and radicalism, revolution, and most forms of resistance would surely be eliminated.[49]

In this sense, CCIH was engaged in a program of "Progressive repression." Worker contentment—in other words, the Progressive elimination of the need to express inferiority through strikes or other ill-advised outbursts—became the primary target of the Commission. But "contentment" was not to be pro-

Figure 5. Housing at the Durst Brothers Hops Ranch in 1914 after the California Commission of Immigration and Housing had rebuilt the workers' camps. (Photo: California Commission of Immigration and Housing.)

duced by attacking the political economic structure of the California agricultural system. Rather, it was to be gained by tinkering with minor aspects of the "environment" in which workers toiled and lived. CCIH sought to make workers content by implementing a benevolent technology and the creation of psychically satisfying environments. Truly, the production of landscape is about the reproduction of power: the construction of model camps along the lines depicted in the *Advisory Pamphlet* represented the shifting of social struggle to a spatial terrain. Social conflagrations like Wheatland were really about environment—not politics, not economics, not power and powerlessness—and changes in the environment would inevitably solve the problems brought to light by the riot.

At the same time, the degree to which CCIH highlighted the spaces of agricultural production and reproduction is important. It illustrates the degree to which the material landscape serves as a crucible of competing social needs and desires contested under conditions of great inequality. The Commission sought to reconfigure both the crucible and its explosive contents by rendering unstable elements neutral, by muting powerful catalysts such as the IWW—all so the crucible itself could be maintained. Changes in the material landscape did indeed imply changes in social relations. The riot at Wheatland had made at least that much clear. In turn, changing social relations—the explosive (if still tenuous) power of the IWW, for example—demanded a reformation of the material landscape.

The changes in the minutia of labor camp environments during the years immediately following the Wheatland riot were not inconsequential. For the first time, specifications for bunkhouses, toilets, dining halls, and camp spatial arrangements were mandated by state law, and there was a state agency dedicated to improving camp conditions. But these efforts of CCIH in creating a landscape as a tool for the benevolent repression of "inferior" behavior were resisted every step of the way—by growers, certainly, but most particularly by the workers themselves, most of whom saw the strike at Wheatland as anything but an expression of deviance. If the landscape is a temporary stasis in struggles over power, if it is indeed an embodiment of power, then we can say that after Wheatland, the growth of state interest in labor relations in the fields of California reformed the landscape's morphology. But that does not mean that stasis was anything more than apparent, anything more than a contested representation of what the landscape *should* be by those who arrogate to themselves the "power to define" what is natural, what is right, what is proper; how social reproduction will proceed; and by what means surplus value will be produced.[50] By writing the words "true" and "natural" across the land, Carleton Parker, Simon Lubin, and CCIH (to say nothing of Ralph Durst or any number of other agricultural industrialists in the state who sought to stabilize the landscape by defining it in their own preferred image) were working against a resurgent, and quite subversive, militancy among migratory workers. As the next chapter shows, these workers were not willing to accept either the CCIH or agribusiness definition of workers' place in the landscape.

3 / Subversive Mobility and the Re-formation of Landscape

Its public pronouncements to the contrary, the California Commission of Immigration and Housing (CCIH) did not put all its faith in the "spatial fix" of environmental change. Rather, it sought also to rationalize the very mobility of labor that made California agriculture possible. The Commission understood—indeed, like numerous government agencies after it, took for granted—that a highly mobile labor force was essential to the rural industries of the state (not just agriculture, but also mining, lumbering, and construction). But Wheatland had shown that the migratory system had grown irrational, that the huge number of migratory workers was becoming dangerous to the development of the state itself. Migratory workers—usually referred to in popular accounts as "tramps" and "hobos"—had attracted national and statewide attention in the past. But with Wheatland and the subsequent threats of the Industrial Workers of the World (IWW), coupled with the growth of mass political movements of migratory and other poor workers such as Kelly's Army in San Francisco, the problem of the mobility gained a new urgency.[1]

Mobility of labor had been entrenched in the California system of agriculture almost from the start. Both the creation of huge landholdings in the early American period and the intensification of agriculture after 1880 had created an agricultural landscape of both stunning monotony—in which holdings of several hundred thousand acres were not unusual and in which whole districts were given over to a single crop—and stunning diversity—where up and down the state crops matured at different times and demanded a short burst of highly intensive work to gather oranges or lettuce or grapes before the crops rotted.[2]

By the beginning of the twentieth century, the template was set. One hundred and fifty thousand or so *temporary* agricultural workers were needed somewhere in the state during the peak season. During a given year, farm industries might employ some 200,000 individuals. Labor turnover was surprisingly rapid. In 1915, monthly turnover ranged from 9.1 percent in the hops camps to 50.1 percent in the general ranch camps. However, these were figures for the whole year; at peak season, turnover was considerably higher than it was at other times of the year. Hops ranches, for example, employed a small number of employees year-round who were relatively well paid and well treated. Turnover among these employees was very low. By contrast, during the harvest, vast armies of temporary workers were recruited, paid as little as possible, and, as we have seen, housed in appalling conditions. Turnover during harvest was great. A 1915 CCIH study showed that 29 percent of male migratory laborers had left their last job "because work gave out." Average jobs for "casual laborer" in the state's harvest lasted only seven days. In orchard work, the average was perhaps ten days. When men could get jobs in canneries (this work was often reserved for women) they might work as long as thirty days.[3]

California agriculture *demanded* a labor supply thus structured. The intensification of production that occurred with the bust of the world wheat market in the 1880s brought with it high capitalization costs. To bring a ten-acre orange grove to maturity in the Los Angeles area cost some $230 per acre in 1885. A 2,000-acre farm therefore cost $460,000 before crops became viable. By 1912, 2,000 acres of oranges cost $778,000 to bring to maturity. Deciduous orchards were nearly as expensive. To compete in eastern and overseas markets, therefore, such a capital-intensive agriculture demanded a concomitantly cheap labor. Large-scale, capital-intensive farming simply could not rely only on family labor: crops would rot before they could all be picked. Nor could it rely exclusively on a local pool of labor for such temporary work. In that case local farmers would have to pay the *yearly* reproductive costs of their workers (and their families) out of *seasonal* profits. As labor economist Varden Fuller put it, California agriculture was capitalized precisely on the assumption of cheap, abundant, and temporary labor. Any other form of labor would threaten the profitability of the system.[4]

The Problem with Mobility

Even before the intensification of California agriculture that began in the 1880s, commentators on the California scene noted the large armies of migratory labor that moved through the state. Henry George pointed to them in 1871:

And all over our ill-kept, shadeless, dusty roads, where a house is an unwonted landmark, and which run frequently for miles through the same man's land, plod the tramps, with blankets on back, the laborers of the California farm, looking for work, in its season, or toiling back to the city when the plowing is ended or the wheat crop is gathered.[5]

Migratory labor often seemed invisible to the population of California as a whole. Once it burst into visibility, however, it was hard *not* to notice. As Carey McWilliams wrote much later:

One can travel the length of the San Joaquin Valley, at the height of the season, on the main highway without being aware of the fact that tens of thousands of migrant workers, an army of 200,000, are somewhere camped, somewhere at work. But, once you know that this curious "hidden" world exists, you are forever conscious of it and your eyes seek out the evidence that this phantom army is there, in the vineyards and orchards, in the camps and shacktowns.[6]

Agricultural labor power in California was quintessentially a commodity. Who embodied it was always less important than the fact that it materialized at appropriate places and appropriate times, and at the appropriate price, to make sure the crops were harvested. Historian Cletus Daniel summarized the facts of labor mobility this way:

By the twentieth century, employment in California's large-scale agriculture had come to mean irregular work, constant movement, low wages, squalid working and living conditions, social isolation, emotional deprivation, and individual powerlessness so profound as to make occupational advancement a virtual impossibility.[7]

Yet this mobility was a double-edged sword, both for the workers themselves and for agribusiness. By dint of their mobility, many agricultural workers remained individually invisible to the powers of exploitation and domination. As Matthew Hannah has explained, modern power demands a fixity in place, so that each individual can be catalogued and accounted for. Surveillance in the modern world is predicated on fixing individuals to specific "addresses," making them accountable for specific spaces. Uncontrolled, constant mobility removes people from the policing gaze of the state (or other powerful interests), making the job of control that much more difficult. With the high degree of mobility that was demanded of agricultural labor, it was quite difficult to pinpoint culpability for any particular action (especially crime) that may have been committed by a worker. The sensational, wild response of both public and private police forces to the riot at Wheatland illustrated this point well to CCIH, and the Commission understood that one of its most important functions in reconfiguring labor camps in the state was to rationalize mobility so that individual workers could become more visible and accountable to structures of power. As will become clear, this understanding led the Commission away from a singular focus on labor camp improvement and toward a greater and greater reliance on undercover work among migratory workers and their organizations.[8]

On the other hand, the problem for the IWW during the years after Wheatland was to maintain workers' individual invisibility, understanding this to be a real source of power, even as they sought to make their common struggle ever more visible. High rates of migrancy were thus both oppressive and potentially oppositional. The IWW quickly found that the anonymity afforded by mobility could be put to productive use.

Patterns of Mobility

Migratory labor streams were not confined to the agricultural valleys of California. Migrant workers—especially single male migratory workers[9]—traveled extensive distances in search of work, following ripening crops, shifting to lumbering, drifting into manufacturing for a time, obtaining work in emergency railroad repair crews, and often traveling across the breadth of the trans-Mississippi west each year (Figure 6). Indeed, in 1915 some 21 percent of male workers surveyed by CCIH had held their last job in a state other than California, and 67 percent considered themselves permanent "floaters" who had abandoned the idea of steady work. The complexity of the patterns established by migratory workers, and the degree to which workers switched between types of employment, is made clear in records kept by the Military Intelligence Division (MID) of the United States Army during its program of World War I domestic espionage.[10]

Robert Blaine was typical of the male workers questioned by MID. Born in Arklow, Ireland, Blaine moved to San Francisco with his family in 1892 and started his first employment in 1900 as a sailor's apprentice in the English Merchant Marine. He returned to California in 1913 and worked as an itinerant laborer in the agricultural fields until 1915. From January to May, 1915, Blaine tramped his way from San Francisco to Charles City, Iowa, where he was an apprentice in a munitions factory for a month. Next he followed crops to Ellendale, North Dakota, where a series of temporary jobs were found for most of the summer. In the fall, he moved on to Minnesota, returning to Algona, Iowa, around April 1, 1916. Blaine worked two months as a hod carrier for "a partnership consisting of an Irishman and a Swede" before moving on to work the harvests in Minnesota and North Dakota. After the harvest, he worked in the stockyards at Sioux

Figure 6. A male migratory worker in the Napa Valley photographed by Dorothea Lange in 1938. On the back of the copy of the photo in the Bancroft Library's Farm Security Administration collection is this notation: "More than 25 years a bindle stiff. Walks from the mines to the lumber camps to the farms. The type that formed the backbone of the I.W.W. in California before [the First World] war. Subject of Carleton Parker's 'Studies on the I.W.W.'" (Courtesy, Bancroft Library.)

City, Iowa, for five weeks. At the end of that stint, Blaine's tramping took him to Milwaukee, Chicago, Rock Island, Kansas City, and eventually Los Angeles. After arriving in California, he worked for six weeks as an irrigator "for an unknown banker" until his foot was smashed as he attempted to cross the Southern Pacific Railroad tracks. Blaine was confined in the Los Angeles County Hospital until after August 1, 1917, but could not work until October.

When he resumed working, Blaine took a job with the state of California as a water-truck driver for about three weeks before moving on to Turlock, where he obtained a job as a teamster for an ice and fuel dealer. Radicalized by his life on the road, Blaine left Turlock for Exeter to work "a week as all around flunky for

I.W.W. camp" (as the MID records put it). Next he picked oranges in Porterville, and then moved on to Sacramento. He was arrested by federal agents "the day of the raid on the I.W.W. headquarters voluntarily appearing, giving himself up." Like all the other men arrested and interrogated at this time, Robert Blaine had never been married.[11]

Such a migratory pattern was quite typical of single male—and many married, male, and both single and married female—workers at this time. Work for migratory laborers was often interspersed with periods of unemployment, and life on the road could be mean indeed. For many workers, however, the years immediately preceding World War I saw a renaissance of power and radical agency, organized in part through the political, economic, and perhaps especially the social initiatives of the IWW and its migratory agricultural labor branch, the Agricultural Workers Organization (AWO). IWW and AWO union halls throughout the west became places of refuge and learning for migratory workers. If migratory life was generally defined by squalid conditions and a seemingly utter lack of power, by the constant pressure to take to the road in search of menial and demeaning labor, then the IWW halls served as a powerful counterbalance in the lives of many migratory workers. One of the primary functions of the IWW hall in each town was to provide a place for learning, for elevation of the mind and means *in spite* of the level to which industrial society sought to drag migratory workers. Through all the sectarian struggles that defined and undermined the IWW after its formation in 1905, one goal always remained paramount: the educating of people to act in their own (collective) economic and political interest.[12]

To this end, Wobblies, and especially western migratory Wobblies, *read*. They debated and they argued. They studied economics and politics. "The typical hall, especially in the West," according to Philip Foner, "usually contained dog-eared copies of Marx, Darwin, Spenser, Voltaire, Tom Paine, Jack London and a wide variety of government documents." Despite his theories of inferiority, and despite his more general distaste for the economic and political ideals of the Wobblies, Carleton Parker grudgingly admired the intellectual culture of the IWW movement. "Presumably they were better acquainted with American social statistics than the academic class," he wrote. And a historian of the IWW in the Pacific Northwest has written:

> Entering a hall in the evening one might see several shabbily dressed young men reading from books taken from the shelves of the library in the room. Others crouched over a makeshift stove brewing a mulligan stew, its ambitious odor permeating the hall. While they tended supper, they argued some point in economics or religion.[13]

For migratory workers, class interests were welded together in the fields, mines, and factories, *and* in the IWW halls and hobo jungles of the American West. The education of the migratory worker was designed both to radicalize and to liberate—but this was a liberty quite different from (and radically opposed to) the psychic liberation that Parker theorized. It was not designed to placate.

Wobblies were often eloquent in their sense of the injustice they were constantly forced to endure:

> You asked why the I.W.W. is not patriotic to the United States. If you were a bum without a blanket; if you had left your wife and kids when you went West for a job, and haven't located them since; if you slept in a lousy, sour bunk-house, and ate food just as rotten as they could give you and get away with it; if deputy sheriffs shot your cooking cans full of holes and spilled your grub on the ground; if your wages were lowered on you when the bosses thought they had you down; if there was one law for Ford, Suhr and Mooney, and another one for Harry Thew; if every person who represented law and order in the nation beat you up, railroaded you to jail, and the good Christian people cheered and told them to go to it; how the hell do you expect a man to be patriotic?[14]

Not just patriotism, but loyalty to any aspect of the bourgeois construction of America was difficult for many Wobblies and other migratory workers. They were an outcaste, and they were almost uniformly despised. They were seen as beggars, mental inferiors, habitual drunks, and lousy workers. By these descriptions, migratory workers were at once erased from view as real, corporeal, thinking humans, and transformed into caricatures, mere pictures of themselves, who deserved no better than to become the drones of an industrial society.

In a society so ruthless in its depiction of migratory workers, justice meant nothing to Wobblies so much as its inverse. If society judged an action as unjust, immoral, or simply wrong, then, for many migratory workers, it became a goal to be achieved, a tool in the cause of justice. If the law was not meant for them, they were not meant for the law. Sabotage, strikes, and revolutionary propaganda, therefore, became sensible and effective weapons in the class war into which workers had been thrust. Issues of "greater good" ruled action. Reading and debating in union halls provided much of the ideological ammunition for this view of the world, but it was through mobility itself that these actions were promoted and made effective.

Mobile Subversion

Mobility cut both ways: it pauperized and it radicalized. The doctrines and ideologies of the IWW (at their best and certainly not always) were designed to reach into and energize seemingly "spontaneous" incipient revolts (like

Wheatland) all across the country. "The iww can work this way because it is not really an organization," Wobbly Arno Dorsch declared. "It is a revolution. . . . It breaks out here and there, where industrial conditions are the worst. That is the secret of iww success. Anyone can understand it. Our purpose is simple. We refuse to continue as slaves." ccih agreed. It found in its investigations that the iww sought not just control of the workplace. The iww seemed intent on expanding unionism into something like a social movement designed to create a set of oppositional cultural forms out of which would be developed a (material, social) space separate from, yet connected in opposition to, the spaces that provide the foundation for industrial capitalism. As the iww declared in the preamble to its constitution, its goal was to create a whole new world "out of the shell of the old."[15]

To achieve this goal, the iww relied largely on "wildcat" strikes called with very little notice, and bolstered by unemployed migrants rushing to the site of the disturbance. For Wobblies, mobility itself became a tool of class warfare. Such strikes, and the subversive mobility that attended them, particularly threatened agribusiness concerns that relied on large pools of temporary labor at critical times throughout the season. While declaring their goal to be the destruction of capitalism, the iww more often engaged in strikes over basic "bread-and-butter" issues—wages, for example, or better housing conditions at a labor camp. Even though the iww often failed to meet even its most basic short-term goals in many of its wildcat strikes, the Wobbly methods of "mobilizing mobility" had profound effects on the nature of industrialized capitalism. As Henri Lefebvre has put the matter more generally, the ability to mobilize new spaces and new spatial patterns—in other words, the ability to create counterspaces in opposition to the domineering power of the capitalist political economy (like union halls and hobo jungles)—"shakes the existing space to its foundations, along with its strategies and aims—namely the imposition of homogeneity and transparency" through which the reproduction of capitalism is ordered.[16]

This was precisely the problem Carleton Parker identified in his studies of Wheatland and the migratory labor system more generally. In a widely read article on the iww, Parker spelled out the threat that the iww presented to settled society:

> This tenacity of life is due to the fact that the I.W.W. not only is incapable of legal death, but has in fact no formal politico-legal existence. Its treasury is merely the momentary accumulation of strike funds. Its numerous locals are the result of the energy of local secretaries. They are not places for the executive direction of

the union so much as gregarious centres where the lodging-house inhabitant or the hobo with his blanket can find a light, a stove, and companionship.[17]

The threat that the IWW posed in the fields of California was precisely that it was spatially diffuse, that it spread invisibly, unaccountably, across the landscape. It was not so much a union as a *movement,* in both senses of that word.

Worker movements, as David Harvey notes, have often been adept at controlling the politics and social relations of particular *places.* Less have they shown the ability to control *space* in the more abstract (but no less concrete) sense. Command over the spaces of production and reproduction of the political economy have been much more the province of the state and capital. As such, various place-based workers' movements have been hampered in their ability to forge connections across capital-controlled spaces. Harvey suggests a "simple rule": "those who command space can always control the politics of place even though . . . it takes control of some place to command space in the first instance." By mobilizing mobility, the IWW sought precisely to take command of space. The mobility of militant labor provided the pathways for connecting sundry place-based struggles, but it also did more. It took hold of the established spatial practices of industrialized agriculture and other resource-based industries in western North America and utilized them for its own purposes. Here lay the very subversiveness of mobility. By connecting place-based struggles, migratory workers were able to transcend the spaces and places of their oppression; they were able—at least potentially—to rattle the patterns that underlay capitalist productivity. In this sense, mobility was both necessary and subversive to the aims and desires of capital and the state.[18]

Mobility, Free Speech, and the Class Struggle

Forced mobility of labor created a moral economy among migratory workers that, like the mere fact of mobility, was potentially subversive to the interests of more settled society. If migratory workers were mostly invisible, illegitimate, or simply taken for granted (at times when they were not radically militant), then this structuring helped to turn the destitution of life on the road in on itself. Migratory workers were forced to look to themselves, rather than to the state or private philanthropy, to develop effective means for coping with (and perhaps transforming) the structures of their oppression. For most migratory workers, the conditions of labor showed that work itself held little value except as a means to gain enough cash to survive another few days. Once workers had made this, they often left their jobs, content to survive as long as possible on the "stake" they had accumulated, and perhaps on meals and lodging provided by charity, returning to work when their funds were exhausted. Such a pattern hardly made for a disciplined workforce.

In hobo jungles and flophouses, the stake was considered, at least in part, communal property. Migratory workers expected each other to share what they had to tide over those who had nothing. The moral calculus of the hobo jungle thus promoted a certain solidarity. In this manner the marginalizing processes of capitalist extractive industries were turned on their heads by migratory workers: marginal workers owed nothing to the economic and political systems through which they were exploited but from which they had been formally excluded. Rather, there was an economic, political, and moral allegiance that workers owed to each other—even if this allegiance was frequently breached in practice.[19]

Wobblies in the western United States built on the solidarity constructed in these "alternative spaces," most spectacularly in a series of "free speech" fights engaged in the city streets where casual laborers gathered between their jobs in the fields, forests, or mines. In California, the first significant activities of the IWW among migratory agricultural workers occurred with the Fresno Free Speech struggle of 1909. Fresno was a central gathering point not only for agricultural labor, but also for workers seeking employment in construction, mining, and lumbering camps in the Sierras. Wobblies had established a small local and engaged in a program of street speaking and canvassing in the flophouses and "jungles" of the city. The organizing campaign met with "unexpected success," and within a few months Mexican Santa Fe Railroad workers and a fair number of farmworkers had been organized. Realizing that the growing power of casual labor in his city threatened local agricultural concerns as well as Santa Fe, the Fresno chief of police revoked permission for Wobblies to speak in the streets, undermining the IWW's ability to organize. The IWW responded by defying the ban.[20]

Responding to a call for help in defying the order of the chief of police, hundreds, and perhaps thousands, of footloose workers rushed to the scene from all over the west to speak in the streets as their comrades were arrested. Many of these workers had experience in free speech battles in other cities, and brought with them experience both in street speaking and in persevering in the face of withering police brutality. The Fresno fight was thus connected to battles elsewhere that had gone before it, and would likewise be connected to later struggles (such as those in San Diego, Denver, Spokane, and Kansas City) through the mobility of radicalized workers.[21]

The right to speak in the street was understood by Wobblies to be essential to their organizing abilities. The ban on street speaking (which did not extend to the Salvation Army), coming as it did in the midst of the harvest season, severely restricted the IWW's access to migratory workers. "If we had the streets so we could get the workers we would build up a good fighting organization," Fresno organizer and future IWW martyr Frank Little declared.[22] And control of the streets was precisely the issue:

> For Wobblies free-speech fights involved nothing so abstract as defending the Constitution, preserving the Bill of Rights, or protecting the civil liberties of American citizens. They were instigated primarily to overcome the resistance to IWW organizing tactics and also to demonstrate that America's dispossessed could, through direct action, challenge established authority.[23]

Control over the space of the streets was thus important, but so was control over the larger spaces of industrialized capitalism within which those streets were placed.

Through its free speech battles, the IWW was able to show workers that they possessed certain rights, and that capital and the state would do what they could to assure that workers did not exercise those rights because doing so would fundamentally threaten the established political and economic order. The exercise of free speech was thus an act of quite basic resistance, and it showed to Wobblies that they could take possession of the streets even if they could not yet take possession of the means of production. It likewise showed to migratory workers that their ability to travel quickly from one social conflagration to the next was itself a source of power; it was a means of subverting the overwhelming power of orderly production and reproduction. Free speech, as always, was about carving out and commanding space: about commanding the space to resist.[24]

Eventually, hundreds of Wobblies in Fresno were jailed, beaten, fire-hosed, and subjected to vigilante attacks organized by the mayor. As in other free speech fights around the west, however, the sheer cost of jailing and feeding arrested workers (who upon release invited rearrest by immediately climbing back up on the soapbox) proved too great, and the city capitulated to the demand by Wobblies that they be allowed to speak unmolested on the streets. In all, the IWW spent less than one thousand dollars on the struggle. Nonetheless, the benefits to the IWW, at least in terms of what organizer George Speed called "education," were immeasurable. Wobblies quickly gained respect among migratory workers for their tenacity in the face of oppression (a valuable commodity, considering the conditions migratory workers daily faced), and for their willingness to fight to the end for what they knew was right.[25]

Organizing Mobility

Wobblies were well aware of the subversive potential of mobility. "Nowhere else can a section of the working class be found so admirably fitted to serve as the scouts and advanced guards of the labor army. Rather, they may become the guerillas of the revolution—the *franc tireurs* of the class struggle," argued one Wobbly theorist.[26] The evident revolutionary potential of the free speech fights and events such as Wheatland and the subsequent campaign for the release of Ford and Suhr provided the impetus for the formation of the IWW's Agricultural Workers Organization No. 400 (the number was chosen to mock "the 400" of New York society), whose express purpose was to organize this labor infantry both for revolutionary long-term goals and to win gains on more immediate "bread-and-butter" agendas. Melvyn Dubofsky attributed the success of the AWO among migratory workers to its willingness to engage, over the long haul, in the hard work of organization. Moreover, the AWO "offered the migratories what they most needed: protection on the freights they rode and in the hobo jungles they called home; higher wages and better treatment on the job; and in IWW headquarters, a place to meet friends, lounge, rest and even read while in town between jobs."[27]

The primary centers of the AWO were the upper Midwest and the Pacific Northwest, but by December 1915, it had established an important and lasting California local centered in Sacramento. Historians of California farmworkers have maintained that the AWO held minimal influence in California, due to local Wobbly hostility to the growing influence of Midwest organizers, and due to the California local's inability to avoid "localism and sectarianism."[28] But this charge ignores the importance that worker mobility played in connecting and strengthening struggles throughout the west. Existing records indicate that a good percentage of male California workers in the pre–World War I years *also* worked in agriculture east of the Rockies while the AWO existed. Many of the most radical workers arrested in California in 1917 traced their IWW membership to locals in North and South Dakota, Kansas, and Minnesota—precisely the states in which the AWO was having the greatest impact. Still other workers traced their IWW membership to the Pacific Northwest, where both AWO and other IWW organizations were quite active.[29]

In California, one of the most important innovations of IWW and AWO organizers was making organization itself mobile. Other unions before them had attempted to organize the harvest workers, but their attempts were usually limited to opening a hall in a harvest town or a nearby big city. Soon after Wheatland, changes in the IWW union structure allowed for the establishment

of "camp delegates" who were given authority to organize on the job, no matter how small that job was, and to open a local that existed on the job itself.
"The camp or job delegates literally carried a union local under their hats" and
organized resistance when and where they saw conditions that warranted it.
These delegates carried with them an important sense of solidarity and militancy right to the place of employment. Delegates thus organized workers
wherever they were found rather than merely following the traditional practice
of organizing against particular firms and jobs. If a job gave out, or if a worker
left a job, that did not imply the end of organizing. The local was no longer
simply local. It was instead a means of spreading power across expansive spaces.[30]

The mystery to urban-based middle classes and reformers of growing
Wobbly power after Wheatland was only deepened when the IWW made its
organization mobile in this manner. The IWW was a union quite unlike the
rather conservative trade unions Californians had been used to. An investigator
for CCIH wrote:

> The extent and activity of this organization's workings are almost beyond belief.
> One sees the notices everywhere. You hear the "Wobblies" spoken of favorably
> in "jungle" conversations. There is widespread knowledge of and interest in its
> doings that is of far more than passing importance in any consideration of the
> problems connected with this organization.[31]

Yet as late as a year after Wheatland, CCIH had little idea of who comprised the
IWW in California or where its power was centered. At least to the eyes of CCIH
inspectors, individual Wobblies seemed to be literally nowhere. Yet they also
seemed to be everywhere. And it was unclear even how many IWWs there
were—though perhaps that did not matter too much. In 1915, there were
probably fewer than 5,000 paid-up members of the union. But as organizer
George Speed claimed, "The sentiment of the great bulk and the great number
of migratory workers is strongly with the IWW." Here, too, CCIH agreed with its
radical adversaries.[32]

Sabotage: Mobility as Strategy

As worrying to CCIH as the growing influence of the IWW was, even more so was
what seemed to be a growth in the use of sabotage in industrial relations
throughout the state. Investigators for the Commission early felt there was a
good deal of evidence linking an IWW conspiracy to many fires and other acts of
destruction in the farming districts of the state. The IWW did nothing to allay
these fears, even if it was a bit coy at times. "Don't Forget Ford and Suhr on the
Job," an influential Wobbly reminded his colleagues. "As Long as Ford and

Suhr Are in Prison, Don't Stick Copper Nails or Tacks in Fruit Trees or Grape Vines. It Hurts Them." Friendly advice such as this was effective only if those who acted upon it could remain anonymous and could disappear when they were done with their deeds.[33]

Threats of sabotage, enhanced by the anonymity that mobility provided, were quickly adopted as a means of struggle by Wobblies after Wheatland. In 1914, picket lines around the hops fields had been somewhat successful in encouraging reform from CCIH, attention from growers, and a reconsideration by the governor of the "justice" meted out to Ford and Suhr. But they were also difficult and expensive to maintain, staffed as they were by workers who were usually desperately poor. The 1914 pickets had also called forth a posse of gunmen hired by the Durst-organized Farmers' Protective League. In 1915, the Dursts, Horst, and other hops ranchers affirmed their intention to rehire this private army at the cost of $10,000 per grower. The IWW, therefore, changed tactics in 1915, emphasizing sabotage and the subversion of mobility. IWW-organized and influenced workers knew that they could not beat the farmers at their own violent game. Organizers thus recommended that individual workers "depend on their own individual action to make every kick count," as Sacramento organizer Charles Lambert put it.[34]

This new strategy worried CCIH, which now sought to undermine worker resistance not just to protect industrialized agriculture, but also to protect the Commission's own investment in labor camp improvement. Ralph Durst was similarly concerned. At Durst's request, George Bell, who had recently replaced Carleton Parker as executive secretary of CCIH, ordered camp inspector J. R. Murrison to work undercover at Wheatland during the August harvest. Simultaneously, special investigator F. J. Cunningham was asked to "drift around to the IWW local in Sacramento and get acquainted with this man Lambert. The Governor feels he is very influential in this year's movement." Even with Governor Johnson considering Ford and Suhr's pardon appeal, the Wobblies resolved to step up the war against the hops growers. "It is no use appealing to the master's sense of justice," Lambert wrote to Ford, "for he hasn't got any, the only thing left is action on the pocket book, he has got a considerable dose of this but he seems to want more."[35]

Making "every kick count" implied maximizing the power of each worker to effect change in at least some small part of the productive system, and workers seemed eager to do just that. Sabotage was the key. Officially, the IWW was coy about the practice and efficacy of sabotage, usually defining it simply as the withdrawal of efficiency. The IWW newspaper *Solidarity*, for example, printed the advice of one California worker that farmhands should "give attention to the case of Ford and Suhr" for a quarter of every hour on the job. The first official endorsement of sabotage had come at the 1914 iww convention, but even here the iww simply made it a policy that "All rush work be done in a wrong manner." But with individual invisibility wrought by migrancy, many Wobblies found sabotage of a more incisive variety quite efficacious. More importantly, Wobblies in California found that just the simple threat of sabotage, coupled with the state's inability to observe all workers simultaneously (since each was as potentially dangerous as the other), was enough to panic growers and reformers alike.[36]

By September 1915, ccih was convinced that the iww was behind a well-orchestrated campaign of arson, and that the campaign reached beyond California and "extended throughout the Pacific Coast States." By this time, ccih had retained the Pinkerton Detective Agency to assist in rounding up suspected saboteurs and to report on the doings of numerous subversive workers. The Pinkertons managed to place an agent, "No. 168," in a position of confidence with prominent Wobbly organizer George Speed, and this agent felt that most of the incendiary activity during the summer had been orchestrated by two men—Williams and Armstrong—who used a certain McGill "as a tool" in their campaign. McGill eventually confessed (four times, each elaborating and contradicting the others) to having set fires in the Stockton area. He claimed "the iww are directing the whole campaign of incendiarism." Unfortunately, McGill was unable "to furnish anything definite in the way of clues" that ccih could follow to break the arson conspiracy. Moreover, at the beginning of October, Pinkerton agents were having difficulty tracing Armstrong and Williams, and suggested to the governor the need for more "inside" work. ccih executive secretary George Bell reminded Lubin that the Commission "already ha[s] such a man" working inside the iww, and the Commission could therefore "save the governor some money."[37]

The inside work never produced Williams, Armstrong, or any other "smoking gun," but it did produce some highly spectacular and speculative reports. ccih investigators, like the Pinkertons, with whom they sometimes cooperated, became adept at finding an iww conspiracy behind every suspicious event. One investigator filed this report upon arrival in Turlock, where he found a grape juice factory ablaze:

> The whole plant was destroyed. It is the opinion of everyone here that the fire was started by incendiary as it began simultaneously in different parts of the warehouse and got to such a quick start that the fire department was unable to stop it. Sunday night another large warehouse . . . was destroyed by fire. . . . I found that there is a noted iww agitator from Sacramento here in Turlock and he is doing a

good deal of talking. . . . There is also another well-known "wobbly" in town, and a great number of tough characters are camping in the jungles nearby.[38]

Reports such as these allowed CCIH and the governor to increase their anti-IWW propaganda in the name of orderly labor relations. Early in September 1915, Governor Johnson publicly identified the IWW with a pattern of arson in the state, and CCIH developed the groundwork for a plan of outright IWW suppression.[39]

Despite these investigations, and despite parallel investigations by the federal Department of Justice at this time, no direct, indictable offense on the part of any Wobbly was ever detected. Nonetheless, the hysteria encouraged by official focus on suspicious fires provided Governor Johnson with the rationale he was looking for to deny a pardon to Ford and Suhr and still remain legitimate in the eyes of his urban labor constituency. By demonizing the IWW as lawless saboteurs, CCIH and the governor were able, at least partially, to delegitimize the aims and desires of the poorest workers in the state. Paul Scharrenberg, secretary of the California State Federation of Labor and a CCIH commissioner, ratified the governor's action. Scharrenberg wrote in the *Coast Seaman's Journal* that it "is better to have two innocent men in jail and suffer the fate of martyrs, for the time at least, than to submit to the rule of the torch." Not for the last time, as we will see in Chapter 7, even the limited subversive power of marginalized migratory workers was becoming too much for the respectable labor hierarchy.[40]

The Return of the Repressors: CCIH and the Federal Repression of Radicals

The IWW's threat of sabotage was at least partially effective during the summer of 1915. E. Clemmens Horst and one of the original Wheatland prosecutors each testified at a special pardon hearing in favor of the release of all remaining Wheatland prisoners. But the threat of sabotage also led CCIH's camp improvement program to be quickly overshadowed by its involvement in labor espionage aimed both at uncovering the source of sabotage conspiracies and finding a means to make migratory workers visible to the eye of power. The CCIH espionage program had started innocently enough: Carleton Parker had sent several of his students into the fields masquerading as "hobos" the previous summer to gather information on the patterns, lifestyles, conditions, and customs of migratory workers. Parker reasoned that the only way to uncover this information was by making his agents as mobile as the workers were. The value of such a program quickly became obvious. By tracking individual workers as they faded from the sight of employers, CCIH was able to keep tabs on militancy and radicalism, and was able to use that information to circumvent planned or rumored strikes and acts of sabotage.[41]

Planning Repression

Many in California saw IWW militancy as more than just a local phenomenon geared toward transforming California agricultural relations. It was seen rather as part of a larger "conspiracy" to overthrow the California and United States governments designed by national IWW leaders (and perhaps funded by German money). Striking in the fields was represented by growers, by much of the press, and certainly by CCIH during these years as not only radical, but also un-American. Reacting to pressure from California growers, and responding to this climate of fear, Governor Johnson asked CCIH to discover the sources and nature of this "conspiracy" menacing California and the nation. By the summer of 1915, in the words of the historian of CCIH, the "entire camp inspectional staff was . . . engaged in labor espionage in conjunction with its inspectional tours." Indeed, for CCIH the logic of labor camp improvement was turned upside down. No longer would environmental change make agriculture safe from radicalism. Rather, improvement itself was understood to be impossible without the simultaneous repression of "agitators." Progressive science was supplanted by Progressive repression.[42]

George Bell removed inspectors Paul Brissenden and Paul Elliel from the Commission in 1915 to ensure room in the budget for Frederick Mills, who had proven his abilities as a hobo-spy, and J. Vance Thompson, the notorious once and future editor of Paul Scharrenberg's *Coast Seaman's Journal* and the president of the Alaska Fisherman's Union. Thompson was made point man in CCIH's IWW espionage program. Quite happy to exaggerate the threat posed by militant workers, Thompson, like many of the other CCIH labor spies, saw in the pauperized army of migratory labor a revolutionary cabal of dangerous proportions.[43]

Though the federal government had determined in 1915 that there was not enough evidence of an IWW conspiracy to warrant action, CCIH was able to renew the federal government's interest in the IWW as the involvement of the United States in World War I deepened in 1916 and 1917. With the United States' entrance into the war in the spring of 1917 and with the subsequent institution of conscription, the farm labor supply in reality, but even more in perception, began to shrink. The IWW continually sought to exploit this situation. In response, California farmers declared that patriotism demanded increased food production, and that willing labor was critically needed to meet new production demands. The state and federal government, growers argued, therefore had an obligation to smash the union.

In March 1917, just before the United States declared war, J. Vance Thompson reported to George Bell that informants had told them that an orchestrated program of incendiarism had succeeded in causing $3 million in damage in Kansas alone during the 1916 harvest. The plan for 1917, Thompson reported, included expanding the fire program to California, Washington, Montana, and throughout the Midwest. Concurrently, "missionaries from Puget Sound" were arriving in San Francisco not only intent on gaining control of the harvest fields, but also on destabilizing Thompson's control of the Alaska Fisherman's Union. Throughout the spring, Thompson continued to report on the growing strength of the IWW in California. In Fresno, the IWW had "become quite active" by the end of May. In Stockton, "a street speaking campaign is on in full swing and sabotage is openly advocated; although merely described as the withdrawal of efficiency." And the menace of the IWW, Thompson felt, was growing increasingly subtle: "There is much organizational work going on and there is more money amongst the migratory workers. They are becoming more prosperous to all outward appearances and more conservative to the public eye," and they thus needed even closer surveillance.[44]

The "more conservative" appearance of migratory workers that Thompson found did not stop them from striking the orange harvest in Riverside County in April 1917. The strike was broken only after a local judge issued an order restraining all picketing. And in June, workers in the cantaloupe fields near Turlock also struck, again with the IWW playing a leading role. For farmers, these actions were evidence of the IWW's subversive and unpatriotic nature, and they proved the danger associated with a possible labor shortage. They placed the blame for farmworkers' increased willingness to strike squarely at the feet of the IWW. For Thompson, these activities inevitably implied complicity with German money and interests—a view he held in common with many "patriotic" Americans as war fervor increased. In spite of protests by Wobblies that life under the Kaiser would be, if anything, worse for the toilers of the world, Thompson declared on June 18, 1917, "the I.W.W.s . . . are giving aid and comfort to enemy interests, and for the welfare of our country some means must be found that will put an end to this situation."[45]

The next day, George Bell codified a plan to eliminate the IWW. His three-part program included, first, "a strong voluntary or forced censorship of the press" which would "suppress every particle of publicity or news" about IWW activities and ideas; second, "the careful investigation and elimination of any industrial conditions that might afford an opportunity for agitation and I.W.W.

organization 'on the job'"; third, a program of increased espionage that in-cluded the infiltration of the national IWW offices, a program of decentralized agitation designed to break the centralized power of the IWW, and an intensifi-cation of undercover work in the fields.[46] In consultation with Simon Lubin, the third component of the plan was strengthened "with a far more drastic recommendation":

> ... members of the I.W.W. against whom there is evidence of intrigue or activity, not merely to agitate for better conditions, but to commit acts of treason and trea-sonably to hinder the operation of industries, or harvesting of crops, necessary to the prosecution of the war, be not arrested after charges, but that they be interned for the period of the war—preferably in camps some distance from the place of operation.

Bell claimed this program would "effectively mystify and frighten them; would avoid making heros of them." At the same time, Lubin and Bell hoped their pro-gram would also forestall increasing vigilante violence in the California fields that threatened to delegitimize all the efforts they had made to improve condi-tions. The end goal of the CCIH program was to immobilize the radically mobile and to replace them with a labor supply incapable of resistance. "It is much better to quietly take the ring leaders away and leave the horde of followers as scattered, ineffectual individuals!" Bell wrote in his outline of the plan.[47]

With their blueprint for repression drawn, Bell and Lubin were able by mid-July to gain the full support of the governors of California, Nevada, Washington, Arizona, Colorado, Utah, Oregon, and Idaho. With the combined influence of the western governors assured, Bell went to Washington to solicit the cooperation of the federal government in the program of espionage and repression. Armed with the plan and the information gathered by Thompson and other CCIH agents, Bell succeeded in convincing President Woodrow Wilson to call a secret conference of the western governors in Portland, Oregon, where a coordinated state-federal program of surveillance and repression could be formulated.[48]

Before the meeting, which was attended by Bell, several governors, and J. Harry Covington, a special federal IWW investigator, President Wilson re-vised the Bell-Lubin plan to develop a "uniform procedure." Wilson's revision left little room for doubt regarding the intent of the federal-state action against the IWW. Wilson declared the following as policies for the western governors to follow if they were to receive federal support:

> 1. Governor to direct his State Board of Health or other departments to immedi-ately inspect and clean up living and working conditions in the camps where migratory labor is employed. . . .

2. Governor to direct Immigration Department of the state government [or appoint special agents] . . . to send men speaking foreign languages to the places where large bodies of foreign men are employed. These agents:

(1) To explain the war situation to these people, and to explain to them that they will not only not be harmed, but will actually be protected by the state as long as they are peaceful, remain steadily at work, and show no tendency to interfere with industry or government;

(2) To urge them not to affiliate with any lawless organization or to take part in any riotous disturbance; otherwise, telling them, they will be liable to arrest and perhaps deportation;

(3) To urge them to learn English, to take out first papers, and to become American citizens. . . .

3. Governor not to call for troops until he feels that it is absolutely necessary . . . [but he should not] rely on more or less impromptu posses, "home guards," etc.

4. Governor to put as many secret service men in the field as possible to supplement the work of cities and counties.

5. *This entire program and matter to be kept confidential, and no publicity given to any actions taken in carrying it out.* [Original emphasis][49]

At Portland, Bell succeeded in convincing the western governors of the worth of the plan, and began the effort to convince President Wilson that CCIH should act as the central clearinghouse for all IWW activities in the west. For Lubin, the IWW suppression program was vital to the legitimacy of CCIH; it was integral to its Progressive mission. "Best congratulations on your success thus far," Lubin wired Bell in Washington on July 21. "Now you must not fail." Bell's mission to Washington and his summit with the western governors would "put us on the map" with both the president and with the new California governor, William Stephens, who was much less sympathetic to the Commission than Governor Johnson had been.[50]

Even before July 26, when the *San Francisco Examiner* made public Bell's mission to Washington (if not the details of the plan), the IWW in California knew that the hour of reckoning was near. On the 23rd, Thompson found that at the San Francisco IWW hall, "nearly every man that appears at the headquarters unknown to Evans [the local secretary] is immediately feared as a government spy, department of justice, or Burnsman." Indeed, Thompson reported that Evans was increasingly fearful that soldiers would any day raid the hall as they had done elsewhere around the country.[51]

When Bell returned to California in August, CCIH set to work implementing the federal-state plan. Though its work in this regard had the support of California farmers, the farm interests in the state were also concerned about what appeared to be a growing labor shortage in the fields. As the summer progressed, farmers called increasingly stridently for the exploitation of alternative labor sources to assure that the harvest could be completed profitably. They were especially interested in the use of contract labor from Mexico. CCIH was convinced neither of the need for Mexican labor nor of the advisability of allowing farm interests to determine if that need was real (in part because it feared such an importation would provide even more ammunition for IWW propaganda). They saw this as an area of CCIH expertise, and one that should be regulated by the state, if the migratory system in California was to be rationalized. Bell and Lubin therefore asked for one final plank in the federal-state program. They requested:

> That the United States Department of Labor, formally authorize this Commission to assure, during the winter and the next planting and harvesting season, the responsibility of determining (a) whether any Mexican agricultural labor should be imported into California under contract, (b) how many such laborers shall be admitted to California if a labor shortage is found to exist, (c) under what conditions and terms such labor should be admitted to California—all decisions based on careful investigations, and to be subject to review by the United States Secretary of Labor.[52]

CCIH never gained formal approval for this last provision, though it did eventually play a significant and rather contradictory role in the importation of Mexican contract labor into southern California during the war (in contravention of the state law that had created the Commission).[53]

Executing Repression: Immobilizing the Mobile

Actually, the federal government used a much more direct form of suppression of dissent than the plan outlined by Bell (though his plan was clearly an impetus to action). Beginning in September, the Department of Justice coordinated a series of arrests and incarcerations around the country, largely on espionage and sedition charges, designed to incapacitate both local and national leaders of the IWW. The suppression of the IWW was effective. By 1919, as CCIH claimed, radicalism seemed to be a dying issue in the fields of California. CCIH was elated—and it was proud of its role in the repression of radicalism and its replacement with Progressive order.[54]

The California repression of the IWW was telling in both its timing and in the public pronouncements made by state and federal officials as it was occurring. On September 2, 1917, the *Fresno Morning Republican* carried a story detailing a program of sabotage supposedly conducted by the IWW in the area. The same day, the Federal Reserve Bank in San Francisco issued a statement declaring that the increasing cost of farm labor (associated with the strikes that had occurred during the summer) "hampers the effectiveness of this country's efforts" in the war. Three days later, the Stockton ɪww hall was raided by federal agents (who arrested, among numerous others, Robert Blaine). The day after that, the Fresno hall was raided, and in the next weeks the raids of ɪww halls and the roundup of suspected Wobblies became general throughout the state. As the dragnet widened, and the Department of Justice franchised its arrest power to local law enforcement agencies, ccɪʜ's role crystallized. Under the tutelage of Bell and Thompson, local sheriffs were guided in their arrests, and taught to create local labor espionage programs designed to assure a tractable labor supply during the war. "The Commission of Immigration and Housing," its historian notes, "not only initiated the federal program, but also through its executive officer, became the coordinating agency for the state program and a liaison agency for the state and federal governments."[55]

The intent of the repression of radicalism among migratory workers was made plain on September 11, when the *Los Angeles Times* reported:

> Because of the hotbed of I.W.W. discovered in Central California and the fact that crops have been maliciously destroyed, the U.S. Dept. of Justice has opened an office in Fresno, with William Freeman, special investigator in charge. Farmers having labor trouble and whose crops are threatened will report directly to the local office. The bureau was opened this morning and one of the first reports was from W. Flanders Satchel, a grape grower, who said that grape pickers had thrown the grapes on the ground and then trampled on them.

The *Times* went on to report that there seemed to be a growing labor shortage throughout the California fields, but with the raids, "the situation is somewhat improved this week." The *Times's* use of "labor shortage" precisely reflected agriculturalists' own usage: traditionally in California, "labor shortage" meant that workers were striking or militant (or perceived as such) rather than actually in short supply.[56]

As the case against militant workers was being prepared during the spring of 1918, California governor Stephens reiterated the reasons for their outright repression:

> There is an organization that has for its purpose the destruction of property, of crops, of human life, of the government itself. That organization is the I.W.W. It must be put completely out of existence. Every person that preaches its doctrines must be dealt with summarily.[57]

The California agricultural pattern had spawned its inevitable outcome: to protect "the crops," which of course were closely associated with "human life," "property," and the "government itself," the rights, desires, and needs of some of the people of the state would have to be "put out of existence." The survival of the state demanded nothing less, according to the governor. Rarely before was the truth of the California Dream so apparent: if California was a yeoman frontier, like Kevin Starr and others say it was, then like all frontiers it was constructed of blood and violence. "California, the beautiful and the damned," indeed.

Mobility, Immobility, and Landscape Morphology

The social relations of labor in agricultural California complicate typical ways of understanding landscape. In the peaceful rural scene, the archetypal subject of landscape representations, "labor is fixed, a subject of representation, while the viewer is mobile . . . ," writes literary critic Elizabeth Helsinger. "To be fixed in place like the rural laborer, [is to be] circumscribed within a social position and locality." The task for CCIH and its allies in the federal government was to provide this social "fixing," in order to protect the productive landscape, while at the same time assuring that, in fact, labor remained *geographically* mobile. With the twin moves of labor camp improvement and increased surveillance over workers, the California Commission of Immigration and Housing did, in fact, fix workers in place, either tying militant workers to specific locations— like the Sacramento jail—so that individuals could become visible to the state, or infiltrating their camps and jungles, their union halls and flophouses so that *individuals* could be made accountable to power. Beginning in the autumn of 1917, any connection whatsoever with the IWW in California could result in arrest, and many workers were detained simply for stopping at IWW headquarters in Valley cities. Highly publicized official raids on IWW headquarters were conducted repeatedly throughout the state. Vigilante raids on the same headquarters frequently supported official state action. All this sent quite a clear message: subversive behavior was not only now effectively seen; it was not at all to be tolerated. Workers were meant to be mobile in the California landscape, but that mobility was to be closely policed.[58]

With militancy eliminated in the fields, and with many agricultural workers moving into the burgeoning war industries, farm interests began to cry even more loudly of impending labor shortages. Many workers refused to work in the fields under the present conditions of outright repression, and opportunities elsewhere allowed them to abandon the environments that had heretofore produced their "inferiority." The rapidly revolving migratory circuits that had allowed the development of industrialized agriculture in California were slowing. Irrational migrancy was not so much rationalized as it was unintentionally hindered. Eliminating the subversive aspects of migrancy had the unintended effect of increasing labor costs to agricultural and lumber interests, who had long relied on a gross labor surplus to meet their needs at prices below the actual cost of their reproduction. The war economy and CCIH threatened all that. Eventual solutions were found, as the next chapter shows, in the enlistment of young women, in child labor, in the use of prisoners, and, most importantly, in the recruitment of Mexican contract laborers who housed in stockades and worked under supervision of armed guards. The "revolutionized" landscape that CCIH pointed to proudly in 1919 was built not just on the science and technology of labor camp improvement, but also on this program of total labor control. An object becomes "real" or "true" as Latour noted (see Chapter 1) to the degree that no one resists against it: CCIH was determined to assure that resistance to its plans of environmental alteration was quite impossible—at least for migratory workers.[59]

Such a program of control had its direct justification in Carleton Parker's science. By defining the migrant worker as inferior, and by diagnosing his inferiority to be part of a nature produced by extant material environments, Parker had been able to declare that "over half" of those migratory workers participating in the various protests of the poor in 1914 and 1915 "had reached an undeniably abnormal mental condition." For Parker, it "was impossible . . . not [to] get a vivid impression of a class inferior, unequal, and with fewer rights than normal American tradition seems to promise its citizens." Since such inferiority led inexorably toward "revolt and guerilla warfare," the revocation of the rights of labor were easily justified. The quarantining—in Foucault's terms, the enclosing—of radicalized migratory labor in 1917 and 1918 was justified with metaphors of social health: labor pathologies had to be controlled at least until the pestilent environments that bred them could be made over. In effect, the incarceration of the IWW and other radical migratory workers served, and was understood, as a social prophylactic, designed to protect the agricultural system and the state that supported it.[60]

The landscapes of productive agriculture that emerged in California during World War I were thus visions of orderly social relations constructed of the contradictory, contested, and fragmentary spaces of production and reproduction. CCIH was most concerned with the spaces of California devoted to labor reproduction, and it continually attempted to stop motion in its tracks, to freeze the constant becoming of the landscape in the name of orderly reproduction, even as it sought to rationalize mobility itself. Labor camps—and their obverse, the hobo jungles and IWW halls—were spaces always in flux, even as the forces of capital and the state tried to freeze them *as* landscape. Hence, in Lefebvre's terms, they were spaces that were "used and consumed by *flows*," flows of labor and flows of capital, but no less so flows of raw unmitigated state power employed to ensure the smooth reproduction of capital in the fields. *That* is the morphology of landscape.[61]

The material landscapes constructed through Progressive and repressive programs of social control that we examined in the last chapter were thus never simply an "expression" or "reflection" of some local "culture," as much traditional cultural geography would have it. Repression excreted and reinforced morphology across a continuity of scales, from the smallest interventions in sanitary living conditions to the larger "view" of agricultural California as a successful capitalist region of production. Landscapes are never transparent—and yet landscapes are always functional to systems of production and reproduction. Gerry Kearns has urged geographers to uncover and theorize "active intention" in the production and use of spatial structures, and to show "the precise consequences of the effort." The "landscape solutions" of CCIH, premised as they were on Carleton Parker's Progressive science, merely served to reproduce inequality in the guise of social advance, even as they revolutionized the thinnest of outer skins on the surface of the state.[62]

The landscape, however, is always more complicated than its morphology suggests, because it is continually translated into a picture of how the world *should* be. And to the degree that workers can claim and reinforce their own radical subjectivity, to the degree they can make themselves *socially* visible within depictions of landscape by becoming individually invisible, by promising sabotage, by striking, they can invalidate claims made by capital and the state on their behalf. In response to this claim of radical subjectivity, CCIH, the Department of Justice, the Farmer's Protective League, and other powerful organizations continually sought to reobjectify workers. Continued profitable production was impossible in California without such a move. But, as importantly, the claim to radical subjectivity by workers, their ability to make their mobility subversive, made such attempted objectifications always open to change and re-vision. With the outright suppression of the IWW during the war, however, such a re-visioning of the spaces of their existence became even more difficult for many workers. And with this advantage, CCIH and organized growers, sometimes in competition with each other, each began the work of solidifying their power in the fields and their power over the spatial practices of agricultural production. They returned, as the next chapter shows, to the work of making a landscape out of the spaces of agricultural production and labor reproduction.

4 / Marked Bodies: Patriotism, Race, and Landscape

Return of the Rural Idyll

With the Industrial Workers of the World (IWW) all but destroyed, growers were able once again to reinvest in images of the California rural landscape as a place of beauty, tranquillity, and neighborly civility. They quickly revived old ideologies of the rural idyll that they had promoted during the shift to intensive farming at the end of the nineteenth century, but now their representations had a clear purpose: they were part of an effort to increase labor supplies in the face of a dwindling supply of male migrant workers. Urban and suburban families, they claimed in articles and advertisements, could find healthful, fulfilling living in the countryside should they choose to spend their summers helping bring in the crop. The work of harvesting was presented as pleasant and life-affirming—the perfect tonic for city families needing a turn in the country. The conditions of labor and life that the California Commission of Immigration and Housing (CCIH) continually uncovered in the fields notwithstanding, growers asserted that workers in the field would find almost vacation-like conditions.

In May 1917, even as Simon Lubin and George Bell were formulating their plan to repress worker radicalism, the Berry Growers Association of Sonoma County placed advertisements in newspapers throughout the Bay Area calling for workers to come to the countryside around Sabastopol to assist with the loganberry harvest. As the *San Francisco Examiner* reported, the ads stated that "excellent camping conditions would be furnished, that the work was pleasant, and that the average adult could earn $2.50 a day and children $1.25." Fifteen hundred workers responded by the June 5 opening date, only to find no camping equipment provided (though it could be purchased at inflated rates from a nearby merchant, who in any event quickly ran out), wages averaging closer to one dollar per day for adults, and bathing facilities furnished by the nearby river. Because of these idyllic conditions, the *San Francisco Examiner* wrote rather sarcastically, "thousands of tons of loganberries are rotting on the vines for lack of pickers." Where growers claimed "labor shortages," the *San Francisco Examiner* found rather a surfeit of labor unable or unwilling to work under the conditions demanded by the agriculturalists.[1]

Some growers did appreciate the necessity of improving conditions on their farms if they were to retain labor as burgeoning war industries provided more and more opportunities to the "casual" laborers of the state. Some even advocated installation of showers or baths, suggesting that such improvements would "make [labor] more efficient and they will stay longer." Others recommended providing fresh hay to sleep on. But all agreed that the life of workers, by dint of their contact with the rural civility of the state's agribusiness, would inevitably be improved. "The fun of the thing comes at night when the day's picking is over and supper is done," asserted one farmer. "All the camp gathers together then and the pickers sing and play banjos, and they make love and gossip—and turn in at all hours of the night, always good-natured and jolly, and carefree for the season at least." Whether this farmer's rural idyll had any basis in reality or not, the California Agricultural Experiment Station reminded its constituents that as new labor supplies were developed during and after the war to replace white male migratory workers, "proper housing and food, including segregation from the low type of transient farm labor," was absolutely essential.[2]

Crops in California were capitalized on the promise of highly mobile, pauperized, and not at all subversive labor being available when and as it was needed. To realize this promise at a time when repression, war industries, and a general economic improvement were depleting the ranks of migratory workers, farmer-industrialists worked ceaselessly to develop new labor supplies. As the United States entered the war, growers turned to a wide array of potential labor power—women, Boy Scouts, schoolchildren, and especially workers recruited from Mexico and held very nearly in bondage. CCIH was skeptical of the need to exploit these groups and was not afraid of saying so publicly. "In California," Simon Lubin declared in a lengthy newspaper account in May 1917, "the cry that there is a shortage of labor for the harvest is by no means new. Season after season the same wail has gone up from the farmer." CCIH was in a good position to assess the current claims, Lubin noted, because of its three seasons of experience working on migratory labor issues. The situation in 1917 was no different from other years "excepting that it may be a little more intensified."[3]

According to Lubin, an *apparent* labor shortage was caused by "(1) inadequate wages; (2) poor labor camp conditions; (3) a lack of a central clearing house for labor intelligence." In essence, Lubin confirmed the IWW's complaints: unscrupulous labor contractors, atrocious conditions, and poor wages made working in the fields intolerable, and growers were thus unable to retain their labor supply. But for Lubin, naturally, the solution lay not in the radicalism of the IWW but rather in a Progressive appeal to the good conscience of growers:

> First, let the employers determine what constitutes a fair and adequate wage, considering the fact that men must travel over considerable distances to reach the job and that they have employment but for a brief period. Then let them pay that fair and adequate wage.
>
> Secondly, let them provide decent living accommodations in their labor camps. In this matter the Commission of Immigration and Housing stands ready to lend every assistance within its power.
>
> Finally, let them support the state labor bureaus and urge upon those in authority to make it possible to enlarge upon the work of these officers so that in reality the state labor bureau may become a genuine clearing house to which all employers and all men who require positions may apply.[4]

The role for CCIH was clear: growers set the agenda, and CCIH assisted. With growers' voluntary cooperation, Lubin was sure that the importation of labor from Mexico was unnecessary. "The Commission definitely recommends that all proposals to import labor be strongly condemned." Growers, however, while wanting to promote the healthy living available in the country, were often not at all ready to cooperate with the Commission. Rather, they saw the destruction of radicalism as an opportunity to solidify their control over labor, both by re-creating an absolute surplus that drove down wages, and by reinforcing notions of inferiority—based on age, gender, race, ethnicity, and natural ability—that worked to naturalize the appalling labor conditions of the state.[5]

Harvest Work as Patriotism

With patriotic fervor enhanced by U.S. entry into World War I, California farmers helped to organize a California Division of the Women's Land Army of America, which sported the motto, "If you can't fight, farm." The economic depression of the early teens, backed by Carleton Parker's theories of natural inferiority, had made single men the desired labor force for agriculture. But with the war and repression, farmers quickly saw the advantage of developing female labor. Women had always worked in the fields (as had children), but until 1917 they had been understood as part of a system of family labor. With the war, growers saw women for the first time as a potentially very important independent labor source. Thousands of young women were recruited during 1917 as part of the Women's Land Army. Encampments with as many as five hundred workers were established in Lodi, Vacaville, Florin, Hamilton City, and Acampo. In the encampments, women workers wore uniforms and marched in military fashion; in the fields they earned twenty-five cents per hour, out of which they paid their own room and board.[6]

Conditions for workers in the Women's Land Army were considerably better than they were for most workers. Following CCIH's *Advisory Pamphlet on Labor Camp Sanitation,* the first encampment, at Vacaville "consisted of tents with board floors and sides, screened mess hall and cook house of knock down construction, shower baths, and modern sanitary arrangements." The *San Francisco Examiner* reported in 1919 that Women's Land Army camps housing one hundred workers cost 4,000 dollars to construct. If a five-year life span for the camp was assumed, and if the costs of contructing the camp were distributed among ten growers, the annual per-grower cost of housing a worker was a mere eighty cents. A more elaborate camp, consisting of bungalows that housed six women each, was also built at this time for a cost of five dollars per worker per season. Yet most farmers considered facilities such as these both extravagant and prohibitively expensive. In the end the Women's Land Army in California did not last the five years assumed in the above calculations. Though at first elated because "these women and girls will help curb the rapacity of certain foreign and alien elements in their demands for higher wages," growers were rapidly disappointed in the Army when it insisted, as the war progressed, on written contracts, guaranteed rates of pay and periods of work, camp inspections, an eight-hour day, and overtime pay—none of which growers were willing to grant to women they felt should simply be glad of the opportunity to work in the fields.[7]

Growers thus also turned to child labor. The agriculture industry had long managed to exclude itself from state and federal child labor laws, and during the war agriculturalists sought to exploit this fact to their advantage. Public and private schools were closed during the harvest, the YMCA and Boy Scouts enlisted, and reform schools and detention centers conscripted. Most of the sources of "boy labor" (as the *Pacific Rural Press* liked to call it) sold the boys' labor power at a loss to themselves: county and state homes and the Boy Scouts usually absorbed the cost of housing and feeding the child workers, thus subsidizing many of the agricultural industrialists of the state. Pleased with the docility of "boy labor," a group calling itself the Farm Workers and Operators Protective Association opened a cantonment for two hundred boys in San Jose in 1918 and announced plans for several others. The intent of the cantonments was to house city boys for the length of the fruit harvest so that their labor would be available to any grower who needed it. And by using child labor in the prune and grape harvest of Napa County (where public schools were closed so that children could work all day), growers reported that they were able to harvest their $2 million crop for only $20,000.[8]

Even with the advantages that children and women offered to farmers, however, growers had not given up on male migratory labor as an important labor supply. Many farmers argued that good male workers could be found if only the state would close the bars and saloons. As a solution to perceived labor shortages, closing saloons was favored "second only to the importation of labor" because, among other things, it would help *increase* and rationalize the mobility of labor. The *Pacific Rural Press* opined that closing bars "will reduce roadside attractions and facilitate transit as well as insure the greater efficiency of labor upon arrival." To bolster the inducement of sobriety, farmers also called for the strengthening of vagrancy laws, the outright conscription of labor, and the "curtailment of non-essential industries," to make labor available at harvest time. For most farmer-industrialists the old problem of migrancy— the proper mix of mobility and immobility—remained the nexus of the farm labor supply problem.[9]

Working with CCIH, the California State Council of Defense announced a plan to solve this problem for farmers without importing labor from Mexico. "By making more mobile the present day supply of labor," the Council proclaimed, "and [by] keeping close check upon the needs in each locality where there is a surplus, there is every reason to believe the present supply is sufficient to harvest the California crops." The goal of this state action was to reinforce the traditional patterns of the California landscape in which workers moved swiftly, quietly, and in poverty against a backdrop of resplendent productivity. Consequently, by reducing the costs of reproducing needed labor, California farmers could, in the words of a University of California labor economist, continue to "sell their crops for less than the actual cost of production."[10]

Marked Bodies: Labor, Race, and Landscape

The connection between landscape-as-representation (the rural idyll of farmer-industrialists) and landscape-as-material-fact (the camp conditions, good and bad, the pattern of crops that demanded high rates of mobility) was, as we have noted, continually made by the people who worked the land. Their bodies, as embodiments of essential labor power, continually negotiated the connections between ideology and spatial form. But these bodies, of course, were themselves ideologically marked, themselves an alchemy of representation and morphological form. For Carleton Parker, migratory male (implicitly white) workers were physically and psychically inferior, marked from the beginning as "permanently undernormal." But theirs were moldable bodies, and under proper environmental circumstances, they could be re-created to form a much more efficient, much less militant, house for labor power. By reforming the environment, a match could be made between the needs and desires of men, and the needs and desires of a productive landscape.

As this dream of the perfectly adapted white male worker faded in the face of IWW militancy, growers re-marked both the landscape and the bodies that moved through it with new ideologies of biological and social fitness-to-serve. Women and children were pressed into service, but so too were old ideologies of race that served to explain why Asian and Mexican workers were desperately needed in the fields. At the height of the war, the cry by industrialized farmers, particularly those in the southern part of the state, for the importation of Mexican workers grew increasingly shrill, no matter how much CCIH argued it was unnecessary. In a rare moment of honesty, a California farmer explained his preference for Mexican workers: "We want Mexicans because we can treat them as we cannot treat any other living men. . . . We can control them at night behind bolted gates, within a stockade eight feet high, surmounted by barbed wire. . . . We make them work under armed guards in the fields." Such bald claims were usually couched in elaborate racist ideologies that explained to farmers why such treatment was both necessary and proper, but the purpose was clear: to create in the bodies of Mexican workers a container for the total control of labor power. Responding to the desires of growers in the south, the Wilson administration defied CCIH (see Chapter 3) and signaled its willingness to suspend the head tax and literacy test for Mexican immigrants in early summer of 1917; and sugar beet growers (who most desired this labor source), working with other agro-industrialists, were able to have provisions for contract labor included in the 1917 federal Immigration Act.[11]

Growers had allies in the semiofficial wartime bureaucracies that had evolved to organize production in the war economy. A special commission established by the Los Angeles Council of Defense and the County Chamber of Commerce claimed that an acute shortage of labor existed in the southern counties. The Los Angeles Commission complained that normally reliable Mexican workers had been fleeing south "as a result of German I.W.W. conspiracies." To aid in the return of these laborers, the Los Angeles Commission convinced the federal government to suspend all contract labor laws in California, giving free rein to employers that sought to bring labor from Mexico into the state.[12]

In Los Angeles, the use of Mexican contract labor was clearly a gambit designed to flood the labor market. CCIH agents were concerned by this turn of events, arguing that "there were no positions open" in the Los Angeles area. No employers reported needing help, according to CCIH investigators, "except at Prada and Santa Ana, where Mexicans are plentiful but staying out for two fifty and three dollars day wage." Calling imported workers "strikebreakers," Los Angeles CCIH bureau chief Ethel Richardson beseeched Simon Lubin, "Can this be stopped?" In a move that did not endear it to many powerful farming interests, the Commission cooperated with the Mexican Consul in Los Angeles to prevent sugar beet growers from recruiting Mexican labor. When agents of the Alamitos Sugar Company attempted to import workers through El Paso and Nogales, the Los Angeles Consul was able to enlist the governors of the Mexican border states in preventing them. "We would scarcely have expected that our most substantial help in a serious matter of this kind," Richardson remarked, "should have come from Mexico." But even as Richardson was informing Lubin of the Commission's success in preventing the Alamitos company from importing five hundred workers, the mayor of Los Angeles was ordering his chief of police to "arrest all Mexicans unemployed, in the Plaza District, as vagrants." Even those who had been unemployed "only a day or two" were rounded up. The Commission spent a considerable amount of time and effort "to get a great many Mexicans out of jail . . . who were there for no cause whatever."[13]

The Commission also found itself in opposition to growers and their apologists in matters of camp sanitation. The Los Angeles Council of Defense declared that Mexican workers certainly should be housed in a manner "sufficient to properly conserve the health and bodily comfort of laborers" but warned that nonetheless temporary agricultural laborers in no way deserved "the same facilities . . . as are now or should be provided for permanent residents in congested districts." The Council was seconded by an assistant to R. L. Adams, the University of California "Labor Agent" whose job it was to advise California farmers on labor policy. The assistant reminded CCIH that "the matter of food production [is] at this time so very critical that the Mexicans should be a secondary consideration." Indeed, he remarked, conditions for Mexican workers were no worse than they had traditionally been and CCIH's policy of seeking enforcement of the Camp Sanitation Act was out of line.[14]

Even though most growers assumed that Mexican workers were naturally suited to and content in agricultural work, they deemed it necessary to house them in fenced compounds out of fear they would flee the beet fields and orange groves for the nearby cities. A University of California professor reported to a farm labor symposium, "I know of one firm who are making a group of their imported Mexicans work for ten or twelve hours a day, handcuffing them at night to prevent their escape." Growers excused these tactics by arguing that their federal permission to import contract labor was contingent on returning the workers to Mexico at the end of the season. The stockades and armed guards merely assured that they could fulfill the terms of this agreement.[15]

While officially opposed to the importation of Mexican labor, CCIH's actions in this matter were quite contradictory.[16] Its camp inspectors helped establish labor camps for imported beet workers, even as it publicly condemned the whole endeavor. A CCIH inspector later recalled:

> The main camp to which the laborers were brought directly from Mexico was known as the Concentration Camp, and was situated in Orange County not far from Huntington Beach. It consisted of a large circus tent with cots for sleeping accommodations, cook house, baths, and toilets according to the requirements of the Commission at the time. The entire camp was surrounded by a barbed wire stockade or fence eight feet in height, and a guard was kept at the entrance night and day to prevent the Mexicans from leaving. After segregating these laborers, they were sent to various ranches in the vicinity to work, and as they were destitute of any camp equipment, the conditions in these camps were deplorable. In many cases, there were no blankets among the workers and seldom a tent, so they simply made the best of sleeping in the open fields. The inevitable result of such a situation was that many desertions took place, whereupon the companies endeavored to check this by placing armed guards over the camps.[17]

CCIH's Spanish-speaking agent, Frank Palomares, was given charge of inspecting both the "concentration camps" and the growers' camps. But his work hinged more on his ability to assure that Mexican workers did not rebel against the conditions they were forced—often at the end of a gun—to endure.[18]

Racism and Landscape

Growers in southern California, responding to the need for a temporary and fully controllable labor supply, had called forth a form of temporary labor *immobility*. But to do so, they had to rely on well-established ideologies of "natural fitness" to justify themselves—for the wholesale abrogation of civil liberties upon which the labor relations of California agriculture was now based (the incarceration of radical white workers, the impounding of Mexican workers, the exploitation of children and women) became a simpler matter if it could be shown that workers were getting all that they "naturally" deserved.

During and after the war, Hispanic workers were particularly singled out as a "natural" labor supply for California agriculture.[19] Growers and their supporters claimed "Mexicans" were naturally docile; they had "no political ambitions," according to Ralph Taylor, long an advocate for industrial farmers. As another agriculturalist put it, the "homing-pigeon" attitudes of Mexican workers (the belief that Mexican laborers simply returned to Mexico whenever they were not harvesting crops) combined with their supposed quiescence to make for a perfect labor source. "The Mexican likes the sunshine against an adobe wall with a few tortillas," this apologist testified before a Senate committee, "and in the off time he drifts across the border where he may have these things." For Dr. George Clements of the Agricultural Department of the Los Angeles Chamber of Commerce, "No labor that has ever come to the United States is more satisfactory under righteous treatment" than that of the Mexican. Between 1924 and 1930 an estimated 58,000 Mexican and Hispanic workers migrated through the San Joaquin Valley each year. Thousands more were employed exclusively in the Los Angeles basin.[20]

Mexican workers in the 1920s found themselves toiling in landscapes that had been defined by race from the start. Landscapes, as Kay Anderson has shown, solidify ideologies—and this is especially true of ideologies of race, ethnicity, and gender. Race, like gender, is a socially created category more than it is a fact of biology. The biological construction of "race" as signified most prominently by differences in skin color, masks the social relations that lie behind it. Yet even though one can claim that there is no biological basis for "race," a historical explication of the development of landscape as part of the historical development of capitalist production must take into account how racial differences are, nonetheless, translated into essentialized differences of innate, biological race and invested with social meaning. It must be cognizant of how "race" is constructed out of very real material circumstances and then set in motion as a set of representations about how the world *should* be. "Race" is thus not descriptive, but is rather, especially as it intersects with the brutalizing processes of California agriculture, *normative*.[21]

Under capitalism, race, like gender, age, ethnicity, and sexuality, intersects in complex ways with class differentiation. As Robert Miles has argued:

> Capitalist production relations do not "cause" racism but they constitute the terrain upon which racism (along with other ideologies) is articulated by real people, not simply to justify certain courses of action, but also to interpret their experience of production relations and the effects of these relations at the various levels of a social formation.[22]

This is an inherently spatial practice: the landscape, when viewed as a reflection of the cultural and biological attainment of a given people (as in Sauer's methodology), reinforces ideologies of difference that underlie the ability of powerful elites to objectify those who exist as "part" of the landscape. As William Cronon has recorded, connecting the look of the landscape to the "natural" qualities of a people is a strong and tenacious part of western philosophy and political-economic practice.[23]

The landscape can thus stand as proof of the very ideologies through which it is seen. As Anderson has written of Vancouver's Chinatown, "Racial ideology has been materially embedded in space . . . and it is through 'place' that it has been given a local referent, become a social fact, and aided in its own reproduction." The material landscape—from the minutiae of labor camp arrangements to the larger view of (white) rural civility—serves as an important medium for the construction of a hegemonic discourse about race: a discourse about insiders and outsiders within a solidifying historic bloc. In the Chinatowns, Japantowns, Mexican Barrios, and numerous racially stratified labor camps throughout California, in the spaces within which agricultural labor was historically reproduced, these processes were readily apparent.[24]

Racialized Labor

The reception afforded Mexican workers during World War I and the 1920s can only be understood as an elaboration of the ways other racialized laborers were historically received in California. Chinese workers arrived in California in large numbers as part of the Gold Rush and as recruits for railroad construction. Subject to racist attacks in the cities and mining towns, early California agriculturalists saw them as a godsend. Growers argued that their short stature and ability to survive on appallingly low wages made them content to do the work that no white worker would do. Chinese workers, farmers assumed, were "consigned to the farm work force by a mechanism of natural selection." When urban (often working-class) anti-Chinese agitation led to the Chinese Exclusion Act of 1882 and the numbers of Chinese workers in the fields began to decline, agriculturalists were concerned they would lose the labor supply that had made their farming possible. Indeed, even as late as the end of World War I, California farmers ritually resolved at their conventions to seek the reopening of Chinese immigration to stave off the imminent demise of the vibrant, yet apparently quite fragile, agricultural economy.[25]

The decline of Chinese labor after 1882 put California farmers in a dilemma. Without inexpensive, tractable labor, their farms could not be profitable in distant markets. Many growers in California thus looked toward Japan, where they hoped to find workers just as "naturally" suited to agricultural tasks as were the Chinese. Farmers eventually turned to Japanese, Filipinos, Asian Indians, and, as we have seen, white men, families, women, children, Hispanics, Mexicans, and any other embodied bit of labor power they could get their hands on, adapting their theories of natural inferiority along the way to suit the specifics of the group in question (Figure 7). Racism thus intersected complexly with the demands of a ruthless agricultural system that, as Varden Fuller showed in great detail, absolutely demanded huge numbers of highly marginalized workers. But racism is a tricky business that rarely runs parallel to the needs and desires of any one social faction. Typical of the complication that race could interject into analyses of the California political economy were Henry George's interventions against Chinese labor. For all his sympathy toward the masses of white migrant laborers trudging through the endless wheat fields of 1870s California, George could not understand the role played by what he called the "degraded" Chinese as quite parallel in economic terms to that of whites. Rather, by 1869, George was among the most vocal of the growing "anti-coolie" cadres that came to dominate labor and progressive politics during the second half of the nineteenth century in California. George warned in an 1869 letter to the *New York Tribune* that the "60,000 to 100,000 Mongolians on our Western Coast" were merely "the thin edge of the wedge" that culminated in over five hundred million people in Eastern Asia. Turning an early and rudimentary social Darwinism on its head, George argued that "Chinamen can live where stronger than he would starve." Like an invading weedy species, Asians would inevitably "drive out the stronger races." With this New York letter, George became one of the earliest to ring the alarm of the rising "yellow peril" of China and Japan.[26]

Henry George's argument, however, was not *solely* a diatribe against people he saw as clearly different and unassimilable to "white" America. Rather, his anti-Asianism was an integral part of a developing economic critique—borrowed largely from John Stuart Mill—concerned with the corrosive power of monopoly in democracy. "Coolie" labor, according to George, made land monopolies possible; and, starting in California, a backwave of "coolie" labor encouraged by profit-hungry capitalists would wash across the western states, erasing any vestige of the democratic initiatives that had swept west with the frontier in previous generations. George's argument was thus political and economic: it was an invective against the processes that George felt would "make the rich richer and the poor poorer; . . . make nabobs and princes out of our capitalists, and crush our working classes into the dust." Yet for all the economic and political critique, George hinged his analysis on the "fact" that the Chinese, as

Figure 7. Filipino workers picking peas in February 1936. Dorothea Lange, photographer. The racial construction of farm labor and ownership has always been complex in California. The workers pictured here, part of a group of sixty, were contracted to, and lived on the ranches of, Japanese farmers. Despite the complexity of racial relationships, the overriding image in California is of racialized labor and "white" ownership. (Courtesy, Bancroft Library.)

"long-tailed barbarians" and "utter heathens, treacherous, sensual, cowardly and cruel," were *naturally* and unequally equipped to destroy the aspirations, and the livelihoods, of the "American" working class. The social relations of capitalist production in California, according to George, were thus invariably racial relations—and in this he reflected quite precisely the workings of the California agricultural political economy.[27]

Chinese Workers, Chinese Landscapes

Faced with the discriminatory effects of racist ideologies, expressed as clearly by the white urban working class as by the growers themselves, Chinese workers in California (and elsewhere in the west) developed fraternal institutions as a means of protection and material improvement. The mostly male population found itself subject to antimiscegenation laws in most states, thereby increasing the social isolation that their fraternal institutions reflected. Defined as social outcasts, and becoming "the indispensable enemy" to politicians and labor unions alike, Chinese workers found themselves ghettoized even in the remotest towns of rural California. Their very ghettoization, coupled with the subsequent necessity to create separate social institutions, of course, merely confirmed to dominant society that the Chinese could never be Americanized.[28]

As Sucheng Chan has shown in a masterful, detailed study of the Chinese role in the development of California agriculture, Chinese truck gardeners, farmers, farmworkers, and cannery workers were engaged in an impressive range of agricultural pursuits the length of the state. "Working as truck gardeners, vegetable peddlers, commission merchants, farm cooks, tenant farmers, and owner-operators of farms," Chan writes, "thousands of Chinese brought new land under cultivation, experimented with various crops, and provided much of the labor needed to plant, harvest, pack, preserve, and sell the crops in almost every major agricultural region of California." Yet reformers and politicians of the first decades of the twentieth century, along with many in agribusiness and urban unions, insisted on seeing Chinese residents of the state only as a "problem." Either they competed unfairly with white labor, or they were unassimilable, or they competed unfairly with white farmers. In such a context, the landscapes created by rural Chinese—either relatively independently, or as a result of oppressive rules and laws developed by dominant society—came to represent for many in the state visual evidence of the "problem" itself. And as is so often the case with environmentalist ideologies, this "proof" was twisted in on itself: as we shall see, agents for CCIH, reflecting a dominant idea of the times, argued forcefully that if only the physical artifacts of the Chinese could be destroyed, then so too could the Chinese be eliminated from view.[29]

The Sacramento-San Joaquin Delta area early became an important center of Chinese agricultural settlement. While large corporate landholdings were the rule in the Delta, an intricate pattern of tenantry also developed. The Chinese were the most important early source of both laborers and tenants. In this region, as elsewhere, Chinese workers lived in camps, in their own towns, in "Chinatowns," and, if tenant farmers, in shacks on the farms they worked. When the Progressive legislature passed the Alien Land Law in 1913 that forbade landownership by any persons "ineligible to become citizens" and that limited leases to three years, Chinese workers and farmers found themselves packed into even more highly constrained towns and districts, living at densities, even in rural areas, that far exceeded most white urban neighborhoods—reinforcing even more strongly the idea that Asian workers were completely unassimilable to white society.[30]

By the end of the first decade of the twentieth century, several sizable

"Chinatowns" had developed in Delta towns, the largest of which was Walnut Grove, a center for potato, onion, and pear production. When the Walnut Grove settlement was destroyed by fire in 1915, many Chinese moved a few miles away and established a town leased (verbally, to avoid the Alien Land Law restrictions) by George Locke. The town of Locke soon became the most important center of Chinese labor in the Delta. The making of Locke as a Chinatown therefore certainly has as much to do with the needs and desires of the larger, dominant society, as it does with the desires of the Chinese themselves. It can hardly be said to represent, in any meaningful sense, some essential aspect of "Chineseness." Yet, to much white society, that is precisely what Chinese settlements like Locke represented: an innate, intractable, unchangeable, natural "Chineseness." Delta Chinatowns (like their counterparts in San Francisco, Oakland, Los Angeles, and Sacramento) were densely packed, and building styles allowed for a great flexibility of uses: family housing, storefronts, opium dens, and boarding rooms could all share the same building. With landownership barred and fair leases difficult to obtain, functional utility was highly valued.[31]

Other Asian Workers, Other Landscapes

In the Delta, as in other parts of the state, Chinese workers and tenant farmers were often joined or replaced by Japanese farmers and farmworkers after 1882. Japanese workers, too, were seen by farmers as "naturally" suited to California's agricultural conditions, and, like the Chinese, they came ready-organized in gangs headed by a single contractor with whom the farmer-industrialists could deal. This arrangement guaranteed that the reproductive costs of labor—housing, food, sanitary conditions—were assumed by the contractor, rather than directly by the farmer. The Japanese, however, proved untrustworthy in the eyes of farmers. Rather than preying on their labor gangs (as was often the case with Chinese contractors and was certainly the case with the commercial casual laborer contractors that arose in rural centers at the end of the nineteenth century to supply white labor to extractive industries), Japanese contractors worked with their gangs, leading them to strike at critical harvest times. Even worse, complained both farmers and Progressive political interests, workers quickly pooled their money to purchase land and directly compete with established white growers. Working with allies in the early twentieth-century Progressive press and state government, agriculturalists led a campaign to exclude Japanese immigration. This campaign resulted in a "Gentlemen's Agreement" between the United States president and the Emperor of Japan that barred Japanese immigration in 1908, and eventually to the 1913 California Alien

Land Law. If anything, the animosity toward Japanese settlers and workers in the state was even deeper than that toward the Chinese.[32]

The Alien Land Law provided a certain amount of difficulty for CCIH (which had as one of its mandates the rational settlement of immigrants on rural lands), particularly as it concerned another Asian group that was becoming important as a source of agricultural labor and as farmers: Asian Indians. The law was clear concerning "Mongolians, Chinese and Japanese"; they were ineligible to own land because of their "race." "Hindus," on the other hand, were sometimes white and sometimes not, depending on their caste and their region of origin. Federal courts had ruled that "Aryan Hindoos" were eligible for citizenship because they were white and thus covered by federal laws; all other "Hindus" were ineligible. By 1923, federal courts had removed even "Aryan Hindoos" from the list of eligible peoples, declaring that even high-caste "Hindus" were not "free white persons" in the "understanding of the common man."[33]

For CCIH inspectors seeking to enforce camp sanitation laws in the Delta or the Imperial Valley where Asian Indians were beginning to operate farms, the Alien Land Law created more problems than it solved. Agriculturalists, whether white or Asian, found it quite easy to use the law to shift blame for unsanitary conditions. Landowners would blame their tenants, tenants their contractors, and contractors the workers as well as tenants and landowners. By law, it was the landowner who held responsibility for conditions in the camps, and the Alien Land Law made it often very difficult to trace ownership. "Always make every effort to determine who the owner of the camp is," CCIH's chief labor camp inspector Edward Brown instructed one of his staff. "Where a Japanese, Chinese or Hindu [is] operating a camp there must be an American somewhere in the deal. This information is sometimes impossible." Yet finding the American owner was vital because that person was the one who "would be responsible for erecting any new structures that are required." The problem of culpability was even further complicated in 1926 when the state attorney general informed CCIH that various court cases had shown that contractors were not employees and therefore the camp sanitation laws did not cover them. White growers quickly sought out new deals with Asian, white, and Hispanic contractors.[34]

Race as Immutable: Destroying Landscapes

Even though concerned about issues of ownership and the culpability they implied, CCIH implicitly—and not infrequently explicitly—accepted the reification of "race" as an explanatory factor in the development and alteration of the labor landscape. Indeed, it simply took such a reification for granted. At the end of the 1920s, Edward Brown wrote, quite unremarkably, "On some farms we find camps for Japanese, Hindu, Mexican, Filipino and American, each with a different method and standard of living." And throughout the decade, CCIH policy reflected this reification. At various times, though they could be quite harsh in their assessment of labor camp operators who provided unsatisfactory conditions to any workers, CCIH inspection staff applied differing standards to camps depending on the "race" of those housed. As CCIH executive secretary Robert Kearney wrote a camp operator in 1926:

> [The Commission] has for many years opposed double deck bunks. As early as 1922 there is a statement in its report that double deck bunks have been practically eliminated. At present there are not more than five camps in the State of California that are using them, and these are occupied by Chinese.

It was clear that CCIH saw its abatement of unsanitary camp conditions as a hierarchical exercise. White camps were deserving of the closest scrutiny; others were less important. When an inspector informed Edward Brown of a particularly good camp in Kern County, he responded that he was "glad to hear that there is one good camp in Kern County, even though it is for the Japanese."[35]

Essentialist notions of race permeated the Commission's workings. Brown had earlier instructed another inspector in the approach to be taken with camp operators who housed Japanese workers:

> I notice that some of the letters [to camp operators specifying improvements to be made] call for the installation of shower baths in the Japanese camps. The Japs have their own type of bath, and until they can be educated to the point of using showers, we can not insist upon operators installing showers for them which they ~~do~~ will not ~~know how to~~ use. [Strikeouts in original]

Most camps, whether for whites or not, of course, did not provide even rudimentary baths or showers, so Brown's concerns seem misplaced, especially since, as Brown wrote for CCIH in an official state publication, "At every camp where Japanese are employed," by *Japanese* farmers or contractors, "a bath is provided." According to one observer of camp conditions during the 1920s and 1930s, "Baths were provided for the Japanese laborers, who are a notoriously clean race—that is, about their persons, not so much where their living quarters are concerned." Or as Brown himself wrote, despite the provision of bathing facilities in Japanese camps that bespoke an attention to hygienic matters, there could nonetheless be found in these camps "open toilets, open drains from the kitchen sinks, unscreened dining and cooking quarters, and living quarters generally littered with boxes, bags, etc." Brown meant this as a condemnation of Japanese workers; but, of course, he could just as easily have been describing the conditions CCIH inspectors typically found in white labor camps. As in Carleton Parker's analysis of white migratory workers after Wheatland, CCIH understood the innate qualities of Asians to be expressed in the landscapes within which they toiled. "Chineseness" or "Japaneseness" could be read right in the landscape; but even more importantly, these landscapes helped form and reinforce those Asian qualities that CCIH and other reformers wanted to eliminate—their unassimilability, for example—and thus CCIH understood that the only way to eliminate the "problem" of Asian workers in California was to eliminate their landscapes.[36]

Responding to urban pressure to eliminate Chinese workers at one of its packing plants at the Delta town of Ryde in 1926, the influential company of Libby, McNeil, Libby felt that the most expeditious means to meet this goal would be to cut "the old Chinese B.H.'s into about half making them into two room apartments." Counting on the success of this strategy, Libby expressed its hope that "they will have no Chinese there in the coming year." In this action, Libby was following CCIH's example. In 1924 the Commission had assisted a Placer County campaign to eliminate the "Oriental" landscape that had grown up in the orchards of the foothills. Designed as a labor camp improvement program, the Placer County initiative simultaneously reinforced racist ideology and subverted the minimal control that Japanese workers had gained over labor conditions in that area. "In the early part of the year," CCIH reported in its *Annual Report* for 1924,

> a number of meetings were held in Placer County, where the fruit growers are trying to break the grip of the Japanese who controlled the picking and packing. The Commission's agent, at the request of the growers, advised them on methods of camp construction for the housing of American labor, most of the existing camps being of the Oriental type. Good contacts were made and the way paved for further work next year when the growers expect to build several camps.[37]

Nowhere in the records of CCIH is it possible to find a description of a labor camp of the "Oriental type," but CCIH inspectors seemed to know one when they saw one, and they also knew that neither Chinese nor Japanese workers could ever be "Americanized." Thus, when CCIH claimed, as it did for the Delta region in its 1924 report, that its "campaign for sanitary camps and adequate housing will eventually conclude in the Americanization of the Oriental delta district," the Commission was advocating the total eradication of "Orientals" from the farms and fields. Any "improvements" in Delta camps and packing towns were celebrated by CCIH as "a very satisfactory achievement" because the Delta area "is mainly Oriental, and Oriental housing and sanitation has existed for years."[38]

CCIH and its industrial constituents continually reaffirmed that it was the

"Orientals" themselves who were responsible for the appalling conditions often found in labor camps that housed Asian workers. One lumber company in the Sierras (whose president was former CCIH commissioner Arthur Flemming) wrote to CCIH in 1922:

> You will be pleased, we are sure, to know that we have burned the Sugar Pine Chinatown in its entirety. Not one of the dilapidated old shacks remains. We intend to make every effort to get along without Chinamen hereafter, and it is not likely that their mode of living will again cause us to conflict with the state rules for camp sanitation.[39]

By such means the "Oriental problem" in the fields and forests was handled. Eliminate the landscape, and the social problems would also be eliminated.

Reform Racism and Representations of Mexican Labor in the Landscape

CCIH's analysis of "Mexican" workers (as all Hispanic laborers were invariably called) paralleled its analysis of Asian and "inferior" white labor, even if the Commission, like other Progressives and reformers, was adept at reformulating that analysis to fit the specifics of the case. Indeed, agricultural reformers, while recognizing the parallels, maintained that the "problem" of Mexican labor was quite distinct from the "problem" of Asian labor. Mexican workers were a growing and increasingly important component of the army of California farm labor during the 1920s. Their labor power was clearly *necessary* in absolute terms in a way that Japanese and Chinese labor no longer was. Thus, reformers, and especially agriculturalists concerned with maintaining their oversupply of labor, could not afford to advocate the elimination of Hispanic workers as they might Asian workers. The "Mexican problem" was instead a problem of reform. Mexican agricultural housing schemes were thus seen by many growers (and certainly by CCIH) as part of a program of "Americanization" designed to create an appropriate and docile labor supply.

Dr. Charles L. Bennett, manager of the San Dimas Colony citrus farm in eastern Los Angeles County, explicated the nature of this ideology in a series of articles published in the *San Dimas Press* and reprinted later in a pamphlet distributed by the state chamber of commerce.[40] "The recently arrived Mexican peon is in a certain state of savagery or barbarism, and can be treated accordingly," Bennett suggested. But he advised against this, arguing that corporations in Mexico were improving conditions for their workers (hoping to stave off emigration to the United States) and thus Mexicans will "soon [be] craving and then demanding the things in use by our own more advanced civilization."

If farmers do not begin to provide some of these amenities, Bennett argued, Mexican workers would have no incentive to come to California and farmers would miss their chance to develop a near-perfect labor source. Rather than become unwitting victims to this rising tide of demand, Bennett advised farmers, they should follow the example of the San Dimas Colony and plan for "labor five years hence, [which] may be white, brown or any other human color."

In orange and lemon groves, where skilled labor is in more demand than perhaps in field crops (with the exception of beets), good housing seemed all the more important to large and small growers alike, according to Bennett. Good housing was a means of stabilizing the workforce and attracting families (and thus gaining access to child and female labor). Besides being more stable and less militant than that of single male workers (because it had more to lose), family labor brought with it the added advantage of not requiring a superstructure of cooks and bunkhouse cleaners. Women were expected to cook and clean for their families, even after a full day in the field. House design and location was thus of paramount importance. Labor housing, Bennett counseled, should be close to (company) stores so that "the housewife does not lose time and energy making her purchases at an unreasonable distance." Grouping houses together with other facilities such as washrooms and stores likewise made "it easier and cheaper to make water, gas and light connections." Perhaps most importantly, houses situated properly "puts the workmen close to the packing houses for supervision and direction." The provision of good, properly located housing fulfilled both a social and an economic good: "The character of housing in any community is a positive index to the grade of progress it has attained." And in return, proper housing would ensure "a readily available and constant supply of efficient help."[41]

For its Mexican "peon" labor, the San Dimas Colony constructed concrete houses with five-inch-thick walls and a frame of reinforced steel. Painting these houses was unnecessary because Bennett's engineers had "found a mixture that could be sprayed on the walls giving a smooth, attractive finish of flinty hardness." The use of concrete walls and floors meant that the company could "turn the hose on them" whenever they needed cleaning. The end result was a house as "sanitary, cleanable, and as nearly indestructible as a house can be." To the objection that these houses were too good for Mexican workers, Bennett replied, "It is true that you cannot make a blooded racer out of a cart horse by putting him in a fine blanket and a luxurious stall. But you can reduce the efficiency of the cart horse by allowing him to stand knee deep in his own filth."

San Dimas Colony's concrete houses were appropriate, Bennett concluded, because they recognized both the previous cultural attainments and the probable level of cultural advancement of Mexican laborers. There was "no mystery about understanding a Mexican," Bennett confidently proclaimed. And, as that was the case, there should be no mystery about the type of housing appropriate for the Mexican, who

> is an empiric agriculturalist, barely emerged from a barbaric past and with little recorded progress. Yet he has natural tendencies that stamp him as a likable human. His very lack of sophistication is an advantage. His tendency is to simplicity and honesty and though he may not have a high resistance to temptation, he is not naturally vicious and he responds with less suspicion to the human touch.

Reform too was ever couched in a language of racism. The conquest of the Aztecs by Cortez was proof to Bennett of Mexicans' low level of pre-Columbian civilization, and they had little advanced since then. In essence, Bennett argued, Mexicans were children: "He is apathetic to propaganda involving any studied principle, his mind not being sufficiently nimble to compass principles." Nonetheless, this quality did not make Mexican workers any less "prone to being stirred up by agitators who throw oratorical sentiment into their exhortations." In response, then, it was incumbent upon farmers who relied on Mexican labor to create environments that satisfied their workers and undermined the abilities of agitators to exhort. Such a program, Bennett confidently predicted (and in this he was seconded by most of the prominent commentators on farm conditions in the 1920s), would allow Mexicans to reach their full evolutionary potential.

Or as Dr. George Clements of the Agricultural Department of the Los Angeles Chamber of Commerce put it in a conclusion to an analysis of Mexican labor quite in agreement with Dr. Bennett's: if treated properly, Mexican workers would become "the most tractable individual[s] that ever came to serve us." CCIH also seconded Bennett's analysis—and his designs for "proper" Mexican housing:

> In Kern County our department has been instrumental in having one of the large cement companies rebuild their entire camp. The old tie and tin type of camp has been replaced by modern well-constructed cement houses for the Mexican employees and comfortable frame structures for the American employees.[42]

Racial Order and the Material Order

In the Imperial Valley, perhaps the place where Mexican workers were most heavily relied upon, CCIH inspector Fred Rugg reported in 1923 that the "majority of the farmers are prejudiced against the Mexican saying that what little education they have absorbed has made them worthless laborers." Whatever the depth of that prejudice, it did not dissuade growers from vigorously protesting any proposed limitations on Mexican immigration. After the U.S. Congress passed the 1924 Immigration Act (which was one of a series dating to 1917), nativist factions in California sought to amend the law to put western-hemisphere immigration on the same quota system that guided immigration from Europe. Against this, California farmers, especially those who grew cotton, melons, and beets, repeatedly called for *increased* immigration from Latin America to prevent the "labor shortage" produced by the restriction of European and Asian immigration.[43]

As it had been during World War I, CCIH remained opposed to Mexican immigration for labor purposes and took a leading role in the immigration restriction movement. The Commission declared that "it believes that un-restricted immigration from Mexico should be stopped" because it was inimical to the social health of the state. Admitting that Mexican laborers "seem almost essential" to agribusiness as well as to railroad construction and repair, CCIH claimed that Mexicans were "causing an immense social problem for our char-ities, schools and health departments":

> The spread of agriculture and vastly increased acreage devoted to seasonal crops require more labor for harvest time and a constant parade of Mexicans is to be found about the state. Sooner or later many of them are stranded without funds . . . with the result that they become charges upon [the] counties. . . . There will always be a need of Mexicans in agriculture and consequent need of watch-fulness against impositions practiced upon them, as well as a need for community protection against disease carriage by them as an *inevitable* consequence of the mode in which they live. [Emphasis added][44]

Absent an explanation of how Mexicans were more of a social hazard than were white migrant workers (whom CCIH records indicate were still in or near the majority of all migrant laborers in inspected camps), presumably CCIH felt that there was some innate, inevitable quality in the Mexican people that made them threatening.

Archbishop Edward Hanna, Simon Lubin's successor as president of CCIH,[45] lobbied the California congressional delegation early in 1926 in support of the Box Bill, which sought to put western-hemisphere immigration on a quota. Hanna informed the California congress members that "Mexicans as a general rule become a public charge under slight provocation and have become a great burden to our communities." Closer to the point:

> For the most part the Mexicans are indians [*sic*] and very seldom become natural-ized. They know little of sanitation, are very low mentally and are generally unhealthy. Their children, however, who are born here are citizens and have all the rights and privileges as such. This second generation has given our school depart-

ment, juvenile and other courts a tremendous amount of trouble and no doubt this will continue.

Just in case the representatives and senators were still unclear as to why Mexican immigration should be restricted, Hanna enumerated the reasons precisely:

1. They drain our charities.
2. They or their children have become a large portion of our jail population.
3. They affect the health of our communities.
4. They create a problem in our labor camps.
5. They require special attention in our schools and are of low mentality.
6. They diminish the percentage of our white population.
7. They remain foreign.

Hanna publicized these opinions in various newspapers throughout the state (and thus drew considerable ire from Mexican-Americans and their supporters).[46]

If Mexican-Americans were displeased with Hanna and CCIH's positions, farm interests in the Imperial Valley were even more so. In 1924, Imperial growers had publicized what they called a "labor shortage," and the public stance of the Commission two years later was not helping matters. The "labor shortage" was for the most part blamed on an "Immigration Patrol scare" initiated when the Border Patrol announced plans to increase scrutiny of migratory workers' immigration documents because it felt it had evidence that many workers in Imperial Valley had entered the country illegally, failing to pay a head tax and visa fees, and to take a literacy test. The growers, fearful of losing their labor overabundance, quickly established a program to assist workers in saving fees and to assist in tests and registrations. When deposits in any bank in the Valley had reached the $18 required for a head tax and visa, the worker was officially registered with the Immigration Service. In the meantime, the Border Patrol promised only to deport those workers whose savings passbooks were not "up to date."[47]

A writer for the state Bureau of Labor reported at this time that to the degree there was a labor shortage in Imperial, it had less to do with the actions of the Border Patrol and a lot more to do with the fact that "better wages, living and working conditions" were drawing Mexican workers to other parts of the state, and CCIH seconded this notion. "The average employer of Mexican labor," the Commission noted in its 1926 *Annual Report*, "when approached by the Commission's inspector regarding camp conditions, usually answers by condemning the Mexican and all his works, but he realizes the necessity of this class of labor during the harvest."[48]

Given CCIH's complex relationship with the "problem" of Mexican labor—

believing in the inevitability of Mexican "nature" *and* in the possibilities of reform; seeing Mexicans as unfit for California citizenship, as mentally and culturally inferior, *and* condemning the actions of growers—it is perhaps inevitable that one of CCIH's proudest, most publicized achievements came with a Mexican labor camp improvement program on the farms of the Guasti Company near Fontana in San Bernardino County. In this program, the racist rhetoric and reformist impulses solidified in the form of model housing. All during 1926, as Archbishop Hanna was fulminating against the Mexican threat to the health of the state, the Commission received complaints about the Guasti camps. Edward Brown reported to CCIH executive secretary Robert Kearney in April that he had finally been able to convince Mr. Guasti to build a whole new camp for Hispanic workers. "If we put this over," Brown enthused, "it will be the biggest individual labor camp construction in the history of the Commission." By the middle of August, the first worker apartments had been completed, and Brown rejoiced:

> The Guasti camp . . . will be the banner labor camp of the South when completed. It is worth a trip to Guasti just to see how some of the Mexican families can be elevated. . . . The kitchens of this new camp are piped for gas. The Guasti Company sells gas to the occupants for so much a month same as installment houses. I assure you that it was a pleasure for me to look into these Mexican kitchens and see the Mexican women instead of being smoked out with an old Dutch oven, standing by gas stoves like noble Anglo Saxons.[49]

Such paternalistic attitudes toward Mexican workers remained fairly constant, even as these workers became increasingly militant beginning in 1928. As one of the branch office chiefs for CCIH's 1927 successor, the Division of Immigration and Housing (DIH; see Chapter 5) wrote in 1932 at the height of Hispanic worker militancy during the Depression, "A great deal of effort must needs be expended to correct their lapses ~~from the straight and narrow~~ and to guide them into the accepted channels of American convention and custom" (strikeouts in original).[50]

The Rural Idyll at Last

The limits of the Commission's—and agribusiness's—reform racism were most quickly reached in the reclaimed deserts of the Imperial Valley, rendering its halfhearted commitment to the rights and needs of workers quite ineffectual. In Imperial, to begin with, agents for CCIH often tied culpability for degraded conditions not to growers, but to Mexican workers, who "with their willingness to live under any conditions imposed upon them by their employers" had "a demoralizing effect on the seasonal camps within which American labor is housed." And then, when Mexican workers did grow militant and refused to live in the conditions imposed upon them, the Commission worked with growers to assure that militancy would not be successful, though it did always attempt to use the fear of militancy as a lever of reform.[51]

In 1926, with an incipient militancy among Mexican workers budding, Edward Brown and CCIH decided that it was time for a "show down" over camp conditions in the Imperial Valley. At the S. A. Gerrard Company, a large diversified grower, inspector Fred Rugg "found nothing in the way of improvement" over the preceding year and eventually had its foreman G. Jones arrested for violation of the camp law. Jones's arrest was not born of concern for the conditions Mexicans were forced to endure in the Valley. Rather it was one of several arrests designed to show that poor conditions led to a decline in "American" workers and actually attracted unnecessary Mexican workers. If camp conditions were improved, CCIH felt, then unrestricted immigration could be shown to be unnecessary: the "labor shortage" would disappear. The Commission thus resolved to discipline the most influential growers in the region. "You must understand," Brown informed Rugg, "there is no company or operator bigger than the State of California."[52]

The landowners and farming corporations of the Valley felt differently, and CCIH saw formidable opposition to both its improvement plans and its desire to block Mexican immigration. One of Jones's associates set the tenor of the battle that was soon to ensue between CCIH and Imperial growers when he told Rugg: "The company thinks you fellows are unreasonable in ordering bunks and having housing for Mexicans . . . [and] the company is willing to spend the money to put the camp law out" of the Commission and into more friendly hands. Pointing to a favorite myth of the growers in the region, Jones explained that the climate made the guidelines of the Commission both unreasonable and unnecessary—and what is more, the Mexican labor had no use, nor desire, for better conditions. "Growers would get together and fight before living up to the requirements of the housing law," Jones told Rugg. Nonetheless, Rugg was able to extract from Jones a promise to provide latrines, if not decent housing, and dropped Jones's arrest. Edward Brown reprimanded his inspector for this action, telling him to "hop to it" and arrest any operator running an unsanitary camp.[53]

Brown's order caused considerable difficulty for Rugg (not least when he had to rearrest Jones) because, following standard CCIH practice, Rugg had already informed Imperial growers that he would not press charges if they promised to clean up their camps over the winter (after the current summer harvests, which were only then just beginning, were completed). When Rugg followed Brown's advice and filed charges against a number of growers, he found that local judges were far more sympathetic to the growers' highly imaginative defenses than they were to the desires of the state immigration commission. Two arrested growers hid behind their contractors: they told the judge that their camps were not covered by the law. They each had only one employee in the camp; the others resident there did not work for them. Since the camp law regulated only camps that housed five or more *employees,* the growers were not in violation of the law. Agreeing with this logic, the judge dismissed the charges against both growers, but not before reprimanding Rugg for making the arrests and reminding him that "conditions in this Valley are different. They, the Mexicans, are on each ranch a short while—they don't appreciate and won't take care of the facilities provided." Moreover, the judge ruled, since the growers were not operating camps, it also stood to reason that Rugg could not have inspected camps operated by the growers. Therefore, it was highly unlikely that one of the growers could have hit Rugg in the face while Rugg was inspecting his camp. The judge thus dismissed charges of assault against an officer brought by Rugg against the grower. Similarly, the judge in the Jones case gave the defendant a suspended sentence on the condition that he make nominal improvements to the S. A. Gerrard camps. Like his colleague, this judge lectured Rugg that "Mexicans in these camps would not use the conveniences provided for them," and thus he "was not in favor of the Camp Law." CCIH "should not expect the farmers to live up to the requirements of the camp pamphlet here in Imperial Valley" (Figure 8).[54]

Here then, is the "rural idyll" growers promised at the end of World War I: it was built on the constant, consistent objectification and racialization of labor. No individuals here, no flowering yeomanry, only the marked, overdetermined embodiment of labor power. By 1926, as much as they may have despised Mexican and Hispanic workers, California growers *needed* them, just as at various times they had needed single white men, Chinese and Japanese immigrants, women, children, and the growing numbers of Filipinos that were also now entering the fields. But need required neither respect nor understanding; rather it required just the opposite: a set of ideologies that explained to the farmers themselves why it was acceptable to so fully exploit those who made their profits for them. In their friendliest guises, as in the recommendations of Dr. Bennett, these ideologies dripped with the paternalism that had long been associated with the exploitation of labor in extractive industries. At their worst, they provided the excuse for the attempted elimination of those—like the Chinese and Japanese—that farmers or other powerful interests no longer needed or wanted.

Both forms of racist ideology were at work in the Imperial Valley. The

Figure 8. Migratory labor "housing" in the Imperial Valley in the 1920s encountered by inspectors for the California Commission of Immigration and Housing. (Photo: California Commission of Immigration and Housing.)

Imperial Valley "represented industrialized farming in its most extreme unalloyed form," according to Cletus Daniel, but because of that, Donald Worster adds, for many "it demonstrated that the entrepreneurial Americans were the master race come at last to command the desert."[55] Entreprenuerial bodies were marked too: they were inevitably white, and most often male. The Imperial was destiny clearly made manifest, the very culmination of the American Dream. As early as 1911, popular literature was picturing the Imperial Valley as a blooming, spectacular, visionary, quintessentially *American* place. It was a place made primarily by white American engineering ingenuity, as the Colorado River was eventually tamed and put to good use. In his novel of that year, *The Winning of Barbara Worth,* Harold Bell Wright displayed the view for us:

> There was more in Barbara's desert now than pictures woven magically in the air. There were beautiful scenes of farms with houses and barns and fences and stacks, with cattle and horses in pastures, and fields of growing grain, the dark green of alfalfa, with threads and lines and spots of water that . . . shone in the distance like gleaming silver.

For Wright, as for his heroine Barbara Worth, building a home in the desert, and making that desert a rural retreat not just recognizable, but enviable in the east for its dedication to the cause of "Good Business," was "the master passion of the race."[56]

For that "master passion" to be realized, for the white race to triumph over nature in California and create such a stunning landscape, the objectification and destruction of racialized other was an economic and social necessity. Mexican workers could not be seen as active subjects. In CCIH's version, they were pawns undermining the ability of "Americans" to secure decent camp housing and good jobs. In the growers' minds, they were simply living as they naturally do, making themselves available to *serve* whites in their quest to make the desert a garden. Mexican workers deserved nothing better than what they were given. *Only* through the objectification of Mexican workers in this manner, it seems, was "our" own Worth to be won.[57]

Whenever CCIH inspectors were in Imperial Valley—in 1926 to analyze the claim of "labor shortage," in 1928 when Mexican workers began a series of strikes notable for their militancy, in 1934 when one of the bloodiest strikes in California labor history drew national attention to the labor relations of the California desert—they stayed at the Hotel Barbara Worth, named for the mythical champion of southernmost-Californian rural civility. It is an odd experience indeed to read the reports by CCIH employees about excruciatingly bad living conditions in the labor camps of the area, vigilante assaults on striking workers and their allies, and punitive raids on strikers' encampments, on letterhead, yellowed from years of sitting in boxes on archival shelves, that features a drawing of Barbara Worth represented as the beautiful, quintessentially western, white, satisfied ranchwoman. Looking like Barbara Stanwyck in *The Big Valley*, Barbara Worth represents—in her body, the way that Mexican workers are made to represent only labor power even as their bodies continually negotiate the bloody terrain that exists between the picture of the landscape that materializes in the heads of growers and novelists, and the reality of their lives in the fields and camps that constituted that picture—not just the destiny and "master passion" of the "master race," but also the conquering of nature through the appropriation of living labor that makes such a passion at all possible. In the loganberry fields of the north during the war, as in the pea and cantaloupe fields of the desert Imperial a decade later, the rural idyll remained a convenient mirage that masked the everyday business of growing staggering profits.

5 / The Political Economy of Landscape and the Return of Radicalism

For some growers in California during the 1920s profits were enormous; but numerous other growers found profit making, like much of the landscape, to be something of a mirage during this period. Beginning in 1921, agriculture in California suffered a debilitating deflationary crisis as the World War I boom finally came to an end. With deflation came a brutal process of capital centralization. This deflation was particularly threatening to smaller farmers; to larger agricultural concerns, deflationary restructuring provided even greater opportunities to consolidate their control over agricultural labor. For farming industries, the land itself is a fixed investment; it is their primary means of production. Returns on investment in land may be realized in two ways, each of which will be at some risk during economically uncertain times. In the first place, land appreciates, and over the long term farmers reap profits from their improvements to it. But in California, as labor economist Varden Fuller showed, the appreciation of farm land values was tied directly to the promise of cheap and assured labor. Without that, agricultural land could not be sold; it was too heavily capitalized. The second way to realize a return on investment was by making the land productive, by farming it. Farming is a unique enterprise, different in many ways from other forms of industrial production. Chief among these differences is that profit from any portion of land is realized only once (or at best twice) each year. Unlike that in a factory, which can engage in continuous production, commodity production on farms is highly time specific. If a harvest is disrupted for any reason, then at least a year's investment is lost. Either way, surplus value in agriculture during times of crisis can be difficult to realize. More than anything else, therefore, the deflationary shakeout demanded an even greater control by capital over the costs of labor power and the forms of labor reproduction.[1]

Growers had two strategies for controlling the costs of labor. The first and most widely accepted technique was to minimize housing and sanitation costs by subcontracting, shifting costs to the community at large, or providing only the most rudimentary facilities on farms and ranches. To do so, growers relied on the daily reproduction of labor occurring through an oversupply of labor (which meant that it did not matter if any *particular* laborer returned each day, as long as *a* worker returned). The reproduction of labor power, a primary "function" of the landscape, itself rests on a need to rationalize *systems* of reproduction because inequality and powerlessness inevitably carry with them the seeds of revolt. If productive landscapes—in the Delta, in Imperial Valley, in the rice-growing regions north of Sacramento, or in the expanding cotton district of the southern San Joaquin Valley—are to be maintained under capitalism, possibilities for workers to revolt must be minimized. This contradiction in the production of labor power provides workers with a significant, indeed essential, degree of power, because their status as threat, especially during times of economic instability, must be neutralized. And this process of neutralization, as we have already seen, was an awful lot of work. It required an exercise in violence to compel labor, an exercise that was often neither politically nor ideologically expedient.

When agricultural labor was militant in California, and when it possessed the power to challenge growers' supremacy in the fields, the first strategy of labor control carried with it significant risks: dissatisfied workers often struck particular growers and whole harvests, threatening a whole year's production costs and profits. At these times, if brute force was not working, or if it was not politically possible, growers turned to their second strategy: providing decent accommodations and work conditions in hopes of minimizing turnover, increasing productivity, and making workers more content and therefore not prone to striking. If anything, this strategy was even more risky than the first, especially to smaller, less highly capitalized firms. The built environment— tents, cookhouses, toilets in the fields—represents an investment in *fixed* capital, a freezing of capital in place for relatively long periods of time (and capital can only attract profits to the degree that it is capital-in-motion). In times of economic uncertainty, like the deflationary 1920s, long-term investments with returns that were not readily visible often proved too great a risk to many growers, small and large alike.

As a "quasi object" that incorporates the power struggles that go into its making, the built landscape is the result of a series of compromised decisions that, in Harvey's words, "litter" a region with evidence of the past needs and desires of capital-in-motion. Labor camps, or other inputs to the reproduction of labor power, are thus a form of "productive consumption"—items consumed so that production may proceed. The built environment "functions as a vast, humanly created resource system, comprising use values embedded in the physical landscape, which can be utilized for production, consumption, and exchange." Harvey argues that at "any one moment the built environment appears as a palimpsest of landscapes fashioned according to the dictates of different modes of production at different stages of their historical development." While Harvey's formulation sounds too one-sided, leaving little room for worker agency to fashion landscape even in resistance, the point is apt. The "geographical landscape that results" from this ceaseless motion of capital, Harvey declares, "is the crowning glory of past capital development. But at the same time it expresses the power of dead labor over living labor, and as such it imprisons and inhibits the accumulation process within a set of physical constraints."[2]

The landscape thus occupies an uneasy position, at once a (compromised) product of past investment, that itself was a response to social conditions of the time, a necessary component of the reproduction of labor power, and a fetter to further accumulation (the triumph of dead labor over living labor) that has to be "creatively destroyed" so that new returns can be realized. For many farmers in the 1920s, investment in the landscape of labor camps was seen as too risky, precisely *because* it froze capital in an uncertain investment. During the economic crises that wracked California agriculture in the two decades after World War I, therefore, many farmers sought to minimize the risk inherent in fixing their capital in land and buildings. Rather, they chose to reinforce the first option of labor control by continually recruiting for more—and (they hoped) ever more tractable—labor supplies in Mexico and, for a while, the Philippines.[3] Doing so, of course, they unwittingly invested in the landscape anyway: Harvey is correct, the landscape *is* a result of the dictates—or more accurately the desires—of capital at particular moments of its historical development. Even if those desires are expressed as *dis*investment, they are still recorded in the spaces in which agricultural laborers lived.

Labor Supply and the Consolidation of Capital

Demands for increased western-hemisphere and Filipino immigration were typically led by large growers and were not universally welcomed by small farmers, who realized that the benefits of immigration disproportionately accrued to large agribusiness concerns. Small farmers understood that a saturated labor market increased the competitive advantage of large, more highly capital-ized farms because the value of the labor power of a farmer working alone, or the value of a family's labor power, was determined by the social value of *all* farm labor. A saturated labor market meant that the value of the labor of an independent operator was depressed.

The competition between larger- and smaller-scale farming operations that increased with the 1921 deflation became acute after 1925. War prices had led to "unwarranted optimism" in the planting of many crops, especially decidu-ous fruits, which came into maturity during a time of deflated farm prices. While "small holdings remained the rule" in specialty crops because of high capitalization costs and because of uncertainty in the long-range market, ship-pers and processors sought to consolidate their control over the production process, and thus to guarantee for themselves some stability during the 1920s. These processors and shippers—cotton ginners, fruit and vegetable canners and packers, large-scale marketers—increased their control over smaller grow-ers particularly by extending long-term contracts and credit, in essence shifting risk to the growers and inaugurating a trend that persisted until well after the end of World War II. To further solidify control and protect profits, the corpo-rations and cooperatives frequently dictated wage levels to which their contract farmers had to adhere. The Division of Immigration and Housing (DIH) found that throughout California control over labor and production conditions in a district was often highly centralized. "This district is practically controlled by the Chowchilla Gin people, the management of which is a subsidiary of the Pacific Cotton Seed Oil Company," an inspector wrote to Edward Brown in 1928, suggesting that the Division should put pressure to bear on the gin com-pany since decisions concerning labor camp conditions were made there and not by individual farmers.[4]

During the 1920s banks became increasingly important as holders of mort-gages, lenders of capital to farmers, and owners of defaulted farms. As farm foreclosures became common after deflation was generalized throughout the agricultural sector in 1925, banks and their allies in the packing and shipping industries argued that no matter what they might prefer, and no matter what may seem right, they had little choice but to minimize labor costs by disinvest-ing in labor camp improvements. "We admit that Bankers, as a class, may not have the gift of prophesy any more than common mortals," the Bakersfield cot-ton company S. I. Merrill and Sons wrote CCIH that year, "but they have a good deal to say about money needed to construct houses for cotton pickers."[5]

Soon to become the largest bank in the world (and a lightning rod for farm reformers in the 1930s), the Bank of America established California Lands,

Inc. in 1929 to manage and sometimes sell the more than 1,000 farms it acquired largely through foreclosure or other financial transactions. Although it was official policy to subdivide large holdings it possessed and sell them to small farmers, California Lands more typically sold to companies such as the California Packing Corporation (Cal Pak, later Del Monte), one of the largest canning operations in the country. Bank of America justified its practice by pointing out that these firms possessed a greater economic stability than did smaller farmers.[6]

The increased economic power of large corporate farmers during the 1920s, with their reliance on imported labor and on labor contractors who made it possible to minimize labor reproduction costs by skirting the Labor Camp Law, was matched by the increasing power of the marketing and production cooperatives. The cooperatives (such as the California Fruit Growers Exchange [Sunkist], the Western Growers Protective Association, the California Walnut Growers Association [Diamond Brand], and the Grower-Shipper Vegetable Association) themselves were clearly controlled by (and served the interests of) large, capital-intensive firms. Small growers were less enamored with the development of cooperative associations as they assumed monopoly power in particular crops: Sunkist and Diamond, for example, controlled between 75 percent and 90 percent of the citrus and walnuts in the 1920s and 1930s. Allied with the marketing and production cooperatives as California agriculture restructured in the 1920s were the Chamber of Commerce and the Farm Bureau Federation, organizations ostensibly dedicated to the promotion of small farmers. The Farm Bureau had been established originally to disseminate Agricultural Extension research and information to family farmers throughout the United States. In California, the extension service of the University of California was closely allied with the Gianini Foundation, the University of California, Berkeley, agricultural economics institute established through the generosity of Bank of America founder A. P. Gianini. The foundation specialized in farm economics and research geared to farming *as a business*. With this alliance in California, the state Farm Bureau Federation had a decidedly "big business" cast. As a historian of farm organizations in California found, the Farm Bureau was led by "large farmers with substantial economic interests, who often had close ties with the marketing cooperatives, even though smaller farmers comprised the majority of its members."[7]

Additionally, the 1920s saw the development of numerous regionally based "labor-exchanges" and "labor bureaus." An outgrowth of government efforts to control and rationalize labor-supply and wage levels during the war, these exchanges set the "prevailing" wage for a given region each season, recruited labor, sometimes cajoled growers into providing accommodations, imported strikebreakers when necessary, and generally coordinated grower activity on all phases of the "labor problem." The most active labor bureaus were those established in the Imperial Valley and in the San Joaquin Valley cotton growing regions. The Agricultural Labor Bureau of the San Joaquin Valley was formed in April 1926, under the auspices of the state Chamber of Commerce and the Farm Bureau Federation, and with the active support of the cotton gins and many large growers in the region. The Bureau hired Frank Palomares, erstwhile CCIH labor camp inspector, as its director. Growers liked to refer to Palomares as the "Padre of the Workers" because of his decade-long work, beginning with CCIH, breaking strikes and defusing discontent among Spanish-speaking agricultural workers. Under Palomares's auspices, growers from throughout the Valley met each year to determine the appropriate wage rates for particular crops and tasks. The Bureau was responsible for assuring that the set wage remained the "prevailing" wage—that is, the highest permissible wage in the district. If wages started to rise, Palomares recruited more workers, threatened growers paying higher wages, and otherwise tried to protect the profit of his patrons. The definition of "prevailing wage" actually changed depending on the context of its use. By the 1930s, county relief agencies in the agricultural areas pegged their relief payments to the "prevailing wage." In this case, organizations such as the Agricultural Labor Bureau worked to assure that the "prevailing wage" was understood to be the absolute lowest wage that farmers could get away with paying.[8]

Palomares possessed a gift of understatement that well exemplified how many growers conceived of their labor supplies. "Our fruit season was somewhat late as well as our cotton season," Palomares wrote in an annual report to the Labor Bureau commissioners. "Labor therefore came early expecting to get into the harvest as in past seasons. The delay caused a little inconvenience but that was remedied when the harvest began." That is, many workers arrived destitute, only to find there was no work yet. Even so, as the season began, Palomares recruited several thousand extra laborers "in order to complete the harvest in record time." Palomares's recruitment skills also became important "during the peak of the packing season," when a "labor shortage" of box makers was discovered. Palomares was able to report to his commissioners, however, that "through the efforts of the Bureau, an adequate supply was obtained from Southern California and the Peninsula [Baja California]." Because of this recruitment effort, Palomares noted, "the wage schedule for box making was maintained." In the fall, Palomares was able to "satisfactorily adjust" incipient strikes in some orchards and cotton fields, "resulting in no loss of pickers and in no changes of the wage schedule."[9]

The consolidation of capital was expressed not only in growing control over labor and production conditions by fewer and fewer firms, but also in farming practices that emerged after the war years. One indication of changing farming conditions in the state was that California agriculture greatly intensified. CCIH was impressed with the introduction of "Fordism" in the fields of California during the 1920s, and the imprint of industrialized farming on the land was great. By 1929, farms comprising more than 1,000 acres constituted only 3.8 percent of all farms in California; but they controlled 63.6 percent of all farmland in the state. Of all farms in the United Sates that grossed more than $30,000 annually, 37 percent were in California; for fruit and truck crops, nearly 60 percent were in that state. Intensive crops made up 78.4 percent of all crops grown in California. Only sixty years earlier, intensive crops had accounted for only 6.6 percent of all California agricultural production. While improved agricultural acreage had little changed since 1910, by 1929 the value of all farm land and buildings had more than doubled from $1.45 billion to $3.42 billion.[10]

With this intensification of production came an intensification of labor at critical harvest times. Excepting field crops (such as grain and cotton), farmers of all crop types reported greater labor demands during the 1920s than they had before World War I. Field crop demands dropped to an average of 88 percent of prewar demand (and would have been much lower if labor-intensive cotton was not expanding in the San Joaquin Valley), but truck crops increased to 233 percent, fruit and nuts to 168 percent, and livestock to 110 percent of prewar demand. A weighted average of labor demand for the decade (considering the effects of acreage and share of labor force devoted to each crop) showed an increase to an average 137 percent of prewar demand. This increase in labor demand did not happen evenly across the year. Rather, innovations in chemical use and mechanization led to a *decrease* in demand during nonharvest times, while harvest tasks remained largely unmechanized. In 1929, some 196,000 farmworkers were employed at some time during the year, with demand peaking in September, when 145,000 *temporary* workers were needed by farms and farm-related industries (Figure 9).[11]

"The Proletarian with a Jit"

The biggest problem that this intensification of farming and labor presented to farmer-industrialists centered on the costs of labor reproduction. Labor was only needed during particular and rather short times. Farmers were thus pre-

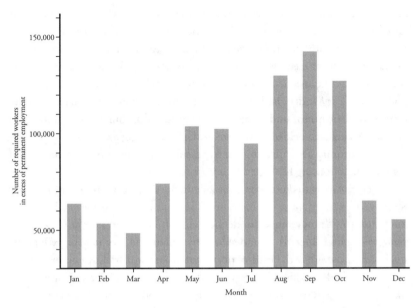

Figure 9. Seasonal farm labor demand in California, 1935-36. Source: California State Relief Administration, *Transients in California* (Sacramento: Mimeo, 1936).

sented with a need to have laborers available in sufficient numbers at particular times in a *yearly* productive cycle, yet they were apparently unable to afford the costs of yearly reproduction. That is, the costs of reproducing workers' labor power had to be externalized by growers in California. In the 1920s, growers reasserted the need for even greater labor mobility as a partial solution to this problem. CCIH concurred that workers had to be sped even more efficiently to places needing their labor, and away again to other districts when their labor was no longer needed. Chief labor camp inspector Edward Brown in 1926 called for the development of a statewide plan for rationalizing patterns of mobility in industrialized agriculture. After conferring with Los Angeles Chamber of Commerce's Dr. George P. Clements, Brown sought a meeting of:

> various groups of people who are now groping in the darkness for a solution to the migratory problem; that is, where large groups of unskilled laborers are congregating where there is no work to be had, the feasibility of shifting these workers to locations where there is ample work and a shortage of labor.[12]

Increased mobility, of course, had to be weighed against the possibility that mobility itself could be made subversive by workers as it had been before World War I. The question thus remained one of rationality—at least as far as growers and CCIH were concerned. For most workers, there was little at all rational about either the system as it then existed or calls for even greater mobility, especially as automobile travel became more and more necessary for migratory workers seeking even a rudimentary living. Little came of Brown's suggestion, as the use of autos, coupled with importation of labor from the Philippines and Mexico, and the work of agents like Frank Palomares rendered labor shortages minor and temporary. The use of automobiles by migratory farmworkers had a decided advantage for California growers: cars could double as homes for migratory laborers, further removing growers from responsibility for providing housing for their harvest workers.[13]

In fact, the increased use of automobiles helped bring about one of the most significant changes in the industrialized agricultural landscape of the 1920s: the growth of "auto camps," both private and "community" (serving several growers). CCIH inspectors found that while others besides migratory laborers stayed at auto camps, the camps' primary purpose in agricultural areas was to house farmworkers. The Commission also found that sanitary conditions in most of the camps were similar to what farmers had historically provided, and thus an issue of great concern in the state. Indeed, the conditions of auto camps, like those of more traditional farm labor camps, tended to change with the waxing and waning of worker power in the fields. In the mid-1920s, when workers' power to transform their conditions was at a low ebb, conditions in many auto camps were as bad as they ever were on the farms. "There is a growing tendency to clutter the state with so-called 'auto-camps' and 'tent-cities,'" CCIH complained as it began to lobby the legislature for the right to regulate auto camps (which was finally granted in 1929).[14]

Agriculturalists, unsurprisingly, pointed to the use of automobiles by migratory workers—especially Mexican—as proof of the prosperity that was possible for crop followers. Conveniently combining racial mythmaking with the California Dream of unalloyed beauty apprehended through mobility, the *Pacific Rural Press* responded to accusations that farmers were actively developing "peon" labor in the 1920s:

> Peons? Isn't the word peon a little out of character when applied to a Mexican family which buzzes around in its own battered flivver, going from crop to crop, seeing Beautiful California, breathing its air, eating its food, and finally doing the homing pigeon stunt back to Mexico with more money than their neighbors ever dreamed existed?

Even more, the *Pacific Rural Press* crowed, the invention of auto camps would finally "Americanize" much of the state (the advantages to Mexicans notwithstanding). "Auto Camps have done much this year to replace Orientals in the raisin district; given a place to camp they may prove the means of making over the foothill orchard district as real American sections."[15]

The Industrial Workers of the World (IWW), somewhat resurgent during the early and mid-1920s, was much less sanguine about the effect that driving was having on migratory workers. "California is noted for its many schemes of graft and the 'auto park' is one of the latest, and best. As always it is the worker who is beggared in the course of the graft." By adopting the car, the IWW argued, fruit tramps (and other agricultural workers) had increased their beholdenness to capital: gas and repairs had to be purchased, and the car parked while the owner worked. "An adaptable capitalism arranges such matters" by creating the auto camp, where lodging for car and driver could be purchased for about a dollar and a half a week. "The fruit rancher seeks the victims of his exploitation most readily in the 'auto park' for he knows that the proletarian with a jit, the migratory by gas, has to work all the time to manage it and therefore has to work at whatever wages are offered." The advantages to growers were obvious: auto campers and tent campers provided their own sleeping facilities and congregated in camps run by third parties or wherever sheriff's deputies would allow them, thereby providing a ready supply of labor while simultaneously lowering the housing burden of many farmers.[16]

Labor Camps in the 1920s

Growers also turned increasingly to labor contractors during the 1920s as a means of lowering their direct costs. In various decisions, California courts had exempted growers from culpability for labor camp and work conditions when contractors were used *and* had exempted contractors themselves from the provisions of the Labor Camp Sanitation Act. Growers were not slow to discover the advantages of these rulings. Whether using contractors or not, many growers simply refused to comply with the camp law, arguing either that there was no need to or that they could not afford to.[17]

Concerned that conditions in the hops fields in 1927 were similar to conditions at the time of the Wheatland riot, Edward Brown ordered his inspectors to be especially vigilant, especially in the camps of Horst and Durst, two of the Commission's earliest model ranches that now seemed to be the worst in the district. Hops growers throughout the northern part of the state had returned to their practices of overrecruiting and providing only the most minimal of conditions. To these growers, CCIH reasserted the dangers to their own self-interest that their camp conditions implied. "This is a practice we do not advise," Edward Brown wrote to various hops growers, "inasmuch as it might lead to dissatisfaction and trouble." If they insisted on recruiting a surplus of labor, Brown pleaded, hops growers had to house them in a legal manner. When growers ignored these requests, the Commission let the matter drop. A comparison of inspection reports and arrests for the Sacramento Valley indicates that no large growers operating "bad" camps (i.e., camps in multiple violation of the law) were arrested or fined.[18]

Large hops growers responded instead by attempting to increase their control over the actions and behavior of workers on their ranches. At the George Hewlett Ranch in Mendocino County, one of the largest in the state, all hops pickers had to register with the management, which gave them identification numbers to be worn at all times. These numbers were designed, workers were told, to "help detect people in your camps who have no business there." Numbered workers would have the advantage of "pleasantly situated campgrounds" and could find "swimming and bathing in the [Russian] river." No other sanitary facilities were mentioned in the Hewlett Ranch advertisement. As they had been a decade and a half earlier in Wheatland, workers were mostly expected to provide their own bedding and shelter, though Hewlett did make a few tents available for rent. Rather than improved conditions, workers in the hops field found heightened surveillance and greater control over their nonwork lives.[19]

Most camps in the agricultural districts were temporary, only operating during labor demand peaks. CCIH was continually frustrated in efforts to improve these camps. Inspections could not begin until the camps were open and had more than five residents, and short seasons rendered the Commission's requests for abatement meaningless. Inspector John Gluth reported to the Commission offices that one operator of a temporary camp—who certainly was not unique in his opinions—"doesn't feel that he should be compelled to furnish bunks or beds for all employees, [or] adequate sleeping quarters and bathing facilities." And like many in his position, this camp operator was never cited nor arrested for the substandard conditions of his camp facilities, despite the fact that whether "temporary or permanent [an] operator who undertakes to run a camp is liable for the provision[s] of the Act." In fact, CCIH was decreasingly able to either force or cajole growers to provide decent conditions in the camps, as capital was centralized in powerful labor bureaus, farm bureaus, marketing cooperatives, and financial institutions; as growers imported huge numbers of racialized workers consigned to inferiority by powerful naturalistic ideologies of racial fitness-to-serve; and as an increasingly hostile state government and legislature sought to undermine the power of CCIH itself. By the mid-1920s the IWW-induced reform of the prewar years, the "revolutionized" landscape, seemed largely a thing of the past. The political economic realities of the post-war deflationary period were incorporated in the details of the landscapes within which migratory workers still toiled in large numbers. But now they did so without even the (compromised) concern of an effective, activist Commission of Immigration and Housing.[20]

The Decline of the Commission of Immigration and Housing

The shape of the landscape is a compromised product of the multitudinous relations of power that structure and are created out of the workings of the political economy. The form of the landscape stabilizes when no one arises to contest the morphology and its representation. For nearly a decade and a half, the California Commission of Immigration and Housing had been an integral part of the equations of power in extractive industries throughout the state, an organization that frequently contested the shape of the landscape. Certainly, CCIH was contradictory in its activities and motivations. Seeking to protect the interests of agro-industrialists and improve conditions for migratory workers CCIH as often as not merely served to undermine the power of workers themselves. Convinced that worker power had been completely subverted by the World War I repression and the subsequent recruiting efforts in Mexico and elsewhere, agribusiness lobbied throughout the 1920s to disempower CCIH, which it saw as its only remaining obstacle to complete control over the conditions of production and reproduction in the fields. As early as 1919, even as it was declaring it had "revolutionized" labor camp conditions throughout the state, CCIH found itself attacked by the very interests it served, as well as by hostile factions in the state, especially the budget-making state Board of Control.

The Board of Control repeatedly slashed CCIH's budget in the early 1920s, and the Commission found itself with fewer resources and staff as it attempted to moderate the effects of massive agricultural growth in the Imperial Valley and a somewhat resurgent IWW in the lumber camps of the north coast and the Sierras. CCIH quickly saw its effectiveness wane in the face of less money and greater demands. Responding not to a public notice, but to a private communication from one of his inspectors, Lubin's successor as CCIH director, Robert Kearney, spelled out the realities of the Commission's role during the 1920s: "It is our duty to enforce the law as it exists, and not to use our judgment entirely on what should or should not be in the camps." Kearney's position was quite opposite the activist stance of his predecessors Carleton Parker, George Bell, and Simon Lubin. By 1926, CCIH had resigned itself solely to the role of camp inspector, even at a time when conditions in the fields were, as CCIH itself put it, "as unsanitary and squalid as has ever existed."[21]

The decline of CCIH as an activist agency involved in labor camp improvement and propaganda may be traced, ironically, to its success in destroying labor militancy during the war. In the summer of 1918, reveling in the fame brought to him by his prosecution of Thomas Mooney and Warren Billings for supposedly bombing a Preparedness Day Parade in San Francisco, the corrupt San Francisco district attorney Charles Fickert charged Simon Lubin with disloyalty and with having connections to such IWW notables as Charles Lambert and J. Vance Thompson (!). By naming Thompson as an IWW member, Fickert was able to allege that CCIH had Wobblies on its payroll—a rather ironic charge indeed. Lubin was placed under investigation and all his calls, letters, and telegrams were monitored. CCIH, meanwhile, scrambled to mitigate the damage Fickert's charges had done to its institutional legitimacy. Even before Fickert publicly leveled his charges, CCIH had been requested by the governor to defend its existence in terms of what it was "costing the State and how that investment is justified in public service rendered and in the actual saving of money directly or indirectly for the people." This request put the Commission in a quandary, as its most notable achievement—its role in crushing the IWW—could not be publicized. Lubin replied to the governor by pointing to CCIH's indispensable role in national wartime affairs: "For four years the State of California has been carrying out those activities which are now declared absolutely essential as a war measure, to anticipate labor difficulties and to increase contentment and patriotism among the residents of labor camps." The very success of these efforts, however, was leading critics of the Commission to doubt whether it was still necessary.[22]

The state Board of Control was CCIH's most persistent critic within the government (it was also the leading state institution of anti-Oriental agitation). Every year, the Board of Control "vigorously fought" the appropriation to the agency on the grounds that its salaries were too high. The Board's parsimonious actions (including cutting the Commission's budget in 1918 without explanation) led to the resignation of an executive secretary because the Commission could not pay his promised salary. In response to these and other attacks on CCIH, Lubin offered his resignation in 1919, which the governor refused. Nevertheless, the combined attacks by Fickert and the Board of Control seriously weakened the ability of the Commission to work forcefully *against* an entrenched agricultural industry riding the war boom (which is precisely why Lubin had always to couch his pleas for better work and living conditions as voluntary measures on the part of employers). From this time the focus of CCIH began to shift from environmental activism to the more bureaucratic position enunciated by Robert Kearney.[23]

In 1921, attacks on CCIH by other state agencies and by organized agricultural interests broke into the open once again with a plan to distribute the Commission's various functions among other state departments, many of which did not even possess the nominal autonomy from industrial concerns that CCIH was able to claim. Intensive lobbying by CCIH and its allies in the waning Progressive movement led to a defeat of the proposal and an actual increase in the Commission's budget. Two years later, however, the new conservative governor, Friend Richardson, announced an "economy budget" that abolished the Commission. CCIH's lobbying this time led to the retention of the Commission but the sacking of commissioner Paul Scharrenberg, who had accused the governor of helping agribusiness in "putting the working man . . . back where he was before the days of Hiram Johnson—at the mercy of the corporations and employers." Lubin protested Scharrenberg's removal, and for his effort the governor removed him from the Commission also—but not until six months later when Lubin was out of the state and had no opportunity to marshal forces in opposition to the governor, or, in fact, even to respond to the governor's action. Indeed, Richardson never officially or personally informed Lubin that he was being fired, making the announcement instead in the press. When Lubin finally did respond it was with all the sarcasm he could muster. "I feel exceedingly grateful to his excellency for having removed me from an embarrassing situation," he wrote to a supporter, "for as long as I remained a member of his official family, many of my fellow citizens might have thought that I was in sympathy with the governor's reactionary and destructive program."[24]

The fate of the Commission as an activist, Progressive agency was sealed in 1927 when its functions were incorporated into a reorganized Department of Industrial Relations. The new Division of Immigration and Housing (DIH) answered no longer to the Commission (though the Commission was retained as an advisory body), but rather to the director of the Department. Though reinvigorated during the Depression, DIH drifted somewhat aimlessly during the late 1920s and early 1930s. As later DIH chief Carey McWilliams explained, "Well, you had governors like Friend Richardson and Frank Merriam and they just weren't interested [in DIH]. The people went through the motions of inspecting labor camps but they didn't really inspect them." Even with its apparent aimlessness, however, DIH remained involved in struggles over labor conditions before World War II, and thus, at least to a degree, in the shape that the landscape would take. But for much of the 1920s, events seemed to pass it by as personnel changes, the growing power of large agro-industrialists and marketing cooperatives, and a hostile state government conspired to keep it ineffectual.[25]

The Return of Radicalism

While CCIH and DIH were hamstrung in the 1920s, labor conditions—housing facilities, sanitary conditions, rates of pay—deteriorated to prewar levels. Growers argued they simply could not afford, and workers—especially Mexican workers—did not deserve, better conditions. Myths of Hispanic docility led growers to believe that workers were fully powerless, and finally fully controllable. CCIH was thus doubly unnecessary. It came as quite a shock to growers throughout the state, therefore, in 1928 when Mexican workers in the Imperial Valley staged a strike against cantaloupe growers that, while ultimately unsuccessful, served as a warning of worker militancy to come. Mexican workers, under the auspices of various mutual aid societies and the Consulate at Calexico, organized La Unión de Trabajadores del Valle Imperial, and by the May harvest, some 1,200 (and possibly as many as 2,700) workers had been enrolled. In response to the formation of La Unión, DIH director Kearney instructed his inspectors to undertake an extensive survey of wage, living, and work conditions in the Valley. Warning that "the reports will be valueless" unless information is gathered "from someone in authority at each camp," Kearney reminded his inspectors that "no publicity is to be given regarding the object of securing the data required." DIH hoped that this information would help avert a strike that seemed inevitable.[26]

La Unión presented a series of wage and work condition requests to growers: an increase of 1½ cents per crate picked, ice water in the fields, and "lumber and brush enough to build sheds for laborers and install closets [latrines] for the service of same." The growers flatly rejected these requests and the leaders of La Unión did not plan to press the matter. A small group of radical workers, however, succeeded in calling out workers on several of the farms at the beginning of the harvest (including S. A. Gerrard and some of the other large growers in the Valley). The growers and their allies in local law enforcement responded quickly and decisively, crushing the strike with threats of brute force. When workers walked off the job, growers responded by evicting them from their labor camps—a strikebreaking tool growers used with increasing frequency in the years to come. When workers refused to evacuate the camps, sheriff's deputies arrested them for trespassing. The sheriff also attempted to stop all meetings of strikers, going so far at one point as arresting strike leaders for congregating outside the courthouse while they waited for a meeting the district attorney had scheduled with them. The strike leaders were only released when the district attorney came looking for them, wondering why they had failed to show for their scheduled meeting. Pool halls, the traditional meeting places for

Mexican workers, were likewise closed by the sheriff during the strike on the pretext that their owners did not hold valid licenses. At one meeting in a pool hall, the sheriff "announced that no mass meetings of foreigners were to be permitted in Imperial Valley due to the tense labor situation." Unamused by this announcement, workers "set upon" the sheriff and threw him out, according to local news accounts. The sheriff returned with deputies and forcefully dispersed the meeting and made several arrests. As a result of this action, according to a local newspaper, "picking continued today by loyal workers." Many of these "loyal workers" were Filipinos (themselves some of the most militant workers during the 1920s and 1930s) whose resentment against La Unión (as an ethnically organized union, La Unión excluded Filipino participation) growers channeled into active opposition to the strike.[27]

Growers, like many townspeople, argued that the cantaloupe strike had been fomented entirely by "outsiders"—by foreigners sent from Mexico City, and by "communist agitators." The federal government deepened this impression when it announced it would investigate all arrested workers for deportation because of their radical attitudes. Growers used the ideology of "foreignness" to great effect throughout the strike, both to muster their own forces and to scare strikers. In one circular, growers reminded Mexican workers of how growers had wielded great influence on their behalf during the "immigration scare" the year before, and how they could just as easily use their power to have workers deported if they persisted in striking. The same circular warned workers that "Imperial Valley planters have mobilized . . . thousands of Mexican laborers who are ready to come to the Imperial Valley at short notice and seize your work." And the sheriff informed workers that any dissatisfaction should be expressed by returning to Mexico rather than abusing the privilege of being allowed to work in the United States. The combined effect of federal and local threat making, the suppression of workers' attempts at organizing, and the importation of strikebreakers quickly broke the strike, but not before growers "suffered the unsettling realization that Mexican farmworkers might not be the docile, uncomplaining beasts of burden they had so confidently described them as being," as Cletus Daniel aptly put it.[28]

The threat of militancy that farmworkers now presented to Valley growers spurred some improvement in camp conditions, and DIH found a greater willingness to cooperate among growers than they had during their campaign to clean up the camps the year before. For those growers who refused to cooperate, however, no arrests for violation of camp sanitation laws were attempted. Such leniency was not readily forthcoming for workers arrested during the strike. Usually charged with "vagrancy"—because they were "outsiders" who were not working—arrested workers found their bail set originally at $1,000 (though it was often later lowered to $500 and $250). Since worker dissatisfaction remained high throughout the harvest, the sheriff attempted to have the trial date for forty arrested workers delayed until the middle of July when the harvest would be complete. The judge refused, and released most of the workers on their own recognizance at the end of May, when conditions had settled sufficiently that it was unlikely the strike would be rekindled.[29]

As the inspectors completed their work in June they predicted that since none of the issues raised by the workers had been settled, "there will be a direct repetition next season of the same labor trouble." Inspectors also increased their vigilance during the subsequent fall and winter cotton and pea harvests, reminding growers that good camps made for contented workers and a steady labor supply. Proper private camps, inspectors pointed out, provided growers with a means for the direct supervision of their laborers, a supervision impossible if workers were allowed to sleep where they may. When growers did not respond, DIH ordered its inspectors to bring as much pressure to bear on them as the local court system would allow, not so much to simply uphold the law, but rather to stave off worker militancy and the violence that invariably accompanied it. C. A. Degnan, southern California regional director for DIH, argued that worker unrest could only be quieted through a program of "wholesale arrests" of recalcitrant growers in the Valley. The primary Imperial Valley inspector disagreed. "There will be more dissatisfaction than ever in terms of . . . contracts and . . . living conditions," he held, but "the Mexicans *themselves* should be held responsible for the cleanliness of the camps" [emphasis added].[30]

The 1930 Strikes: Enter the Communists

The sense of crisis and its accompanying array of repressive measures and subversive countermoves signaled in 1928 deepened during 1929 as Mexican workers in Imperial Valley resumed organizing and militating against the appalling conditions within which they were forced to labor. These organizing efforts came to fruition on the first of January, 1930, when lettuce pickers in the Valley struck ranches near Brawley. The strike spread quickly, until some 5,000 farmworkers in the Valley had left their jobs. The growers responded as they had before, rallying the forces of various state, federal, and local agencies to crush the strike. Growers had a newspaper reporter arrested for reporting that there was a strike (when growers steadfastly refused to call it such), and they enlisted immigration officers in an effort to deport Mexican strikers. These efforts nearly crushed the strike in its first week. But the battle was extended when three organizers for the American Communist Party came to the

Valley. The three quickly assumed control of the conservative and reluctant Mexican Mutual Aid Society (successor to La Unión de Trabajadores del Valle Imperial), and formed the first California local of the Agricultural Workers Industrial League (AWIL), which was allied with the communist Trade Union Unity League (TUUL). While AWIL reinvigorated the strike, and reinforced the militancy of Mexican and Filipino workers (while getting them to cooperate over grower-reinforced lines of ethnicity), it also provided growers and their allies an excuse to reformulate the dispute not as one over wages, conditions, and worker power, but as a question of Americanism, loyalty, and subversiveness. The growers and local authorities, under the direction of Sheriff Gillett (who boasted on his stationery that his was the "lowest-down sheriff's office in the world"), arrested all "agitators" and eventually apprehended the three communist organizers and held them for vagrancy. While the organizers were in jail, the sheriff attempted to get them to confess to acts of sabotage that would allow for convictions under the state criminal syndicalism law. Sympathetic observers such as members of the American Civil Liberties Union, who came to the Valley to investigate abuses of workers' civil rights, were also arrested or physically abused. And at the height of the strike, growers established a *cordon sanitaire* around the Valley to prevent shipments of relief supplies to striking— and starving—workers. Deprived of leadership, outside assistance, and supplies of food, the strike collapsed on January 23 with none of the workers' demands met. The final demise of the strike was hastened by the Mexican Consulate at Calexico, which cooperated with the growers in a program of Mexican repatriation that included (false) promises of free land to workers who gave up the strike and returned to Mexico.[31]

After the defeat, and responding to the Mexican Consulate's treacherous undermining of Mexican worker solidarity, AWIL refocused its efforts on creating class solidarity between Mexican and Filipino workers. Filipinos had a reputation for radicalism, and many growers earlier in the decade had been angered that "un-American" Filipinos could not be deported while the Philippines was still a colony of the United States (indeed, one impetus for granting the Philippines independence was precisely that it would curb Filipino immigration). AWIL sought to organize that militancy as an important reinforcement for the Mexican workers, who comprised a majority of the Valley labor force. With the combined strength of Filipino and Mexican workers, AWIL organizers felt confident in calling a second strike for the Valley designed to tie up the spring cantaloupe harvest.[32]

As the planned cantaloupe strike neared, Imperial growers, organized through the Western Growers Protective Association, secretly petitioned California governor C. C. Young to mobilize the National Guard to force workers into the fields and protect the harvest. Concurrently, county law agencies contracted with Captain William Hynes, leader of the Los Angeles Police Department's notorious "Red Squad," to infiltrate and disrupt the proceedings of AWIL and to formulate a case against militant workers under the criminal syndicalism laws. On April 14, 1930, several worker rallies and organizing meetings around the Valley were raided and the organizers arrested on charges of conspiracy to destroy the cantaloupe crop. Bail was set at $40,000 each. Growers and their allies took the new labor militancy seriously—to the point of militarizing the landscape in order to protect the agricultural system as it then existed. And their efforts worked. The spring cantaloupe strike was broken even before it began.[33]

Country Comfort

The growers, prodded by increased militancy, expressed their concern in more benevolent ways too. DIH dispatched an inspector to the region who found that during May, when a strike was still possible, growers were quite receptive to "the permanent housing idea" as a means of controlling worker activities. But by autumn, when the militant moment had largely passed, DIH found grower interest in camp improvement considerably diminished. Now it was "unreasonable to expect large permanent improvements." Ignoring these messages from DIH, and ignoring the appalling conditions that were always near the top of worker complaints during labor disputes, Department of Industrial Relations director Will French reported to the governor in a relentlessly upbeat report, that throughout the state there was "Comfort for Country Workers."[34]

DIH inspectors were hard at work delineating the outline of "country comfort." In the rice fields of the Sacramento Valley, conditions "were very poor," as workers were made redundant through the introduction of harvesting machinery on some of the larger farms and justices of the peace refused to "enforce any tyrannical law which required a farmer to provide housing for bums who slept under bridges and in jungles all year, but, when hired by a farmer demanded clean living quarters." And in Kern County, regardless of the fact that some growers cooperated with DIH and provided "at least minimum quarters" for their cotton pickers, workers staged a wildcat strike in October demanding "better housing, increased rate for picking, [and] elimination of child labor." The strike was broken when "several arrests were made." There is no evidence that any of the strikers' demands were ever addressed. After reading (or perhaps simply ignoring) the reports from DIH, Will French informed the governor that "California camps are now clean. . . . The conditions have been revolutionized in recent years, and employers have gained by the satisfaction of their employees, and the latter now feel that they are not outcasts of society."[35]

In the grape harvests around Fresno, Eva Barnes, a social worker who worked closely with DIH throughout the 1930s, reported that most workers were housing themselves "usually in a grove, most of them have tents, others do not, but fix a rude shelter from limbs of trees." In many crop districts, growers were finding that an oversupply of destitute labor, forced to follow crops by the economic decline that followed the stock market crash, allowed them to forgo the construction of labor camps on their ranches. Growers relied rather on expanded squatter settlements, auto camps, and hobo jungles to act as localized and efficient labor markets. Although often expressing concern over the rapid growth of these settlements, and just as often threatening to close them down and force residents out of their counties, health officials realized that growers were increasingly dependent on makeshift encampments during times of depressed commodity markets. Encampments were thus tolerated as long as disease and worker militancy remained checked. When conditions warranted—threats to health or labor stability—pretexts such as a lack of proper toilets were used by county health authorities to close the camps, though officials rarely exercised the same power on camps owned by growers.[36]

In Fresno, a large camp developed where Madera Avenue crossed the San Joaquin River. The camp housed about three hundred people in sixty tents and shacks. Most of the residents refused to use the filthy toilets, and the DIH inspector for the region found residents "dressing and undressing out in the open for a swim in the river." The property on which this settlement developed was owned by the Farm Bureau Federation, and residents reported that they were expecting to begin harvest work within a few days. The camp inspector despaired that he was entirely powerless to mitigate conditions because squatter settlements did not fall under the purview of the Camp Sanitation Act (and the Farm Bureau Federation did not admit responsibility for all the workers massing on its land).[37] Such was the shape of Will French's "country comfort," and such were the conditions that lay at the roots of the decade of violent class war that ensued after the early battles in the Imperial Valley.

6 / The Disintegration of Landscape: The Workers' Revolt of 1933

Though they never would have put it this way, growers in the Imperial Valley and elsewhere in the state at the dawn of the Depression were trying to create and maintain the rural spaces of the state *as* a landscape in the traditional, historical sense of the term. Their goal was to assure that workers remained complete objects, that they were subjects not unto themselves, but only of the paternalistic gaze of landowners and industrialists. Growers wanted to assure that rural California remained *simply* a picturesque view, one composed at once of the ordinary—a peaceful, prosperous everyday life—and the extraordinary—a highly technologized, overwhelmingly productive agricultural wonderland. To maintain this view, growers had no choice but to rely on the labor power embodied by thousands of destitute (and increasingly militant) workers. Growers throughout the state during the Depression insisted that their duty was only to profitably grow crops during trying economic times. But to perform this duty, they were once again confronted with the same problem that faced growers and reformers after Wheatland: how can workers be "fixed in place" even as their labor power is made increasingly mobile? As Elizabeth Helsinger put the point for industrializing England, "the capitalist economy needed a large and mobile labor force, as the political economists recognized, and held out promises of social mobility to fuel it. In this sense, the assumptions of the landscape view had always been at odds with the mode of its production and that of the rural economy it depicted." The difference in California, of course, was just how chimerical even the promise, let alone the reality, of social mobility was for the vast majority of migratory workers. To reinforce rural California as a land-

130

scape, to depict it as the sort of ideal countryside that could be celebrated both for its prosperity and its peace, therefore, growers had to find a way to immobilize the *image* and *agency* of workers, even as they mobilized their labor. And if this need meant the brutal repression of every vestige of agricultural workers' rights, then so be it.[1]

For their part, workers fought hard during the 1930s to dissolve and disintegrate the landscape by once again making their mobility subversive, by claiming a radical subjectivity, by creating spaces of resistance that refused incorporation into the sort of pastoral imagery that made them all but invisible as real, corporeal people. So the 1930s saw not just the creative destruction of the landscapes that growers tried so hard to construct and maintain; this decade also saw repeated attempts by growers to subvert the power of workers and reestablish the spaces of the countryside as a landscape, as a representation of rural harmony and order.

The desires of workers and growers were invariably at odds, and throughout the decade capital and labor engaged in numerous pitched battles over precisely the issue of how the social spaces of agricultural capitalism were to be made and represented. Lefebvre argued that determining the space of capitalist production "is not the work of a moment for a society," but is rather "a *process*." Yet there are clearly "moments" when this work is both more important and more problematic. 1933 was certainly one of these times. By then the combined effects of the restructuring of the 1920s (which was coupled with declining profitability for many farmers during the deflation), the bankruptcy of local relief agencies as they tried to cope with enormously expanded unemployment, unemployment itself that sent thousands of destitute families into the fields in search of any work at all, and the reinvigoration of militancy among workers led by a resurgent Communist Party, created fertile conditions for rural discord and strife. The strikes of this period marked another watershed in the production of the California agricultural landscape, but they also exposed the structure of the landscape as it then existed. As Paul Taylor and Clark Kerr put it in their investigation of the bloodiest of all the strikes in 1933, "As the faulting of the earth exposes its strata and reveals its structure, so a social disturbance throws into bold relief the structure of a society, the attitudes, reactions and interests of its groups."[2]

Early Fractures in the Strata

The population of Filipino workers in the fields had steadily increased during the 1920s. Growers saw Filipinos, like the Chinese and Japanese workers before them, through contradictory lenses. On one hand, growers hoped that like other Asians, Filipinos might prove to be "naturally" adapted to agricultural work. Or if not that, then they hoped that racist reactions to Filipino immigration would make them powerless, tractable labor, good not only for their labor power, but also for the threat they posed to other workers. On the other hand, Filipinos proved quite militant during the 1920s and 1930s. Camp inspector Milton Edwards spent December of 1932 in the Salinas Valley assisting Rufo Canete (a scrupulously honest labor contractor and the president of the new Filipino Labor Union) build a new camp for one hundred single male Filipino workers. Rather than being forced to abide by the repressive rules and scrip pay that dominated grower camps, workers could use Canete's camp as a base from which they could contract with various growers in the region. Edwards informed the Division of Immigration and Housing (DIH) that it should "expect another big Filipino camp to be erected" in the area in addition to the Canete camp. "They are all buying their own property," Edwards reported, as Filipino workers searched for greater control over the conditions under which they sold their labor.[3]

A model camp when it was finished at the end of 1932, Canete's supply camp by March 1933 had become a source of difficulty for local growers and packers, and a source of power for Filipino workers. Field workers struck a number of the larger growers in the area in an effort to raise wages from fifteen cents to twenty cents per hour. One of the struck companies, H. P. Garin, was fairly typical of the large companies that had come to dominate production in the Salinas Valley. Diversified and vertically integrated, H. P. Garin operated mainly on leased land, which gave the corporation a greater degree of flexibility in cropping decisions than many farmers possessed. But in addition to the more than thirty farms that the company leased during the 1930s, H. P. Garin owned 1,300 acres of its own farmland around the state: in the Delta, Brentwood, the Imperial Valley, and the Salinas Valley. The company grew lettuce, peas, carrots, melons, apricots, peaches, nectarines, garlic, tomatoes, barley, and sugar beets, each of which was farmed on a different lease arrangement depending on market and labor conditions. In 1937, the company's payroll for picking and packing reached nearly 1.5 million dollars. This pay was distributed among an average of 1,240 employees each month, and a peak employment of 2,150 workers during July. The figures for 1933 were probably quite similar. Other corporations involved in the strike were the Hardin Company, Church and Knowlton, and Spreckles Sugar.[4]

Even though some firms capitulated to the Filipino workers' demands, H. P. Garin refused, evicted workers from its labor camps, and imported Black and Mexican laborers from outside the region. Most of the evicted Filipino workers resettled in Canete's camp. Alarmed by the growth of this camp (which was legally an auto camp and thus under the jurisdiction of DIH), the Monterey County health officer wrote to DIH about the growing danger to social and labor stability that the camp represented. The health officer's concern was spurred by a complaint made to him by a manager of a struck farm. Inspector Edwards, who was personally quite sympathetic to the Filipino workers, found that the overcrowded conditions in Canete's camp were "temporary," and that Canete was providing not just housing, but also food and other necessities to striking workers. He refused to abate Canete's camp or to press charges under the camp laws. "The real overcrowding," DIH's chief camp inspector Edward Brown wrote in his report on the strike, "was in the camp from which the Filipinos were ejected, caused by the introduction from the H. P. Garin Company of what the Filipinos call strike breakers." But in the Garin camp, too, DIH refused to order improvements or make arrests. With the continued importation of strikebreakers protected in part by DIH inaction, the strike quickly fizzled. For Brown, the true import of the strike was that "the Filipino group . . . is showing marked advances in their Americanization" through its retention of legal counsel and through the construction and policing of their own camps. And for these reasons also, many Salinas and Watsonville merchants supported the demands of the strikers, though their support rarely translated into active opposition to the companies.[5]

The Salinas growers, of course, operated with different assumptions about the verb "to Americanize": first and foremost it implied the willingness of workers, no matter what their "race," to lie docile before the dictates of "law and order" in the field. When Filipino workers remained militant, even with the defeat of their strike, growers more clearly associated "Americanism" with "white" rather than with the ability to retain legal counsel. During a brutal struggle in August and September of 1934, the Filipino Labor Union led some 6,000 Filipino lettuce pickers and white packing house workers out of their Salinas Valley jobs in a demand for increased pay and union recognition. The growers organized the Filipino Labor Supply Organization as a "company union" and stepped up efforts to import not only Filipino, but also Mexican, Japanese, and Asian Indian strikebreakers. Growers posted signs in the streets of Salinas during the strike reminding Filipinos of what it meant to be American: "This is a White Man's Country. Get out of Here if You Don't Like What We Pay." Recognizing Canete's camp as an important source of power for striking Filipino workers, vigilantes raided it in September: "75 armed marauders converged on three sides" of Canete's camp and "fired hundreds of shots into four bunkhouses and the owner's home, then set fire to the buildings." The police followed this action by raiding the union headquarters and arresting Canete. The strike was quickly put to an end.[6]

The Filipino strikes in Salinas in 1933 and 1934 were just two of a growing number of labor disturbances that marked the first years of the New Deal. By 1933, wage rates in agricultural work throughout the state had reached their lowest point since before 1910, according to information growers themselves furnished. Even as daily and hourly wages began to recover in 1934, yearly total agricultural earnings for workers continued to decline through 1936. Workers could expect fewer months of work each year (and fewer days each month, too) as growers struggled to keep wage bills down by importing workers and drawing on growing numbers of economic refugees from other states. In 1935 a farmworker could expect to make only 280 dollars a year in agricultural pursuits, down from 360 dollars in 1930. And this worker would find only 5.9 months of work each year.[7]

After two years of relative inactivity following its defeat in Imperial Valley in 1930, a reconstituted communist agricultural workers union under the able leadership of Caroline Decker, Dorothy Ray, and Pat Chambers (among others) emerged in 1933 as a powerful force for change. Renamed the Cannery and Agricultural Workers Industrial Union (CAWIU), the communist union led what historian Cletus Daniel called the "great upheaval" of 1933. It surely was that. In his study of agricultural unionism, Stuart Jamieson tallied thirty-one strikes in California in 1933 involving some 48,000 workers. By comparison, there were only thirty agricultural strikes in the rest of the United States that year, involving only 8,000 workers. The next most contentious year in California was 1936, when twenty-four strikes involved 13,500 workers. Major strikes were conducted in 1933 among pea pickers in Alameda and Santa Clara counties in April; cherry pickers in Santa Clara in June; berry pickers that month in El Monte; pear pickers in Santa Clara and sugar beet workers in Oxnard in August; peach pickers throughout the Central Valley the same month; grape harvesters in Lodi in September and October; and, also in October, cotton pickers the length of the San Joaquin Valley. The majority of these strikes were led by, or involved a majority of, nonwhite workers—Filipinos as in the Salinas Valley, Mexican workers throughout the state—giving lie to the common assumption that before the rise of the United Farmworkers in the 1960s farmworker militancy was the exclusive purview of white workers.[8]

The earliest concerted CAWIU organizing and strike effort began in December 1932 among the orchard pruners working on the Vaca Valley ranch of newly elected New Deal congressman Frank Buck. In previous years, Buck had engaged the services of Frank Palomares, of the California Commission of

Immigration and Housing (CCIH), to dissipate trouble among his Hispanic workers. But much of Buck's labor was locally based during the 1932 election season, and he found it more expedient to promise a pay raise if he was elected. Following his electoral victory, however, Buck instead lowered wages. Other growers in the region followed suit. CAWIU had been organizing both farmworkers and the growing number of unemployed workers in the area, and called a strike in response to the pay cut. When the new wage went into effect two weeks after election day, some four hundred Mexican, Filipino, Japanese, and white workers walked off their jobs. Among the demands the union made were an increase in wages to the preelection promise, no discrimination on the basis of race, sex, or union affiliation, and no eviction from labor camps pending settlement of the strike.[9]

Crushed by vigilantes (including a local judge who suggested ranchers should adopt the system of justice "used south of the Mason Dixon line"), and facing employers who, unlike at harvest times, were under no pressure to rapidly end the strike, the strike eventually collapsed. Mass picket lines and street blockades proved ineffectual against employers who were not haunted by images of a year's investment rotting on the branches. Yet the depth of militancy among workers and the communist union was obvious. As one striking worker said to an organizer after the strike had failed: "We would have starved working so we decided to starve striking." And so began the New Deal in the California fields.[10]

Struggles against Landscape

Learning from the failure of the Vaca Valley pruners' strike, CAWIU organizers vowed to redouble their organizing efforts, focusing first on the April pea harvest in Alameda and Santa Clara counties. Organizers sought to exploit the labor camp system developed over the years by growers. They recruited strike committees at each camp, thereby decentralizing organizing and agitating efforts. A vigilante move against any one camp, organizers held, would not jeopardize the strike as a whole. Each camp committee elected representatives who formed a general strike committee to coordinate overall activities. Organizers focused not just on grower-controlled private camps, but also on the more numerous, informal "supply camps" in which workers awaited the beginning of the harvest and from which they radiated out in search of work. Growers in Alameda and Santa Clara relied heavily on these supply camps in the rather new pea crops because they both diminished direct grower costs, and provided a ready access to a surfeit of workers who assured that wages did not begin to rise unacceptably. They also allowed for greater flexibility in cropping patterns for growers. Pea acreage fluctuated greatly each season depending on market conditions, and the use of supply camps (and contractors) allowed growers to externalize the cost of maintaining a labor supply.[11]

During the second week of April 1933, camp delegates formulated their demands for the impending harvest: thirty cents per hamper (or a penny a pound, which was an increase from the seventeen cents per hamper the year before) or thirty-five cents an hour. They also demanded a closed shop controlled by the union rather than by contractors who worked in collusion with growers. A strike was called for April 14, and when the growers refused the union's demands, 2,000 workers quit work. Striking workers were evicted from growers' camps, just as they had been in the Filipino workers' strike in Salinas the previous month. As in Salinas, workers congregated in overflowing supply camps, or established new encampments wherever they could. This time, however, with communists clearly involved, DIH was less than sympathetic. Chief camp inspector Edward Brown and senior inspector Milton Edwards began an immediate and careful inspection of the strikers' camps. The *Oakland Tribune* reported on April 13, the day before the strike was to begin, that DIH was issuing condemnation orders to several of the more militant supply camps. DIH was additionally concerned that most of the supply camps were located along public highways—convenient to growers looking for labor, but also convenient to picketers seeking to widen their strike. The location of these camps, DIH argued, was a prime reason that the strike was able to be called at all.[12]

While the strikers' camps provided solidarity, they were not always particularly comfortable places to live. Orrick Johns, one of the CAWIU organizers in Alameda, described the largest strike encampment as consisting of "a hundred broken down automobiles in each of which four or five people slept. There were a few tents and some cauldrons where the daily stew was cooked." The camps were placed under constant surveillance by deputized vigilantes, and the vigilantes were not particularly shy, threatening to beat any strikers who dared venture outside the camps alone and unarmed. Despite constant threats from growers, law enforcement officials, and DIH, strikers held nightly rallies with a flatbed truck serving as stage, and the striker-controlled camps became central organizing points for the development and extension of the strike.[13]

Realizing the potential power of these encampments, deputies invaded a militant camp at Decoto on April 15, bombing strikers with tear gas and flailing at them with billy clubs. Within minutes, the entire camp population had been dispersed. Simultaneously, the American Legion and other "patriotic" organizations broke up picket lines and strike meetings all over the two counties. Law enforcement officers were not particularly concerned about the rights of speech and assembly for strikers. A sheriff in the area later commented to a police convention, "Between you and me, what the hell is the Constitution?" More subtle means of intimidation were employed by DIH. Detailed inspections were conducted on all the major strikers' camps, and the communist *Western Worker* published the results of one such inspection. Milton Edwards had found the camp of Eugolio Martin in Hayward in violation of the Camp Sanitation Law, and DIH demanded that it be immediately closed. The letter sent to Martin by Edward Brown listed several rather typical complaints about camp conditions: lime needed to be used in the toilets; toilets needed to be segregated by sex and cracks in their walls filled to keep out flies; garbage cans needed to be covered; and the camp needed to be cleaned. Most importantly, Brown informed Martin, "the camp should be laid out in a more uniform order; the tents should be arranged in rows with adequate space between them." The *Western Worker* complained that strikers' camps were being unfairly singled out for having conditions that were no worse, and often quite a bit better, than growers' camps. The communist newspaper was largely correct.[14]

DIH found an ally in its effort to undermine the pea pickers' strike in the Alameda County welfare authorities, who promised to release from the relief roles any "able bodied man who refused to work" in the struck pea fields. Not content with the official strikebreakers the county was willing to provide, growers also recruited scabs from outside the area and housed them in camps that were certainly no better than the strikers' camps DIH ordered closed. Unable to maintain picket lines because of constant physical assaults and dwindling strike relief supplies, strikers saw more and more fields harvested by scab labor after the violent attack in Decoto. By April 30, the strike collapsed with few gains made.[15]

The strike was not a total loss for CAWIU, however, because it learned, if nothing else, that class war in the fields is like war more generally: it is a struggle for the control of space, for the domination of territory. With this understanding, and despite a fairly poor record of formal success during 1933, CAWIU instigated a farmworkers movement unparalleled since the days of the Industrial Workers of the World (IWW) in the threat it posed to the interests of capitalist agriculture in California. As in the aftermath of Wheatland, growers and agents of the state realized that a new set of relations obtained in the fields, and if they were to regain and solidify their control of the California landscape, vigilante actions would have to be matched by a rearrangement of the spatial substrata that supported the production and reproduction of agricultural labor. If for no other reason, the spaces of agricultural labor reproduction would have to be remade simply to minimize the possibility for agitation on the part of workers.

But this was a painful lesson to be learned, and it was not really clearly articulated—significantly, by law enforcement personnel in Alameda—until 1934. In the meantime, the fields of California exploded in a flurry of strikes.[16]

Conditions in San Joaquin

Over Altamont Pass in the San Joaquin Valley, it was grower practice before each harvest to establish a set of valley-wide, crop-based wage rates to which all growers were expected to adhere. Before the summer fruit harvest in 1933, growers met, as they traditionally did, under the auspices of the Agricultural Labor Bureau of the San Joaquin Valley. Ignoring the strikes in earlier harvests throughout the state, growers adopted a uniform wage range of 15 cents to 17½ cents per hour (depending on the nature of the work done). Some growers themselves criticized this low wage, fearing it would only fuel current unrest. According to Bureau director Palomares, Bureau policy had always been to hold open wage meetings in which a variety of opinions were heard, and a consensus wage developed. In actual practice, while the meetings may have consisted of four hundred to five hundred growers, but they were clearly controlled by large growers, canners, and ginning interests—and worker representatives were never invited. The large growers and their allies in the packing and ginning industry were clearly convinced that a growing oversupply of labor, organized by Palomares, would be enough to minimize worker agitation.[17]

CAWIU was determined to see that such arrogance did not go unpunished. Assessing their own successes and failures to that point in the 1933 harvest season, CAWIU leaders were meeting at the same time as the San Joaquin fruit growers. Following a disastrous defeat in the berry harvest at El Monte, CAWIU resolved to, among other things, democratize leadership, "aggressively work to bring women, youth, and children into its ranks . . . on a permanent basis," and tie workers' struggles to those of the unemployed, a project of great urgency since unemployed workers were often compelled by hunger or by relief officials to scab in struck fields. The combination of renewed CAWIU commitment and grower recalcitrance over wages led to a "rapid-fire sequence of strikes that were to keep the agricultural regions of California in nearly constant turmoil for almost three months."[18]

Late in the summer, fruit pickers at the massive Tagus Ranch in Tulare faced a flat rejection of their demands for 30 cents per hour and called a strike for the middle of August. Tagus Ranch was famous throughout the state not only for its impressive vertical integration and diversified production, but also for being one of the most aggressive proponents of welfare capitalism on the farm. Charles Merritt, the manager of Tagus Ranch, had developed extensive company housing, playing fields, and a schoolhouse for the children of employees. Tagus Ranch also ran a company store and paid its wages in scrip rather than legal currency. Between 1932 and 1933, prices at the company store increased 10.03 percent, but Merritt insisted in the summer of 1933 that wage rates had to remain at their 1932 level—which was what San Joaquin growers had earlier decided at their meeting—if production on the farm was to be economically feasible. To assure wages remained low, Merritt hired 1,200 migratory workers to supplement his normal payroll of several hundred. And to accommodate these workers, Merritt, working under the direction of DIH agents, had in earlier years designed his camps in a manner that would be sure "to keep the undesirable laborer out." Merritt was confident in the ability of his labor camps to protect his labor supply. Indeed, he had never needed to recruit laborers through Palomares's Labor Bureau, even though he was its president and instrumental in setting and enforcing "prevailing" wages. For the destitute workers of 1933, however, decent housing meant little when the wages paid were so inadequate.[19]

When the peach harvest began on the Tagus ranch, and Merritt refused to raise his 15 cents-per-hour wage (despite a recent victory by fruit pickers in San Jose that won a rate per hour of 25 cents to 27½ cents), 750 workers struck the ranch on August 14, 1933. Organizational efforts had been underway on the Tagus Ranch and in nearby Tulare for several weeks at this point, and CAWIU, under the direction of Pat Chambers, felt confident of victory. Workers at Tagus demanded 35 cents per hour, and an end to both the scrip system and the company store monopoly. CAWIU was striking a company town, and like similar strikes in the industrial east, the first line of defense for the Tagus management was to evict the strikers. But like an industrial strike, and quite different from most agricultural strikes, the Tagus Ranch strike had a single, albeit expansive, geographical focus. Mass picketing around the perimeter of the ranch proved effective in grinding work to a halt, especially in the more outlying Tagus orchards. The strikers were also aided, perhaps, by the Tulare district attorney, who, in an uncommon move, refused to outlaw picketing on public property. In response to the evictions, and with picketing proving effective, Chambers threatened to widen the strike to other area growers.[20]

The Tagus strike enjoyed an unlikely boost when peach pickers walked off Cal Pak ranches in Merced (about a hundred miles to the north), making demands similar to those of the Tagus strikers. Nervous over the possible loss of its peach crop (and with the strike spreading to the company's canning operations), Cal Pak accepted a compromise brokered by Department of Industrial Relations director Timothy Reardon that raised wages to the twenty-five-cent level already achieved in the San Jose orchards.[21] With the Cal Pak capitulation to this wage, ten cents higher than the set "prevailing wage," pressure was placed on Merritt and the Tagus Ranch by Reardon and other government officials, and by August 18 wages were also raised there to the twenty-five-cent level. Following the successful peach pickers' strikes in Merced, Tulare, and San Jose, strikes became general in the peach orchards, and twenty-five cents per hour became the standard wage. For the first time in its history, the wage level established by the Agricultural Labor Bureau of the San Joaquin Valley was rendered meaningless by militant workers. Indeed, in the Butte area of the Sacramento Valley, peach pickers were able to extract a thirty-cents wage from many growers.[22]

Buoyed by its success in the peach orchards, CAWIU widened its campaign of agitation to encompass the grape harvest that was just then coming due. The state labor commissioner announced on August 21 that strikes were impending in most vineyards unless growers matched the twenty-five-cent wage established by peach pickers. In Fresno, growers nevertheless announced a twenty-cent wage, and pickers went on strike. Confident in its power after the peach victories, CAWIU neglected the hard work of organizing, and the strikes were crushed when the entire strike leadership and many rank-and-file workers were arrested and charged with crimes ranging from vagrancy to criminal syndicalism. Despite its faltering fortunes in Fresno, however, CAWIU continued to expand its agitation and turned its sights to the grape harvest in Lodi—and here the heat of the struggle was turned up another notch.[23]

The Lodi strike posed a considerably greater challenge to CAWIU organizers than had their peach victories, which were more clearly focused on single, large corporations. On September 13, as the Fresno initiative was floundering, workers in Lodi, with CAWIU backing, voted to demand fifty cents per hour and an eight-hour day. Local growers, realizing fifteen cents per hour was unrealistic in the wake of the CAWIU victories and the general rise of worker unrest, had set wages at twenty cents. Determined not to repeat the Fresno fiasco, CAWIU increased its organizing efforts as the harvest approached. When the Lodi strike began in earnest on September 27, five hundred to seven hundred workers walked off their jobs on over 150 vineyards. Within days the strikers' ranks swelled to perhaps 4,000 workers. Growers responded with all the force and ingenuity they could muster. The sheriff deputized American Legionnaires and growers, and relinquished his authority to "Colonel" Walter E. Garrison, a local grower, retired military man, and future president of the reactionary Associated Farmers of California, Inc. Garrison declared all picketing to be "disturbing the peace" and instructed his deputies to arrest all picket captains whenever they seemed to be interfering with harvest operations. Several were arrested within the first hours of the strike, and most of the strike leadership was apprehended in a raid on the union hall on September 29. Garrison also forced all local relief recipients off the roles and into the struck fields. While these moves had the effect of curtailing picketing at the three largest ranches (which CAWIU had targeted in hopes of not dissipating what little power it had), they did not break the strike.[24]

Striking workers regrouped and implemented "guerrilla" picketing strategies designed to quickly envelop a working field and call the workers out. Using small groups of strikers at numerous places, the picketers hoped to outrun the vigilantes and thereby bolster and widen their strike. Vexed by the willingness of strikers to persist in the face of the overwhelming odds (and violence) against them, growers and their allies in the sheriff's department and state mediation service met on the night of October 2 and devised a plan to "deport" striking workers. Bands of vigilantes made early morning calls on strikers' camps, rounding up striking workers at gunpoint and pushing them toward the edge of the county, scattering them across the agricultural landscape. The mobility of labor in California had reached its logical conclusion.[25]

The Corcoran Cotton Strike: Making Space for Radicalism

No sooner had the strike at Lodi been violently ended than a far more significant strike began in the cotton-growing districts of the San Joaquin Valley. Centered on the small town of Corcoran, this strike, like the Wheatland uprising a generation before, caught the imagination of contemporary observers and activists, and has lived on in the writing of numerous historians, social scientists, social critics, and novelists to a degree unsurpassed by any other agricultural revolt of the period. The final settlement in the strike was the outcome not just of vigilante growers and militant strikers, but also of federal and state government functionaries, social reformers, labor historians and economists, relief workers, health officers, and city reporters who knew a good story when they saw one. Each of the interests involved in the strike, from the cotton pickers to the reporters, sought to leash the struggles in the San Joaquin Valley to its own agenda, and each was instrumental in creating the multifarious representations of the event that were as determining as the struggles themselves. Even so, throughout the strike, an underlying process of material spatial production gave form to the specific struggles over wages and living conditions. And, like Wheatland, these spatial productions themselves would lead to a refiguring of the spaces of agricultural production in California. They would also provide the basis upon which the disintegrated California landscape would be remade.

The best estimates suggest that at least 75 percent of the 15,000 cotton workers in 1933 were Hispanic (and most of those were probably Mexican nationals). The remainder were early Dust Bowl arrivals, longtime white migratory workers (including families), and southern African-Americans that growers had imported to work the expanding cotton harvest. Before the cotton harvest began, mostly white CAWIU organizers had undertaken an intensive organizing campaign, conducted largely in the "tents, hovels and holes in the walls" workers lived in before the season started. The goal was to create a militant and decentralized strike leadership that would not be threatened by the arrest of any key leaders. According to Caroline Decker, one of the primary organizers in the fields during 1933, the main strike leadership was recruited from strikers who had gained experience in the earlier Tagus Ranch battle, but new leaders were developed also.[26]

Though aware of the organizing campaign, and despite the victories in the nearby peach orchards, cotton growers were confident they could maintain low wages when some six hundred of them met under the auspices of the Agricultural Labor Bureau of the San Joaquin Valley on September 19 to set wages for the upcoming season. The weakness displayed by CAWIU in Fresno was enough to convince growers that only a small amount of force would be enough to control the "agitators." Two days before the growers met, CAWIU delegates, "elected by 12,000 laborers in the Valley," drew up their own wage schedule and list of demands for the harvest: one dollar per hundred pounds picked, no discrimination on the basis of sex or race, hiring through union locals, and decent living conditions free of charge. At the growers' meeting, CAWIU's Pat Chambers was allowed to read the union demands, but no discussion was permitted. Growers voted to set wages at sixty cents per hundred pounds, an increase of 50 percent over the previous year; but even at these rates, the average daily wage per worker was less than two dollars, and there was little chance that the season would last longer than four months, less time lost due to fog and rain. For many cotton pickers, the small amount made during the cotton harvest was the only guaranteed income they would have all year. In response to the growers' offer, and leading workers that were, if anything, even more militant than the communist leadership of the union, CAWIU called a strike for October 4.[27]

When the strike started, growers responded by evicting striking workers from their camps. The growers' actions were probably illegal, though the law concerning grower-provided accommodation was murky enough that growers could successfully argue that housing was a form of wages, not rental property that required proper notice for evictions. Growers felt that "the shelter, fuel, light and water furnished was part of the pay for their picking cotton, so if they refused to pick they should not get this pay any more than they should get money." The Kings County district attorney told Paul Taylor (who had been sent to study the strike by the University of California and the United States Resettlement Agency), "I don't know whether the growers had a legal right to evict the strikers or not but the logic of the situation was all in their favor." Rights are never inalienable, but are always backed by force, and the growers knew they had the force of the law officers (if not the law) on their side. "The sheriff and I told the growers not to worry much about the pickers' rights any way," the Kings County district attorney told Taylor. "The growers had all the logic on their side. If it isn't the law, it ought to be."[28]

The widespread evictions—a common practice that should have been antic-ipated—threw the plans of the CAWIU leadership into disarray. They had counted on implementing a decentralized, grower-camp–based strike strategy that would not allow growers to attack all strikers at once. The growers' camps, CAWIU leaders argued, could be grounds for power. Rather naively, CAWIU informed workers that if they were to "remain in the cotton camps after striking . . . the growers would find it impossible to evict them for several weeks, if they went to court for redress." During this time, union leaders felt they could employ the strategy that had been effective at the Tagus Ranch: each camp local could picket the grower they worked for, assuring that the cotton in their area remained unpicked.[29]

But this strike was *not* like the Tagus strike. It extended for more than a hun-dred miles up and down the Valley and concerned many hundreds of individ-ual growers. Given that spatial extent, Paul Taylor and Clark Kerr argued in their investigation of the strike that decentralized, localized struggles would have been doomed to failure as local agreements or repressions were promul-gated. The eviction of striking workers from grower camps—which were quite brutal affairs with machine gun–toting guards overseeing the unceremonious dumping of strikers' possessions along the side of a public highway—actually *strengthened* the strike by forcing strikers to regroup in several encampments and in supportive barrio neighborhoods in Valley towns.[30]

The Corcoran Strikers' Camp

The central and most important encampment was developed on four acres of land leased by a small grower named Morgan in the town of Corcoran (Figure 10). In addition to farming a small amount of cotton, Morgan operated a small free campground at the side of his gas station, and he was known to be friendly to Mexican workers and sympathetic to their strike. When the strike began, there were sixteen families on his property. By the end of the strike, the popu-

Figure 10. The main strikers' encampment, Corcoran, California, October 1933. Tents were arranged in rows, a fence was maintained at the perimeter (*foreground*), and the stage of *Circo Azteca* served as both the cultural and political focal point of the camp. The encampment was a clear representation of growing worker power—to workers, growers, and law enforcement alike— at the end of the most militant year in California farm-labor history. (Courtesy, Bancroft Library.)

lation had grown to over 3,000. Strikers in the Corcoran camp and other similar camps throughout the Valley expressed a remarkable degree of solidarity. The camps were necessarily integrated, erasing many of the ethnic and racial divisions that had been so painstakingly constructed in growers' camps. Caroline Decker claimed soon after the strike, "Even the capitalist press had to admit our solidarity—Mexicans, whites, and colored workers, living, eating, picketing, and going to jail together—forgetting racial prejudice." Realizing the potential power such a centralization of militant strikers represented, growers immediately started agitating for the closure of the Corcoran camp. But, faced with 3,000, rather than a handful, of striking, angry workers, growers were reluctant to exercise the violent force they usually so freely engaged to break worker solidarity. Likewise, DIH was reluctant to act as it had during the Alameda strike, though it did send investigators to the area. Interestingly, DIH's noninvolvement in the strike—not taking a leading role in attempting to close the strikers' encampments—later became a focal point for some Valley growers who argued the Division ought to have its budget increased so that it could be more effective in controlling the health menace of striker camps.[31]

It may have been that DIH was less involved in this strike than it had been in others because CAWIU activists had learned important lessons in earlier strikes about how health and sanitation issues could be a tool for strikebreaking, and they were thus concerned, as the Corcoran camp burgeoned, to lay out the tents and other shelters in as orderly manner as possible. Shelters were arranged in rows along roads named after row delegates, toilets and garbage pits were carefully sited, and a perimeter fence was built (and guarded) to protect against intrusions. Strikers established two schools for their children and employed Corcoran teachers to carry out instruction. A nurse from Oakland was hired to oversee medical problems and supervise camp sanitation (and he always worked with the county health officer in these matters to assure full compliance with the law). The camp was centered on a community kitchen, and an assembly area in which nightly rallies were held was built at the center of the camp. Finally, but of great importance, *Circo Azteca,* a traveling troupe that followed the crops and played in the various camps and barrios, set up for what turned out to be a long run of nightly performances. Like *Teatro Campesino* in the 1960s, *Circo Azteca* celebrated both the traditional folk and the popular culture of the migratory workers, helping to maintain cultural solidarity during the bloody days that followed.[32]

Through the almost accidental creation of striker encampments like the one at Corcoran, CAWIU and the cotton workers of the Valley changed the calculus of power in the cotton strike (and in labor relations in the Valley more generally) not least because the Corcoran camp was more sanitary and better maintained than most growers' camps in the region. Because it was a center of power, growers knew the camp would have to be destroyed. "The camp wasn't so bad," according to the Kings County district attorney (who was no friend of the strikers). "It was just about as sanitary as other cotton camps and these growers . . . kept wanting it to be condemned for being unsanitary. . . . They just had it in their minds that if they could get the camp broken up the pickers would go back to work at sixty cents."[33]

Growers accused the union of imprisoning workers in the Corcoran camp to keep them from willingly returning to the fields. Growers were convinced that it was only outside agitators that kept the workers from doing what they were naturally suited to do: pick cotton. And, of course, they were convinced this was particularly so in the case of Mexican workers who comprised the majority of the strikers. As a central focus of strike agitation, as a free space for exercising the rights of speech and assembly, and as a place where workers could recreate and have a social life on their own terms rather than in conformance to the rules posted by growers in their camps, the Corcoran camp rankled growers and their allies in the conservative press. The camp was a clear symbol of the subversive power communists were claiming among the (presumably otherwise content) workers of agricultural California. Chapin Hall, sent to Corcoran by the anti-union *Los Angeles Times,* became an important mouthpiece for grower interests. His dispatches from the strike reveal the symbolic power the strikers' encampments possessed. He reserved particular animus for the camp at Corcoran:

> This camp is the danger spot. I visited it today, and it is a dreadful place. I don't wonder that the residents of the town are terrorized. No one in the state employ with jurisdictional authority should consider that mass of corruption with anything but shame.
>
> Thirty seven hundred men, women, and children are herded in a ten acre barren field on the edge of town. There is no shade and the sun is cruel. At night it is cold. The equipment consists of a few ragged pup tents but mostly a shakedown on the ground. There are no sanitary precautions. No water for bathing; not much more for drinking. Three or four latrines for 4,000 persons. Long lines of misery marked humanity await their turn. There is grave danger of epidemic. Promiscuity is unlimited. . . .
>
> At the main entrance and at various gaps in the barbed wire fence Mexicans armed with clubs keep people out and in. Inmates practically prisoners. They are harangued at frequent intervals by wild-eyed orators with the gift for gab, and at night picked crews are loaded onto trucks and started on their raids of sabotage and violence.[34]

Hall's breathless prose precisely reflected the imminent dread with which growers and others in the Valley held the encampments. And Hall was seconded by a growing mob of angry farmers who gathered each day at the entrance to the camp demanding its closure.

Morgan, the lessee of the Corcoran camp land, felt the pressure. He told Paul Taylor that the growers "call it Morgan's strike. I ain't so popular around here." He was certain that none of the Valley banks or gins would provide him crop loans in the coming year because of the role he played in the strike—and he too would be forced into the migratory life. Even the local Parent-Teacher Association got into the game, becoming on October 18 only one organization among many to pass a resolution declaring the camp a "health menace." The *Hanford Journal* described the camp as "a menace in more ways than one," and suggested that DIH was not playing its proper role: "State labor camp inspectors would not allow comparable sanitation conditions in the cotton camps on ranches. It is unbelievable they will permit the Corcoran tent city for long."[35]

State camp inspectors *did*, of course, allow such conditions on growers' ranches—and worse conditions, too—and they often freely admitted as much. During the Depression, DIH inspectors were quick to advertise their leniency in inspections of growers' camps, allowing conditions to persist that were in violation of the law and that were perhaps a health threat to the surrounding communities. Though camp inspectors were not to be heard from during the strike, the director of the Department of Industrial Relations (within which Immigration and Housing was a division), Timothy Reardon, became involved in the strike right at the beginning and did publicly declare the Corcoran camp unsanitary.[36] But like other government officials, Reardon found himself unable to act against the camp in the face of the fierce solidarity of the strikers.

Local authorities also blustered against the camp, but they too found they lacked the power to effectively act against it. On October 12, Clarence Wilson, the Kings County district attorney, ordered the camp evacuated within five days if conditions were not improved. Along with the state public health officer, Wilson inspected the camp and demanded the construction of more toilets, a more sanitary means of garbage disposal, and the installation of a water storage and distribution system. When strikers had not fully complied by the deadline (as Wilson knew they could not), Wilson gathered the support of George Creel, the National Recovery Administration chief for California and President Roosevelt's representative during the strike. Creel urged Governor Rolph to instruct state health authorities to dismantle the camp. On October 19, the head of the state Board of Health inspected the camp again and demanded that the improvements outlined by Wilson be made. Three days later, this official reported that the camp was now in better condition and more sanitary than the "average temporary camp in the state." Peaceful means had proved inadequate to the task of breaking the main base of worker power during the strike.[37]

Private Property, Public Space: Reestablishing Control

And power was precisely the issue. Growers realized immediately the value of controlling labor in their own camps. Resistance, they learned, needed space, and the power to control resistance needed control over the spaces in which the workers lived as well as worked. Strikers learned this also. Not only was the cotton strike distinguished by its encampments, but it also was marked by CAWIU's effective use of public spaces like parks and streets to organize picketing and hold rallies. In a strategy that became the cornerstone of the growers' war against militant workers throughout the decade, growers responded by asserting their control over the public spaces of the towns and countryside—often quite violently—and to circumscribe the uses to which public space could be put. While growers tried to close the encampments, they also attempted to reclaim the parks and streets of the Valley for what they deemed "proper" use. Proper use certainly did not include the strike parades, organized pickets, or "haranguing" of workers from soapboxes that strikers were using to widen and solidify the strike.

If strikers' camps and the use of public space for strike agitation became the cornerstone of CAWIU strategy, then growers centered their power on the ideology and reality of private property. The accumulation of private property, from early, graft-ridden land-grant programs to the more recent mergers and takeovers of the 1920s and 1930s, had facilitated the construction of the Central Valley *as* a landscape. It had made possible the grand scale of California agriculture. (And, in turn, as Marx rightly held, the accumulation of property was only possible if there was a simultaneous production of a large army of "free labor" to work it.) Private property was sacred to the growers of the Valley, and its very sanctity became an excuse for the rather public oppression of the very workers who created the reasons for owning such property: profit. For this reason, the Corcoran camp became a thorn in the side of the ideology of private property because it was the workers themselves—the growers' precious "free labor"— who sought to privatize space as a means of challenging the property system (and its legal support) in the Valley. By privatizing space, workers refused to accept *their* status as mere private property, simple embodiments of labor freely owned by someone else.

As strikers picketed along the roads and highways that crisscrossed the hundred-mile corridor of the strike, growers responded by reminding each other of the sanctity of their kind of private property. Under state trespass law, the *Bakersfield Californian* told its readers, "a man has the right to resist the unlawful invasion of his property with force if necessary." The *Californian* further noted that even in the first days of the strike, "farmers are reported to have armed themselves with guns to prevent the invasion of their fields and intimidation of their cotton pickers." Local papers warned that the strike was the beginning of a communist conspiracy to overthrow the government and confiscate the private property of the citizens of the Valley.[38]

To maintain the strike across such an expansive area, CAWIU unions used the encampments to organize the same "guerilla" picketing tactics they had debuted in Lodi. Strikers cruised the highways searching for fields being picked. When they found one, a picket line was quickly thrown up and strikers argued with the nonstriking workers, cajoled them, threatened violence, and sometimes got in fistfights with them—all in hopes of shutting down this small part of the harvest (Figure 11). Elsewhere, groups of strikers blocked highways, making it impossible for trucks carrying fresh supplies of scab labor to reach their destinations. Growers responded by moving their picking crews to sections remote from public highways, or by calling them in from the fields whenever pickets were feared. They also closed roads that went past their farms, declaring them to be private. Officers and deputized growers freely used tear gas, and occasionally gunfire, to rout the strikers. And, if that was not enough, they also sought legal injunctions that effectively restricted the use of public space for demonstrations and parades.

The strike quickly became a war for territory, with growers controlling most

Figure 11. A picket line at a cotton field in the San Joaquin Valley, October 1933. The "flying pickets" and other spatial strategies employed by the union were effective in maintaining a strike that extended for more than one hundred miles up and down the Valley. Like the Corcoran camp, picket lines like these were important symbols of worker power during the 1933 strikes. (Courtesy, Bancroft Library.)

of the theater, but with strikers effectively undermining their control over the space by engaging in both guerilla attacks and frontal assaults. With little sign that worker solidarity was diminishing, growers met on October 9 to plot a new strategy. They decided that efforts to break the encampment had to be re-doubled, and the streets and vacant lots of the Valley had to be reclaimed. One widely practiced strategy saw growers (and quite often deputies) zigzagging across the highways as they attempted to force picketers off the road and onto private property. When this was successful, picketers could be arrested for tres-passing, or, the strikers feared, shot by the offended property owner.[39]

One of the sheriffs in the region laid out the nature of the struggle in the starkest terms: the public good represented by all that the cotton growers had done to build the Valley was gravely threatened by the strike, and the picketing had to be stopped. By definition, picketing was intimidation. "Mass picketing is illegal and I am not afraid to go before any court and prove it." Given the state of jurisprudence concerning picketing at this time, he probably would have won.[40] Other pronouncements by local law officers were no less subtle, but probably less enforceable. "Soap-box orators haranguing cotton pickers must do it in one language—American," reported the *Tulare Advance-Register.* "That is the new rule Sheriff W. V. Buckner laid down. He invoked it yesterday at Corcoran. A Mexican speaker had mounted a truck there and was hitting it off a hundred miles an hour in the Spanish tongue. His hearers, for the most part, were Mexican." Not speaking Spanish himself, the sheriff suspected the speaker was inciting the crowd to riot, and therefore ordered all speeches to be in "American."[41]

Arvin and Pixley

In the fields outside Arvin, a small town south of Bakersfield not far from where the Joads found a modicum of peace and comfort in a government-run labor camp, strikers massed on the edge of a field on the Gary Mitchell ranch. It was the morning of October 10, 1933, the day following the growers' strategy meeting, and growers were determined to break the strike using "any force necessary." Finding strikebreakers at work in the Mitchell field, strikers marched, blew trumpets, and yelled into the field trying to persuade the workers to throw down their bags and join the strike. There were perhaps 250 picketers, and they were unarmed, except for grape stakes upon which signs had been nailed. The property line of the Mitchell ranch was guarded by some thirty growers, heavily armed with rifles and shotguns. The growers proclaimed their intent to protect the sanctity of private property (including "their" labor), no matter what the cost. The picketers, knowing the growers would not hesitate to use violence, were careful to remain on the highway right-of-way. For five hours the opposed groups faced off across the void that separated them and traded insults and threats. The "growers were just hoping one [of the picketers] would put out his foot across the line and he would have been plugged full of holes," an under-sheriff at the standoff later recalled.[42]

Finally, around three o'clock, fighting erupted all along the line, with growers using the butts of the guns and pickers responding with their grape stakes. At the height of the battle, a shot rang out and a Mexican picketer collapsed dead. All the growers started shooting, sending a fusillade of perhaps one hundred shots at the strikers, who quickly fled the scene. As the strikers retreated, deputies shot tear gas bombs into their midst. After most of the picketers made it back to their encampment in the Mexican section of Arvin, growers told the deputies that the dead picketer had been shot by a fellow striker perched in a nearby tree. The deputies arrested nine strikers and charged them with murder. A coroner's inquest later established that none of the strikers carried guns and that all the shots had come from the growers' side of the battle line. Nonetheless, no grower was ever arrested or indicted for the shooting.[43]

Later that day, an even bloodier battle took place to the north in the town of Pixley. Sixteen picketers, accused by growers of invading private property in an attempt to disrupt picking, were being held by armed guards on a nearby cotton ranch. A mass rally in defense of the detained strikers was called, and a large number of strikers gathered at the union hall in town. The crowd grew until it spilled across the street and into the vacant lot on the other side. Pat Chambers was in the midst of addressing the crowd when an organized posse of forty well-armed growers approached the meeting in a caravan of automobiles. Local authorities, well aware of the approaching armed posse and its intent, did not act to halt its progress. After assembling near the mass meeting, the posse warned the strikers to leave the area or face the consequences. Chambers quickly ended his speech and urged all workers to move quickly into the union building. As the workers ran toward the hall, a grower shot his rifle. A striker rushed the firing grower and pushed the barrel of the gun down. A second grower clubbed the worker on the head. As he lay on the ground, helpless, he was shot to death. The rest of the growers opened fire on the fleeing strikers, killing another and wounding eight. With the workers hiding inside the union building, growers shot through the windows. When their ammunition was spent, the growers returned to their caravan and fled the scene.[44]

The massacre was well witnessed by several state highway patrol officers and sheriff's deputies. They neither protected the workers nor pursued the growers when the shooting stopped. When they were finally convinced to respond to the killings by outraged local residents and workers, the officers caught up with the caravan and disarmed some of the posse. But they did not arrest any of the growers. A nationwide public outcry the following day forced local and state law enforcement agencies to respond, and eight growers were eventually arrested. Their $15,000 bail was quickly paid by sympathetic ginning companies. Growers were certainly not vanquished by these arrests. On the contrary, they demanded (and received) the arrest of Chambers on charges of inciting the violence at Pixley. Chambers was eventually charged with criminal syndicalism, reviving an old law that had been used effectively to help break the leadership of the IWW. The formal charges against Chambers, in fact, were made by a grower who had been involved in the Pixley massacre.[45]

Settling the Strike

Following the massacres, demands quickly reached the governor from all quarters that the farmers be disarmed. The governor, unsure how to respond, increased the number of highway patrolmen in the area, but did little else, especially as his own informant on the scene, the chief of the highway patrol, laid blame for the violence squarely at the feet of "outside agitators." He argued that the violence of the farmers was largely justified.[46]

The federal government took a more proactive stance. As city reporters poured into the Valley following the murders, and as public support across the state and elsewhere in the nation for the strikers grew, the federal government considered providing food aid to the strikers while it worked to mediate the strike. On October 12, at the behest of the federal government, Governor James Rolph ordered emergency food rations to be provided to strikers throughout the region. George Creel of the National Recovery Administration used the food relief to lure both sides of the strike to a meeting before a fact-finding committee. Creel promised growers that if they accepted the fact-finding, the federal government would see that strikers returned to the fields at sixty cents per hundred pounds pending settlement of the strike. The growers accepted the proposal. Creel knew the prolonged strike had left thousands of workers nearly starving, and he made acceptance of relief by strikers contingent upon accepting the fact-finding proposal and returning to work in the fields. Along with Governor Rolph, a federal conciliator, and the San Joaquin Valley Farm Bureau Federation, Creel signed a notice informing all cotton growers and pickers that they were "to proceed with the picking of California's cotton crop beginning Monday, October 16, 1933." Unwilling to scab on their own strike, pickers refused to return to work—and so they also refused the desperately needed food aid.[47]

The federal government relented and agreed to provide food relief even if the workers did not return to the fields. But the relief still came with other unacceptable strings attached. Mexican workers were questioned about their citizenship status, and automobile license numbers were requested. Unwilling to give this information for fear of deportation or later retaliation, starving strikers in Corcoran boycotted all relief distribution. Forced by the intransigence of the strikers, and their growing public support, relief administrators eventually also dropped the surveillance requirements, and within days, relief distribution centers were established in all the strikers' camps and most of the cotton belt towns.[48]

Both sides did attend the fact-finding hearing, but both argued that any decisions made by the committee were nonbinding. On October 23, the committee (headed by Archbishop Hanna, who still held a position on the slumbering California Commission of Immigration and Housing) determined that seventy-five cents was a reasonable rate for each hundred pounds of cotton picked. Creel immediately promised growers that if *they* accepted this rate, the federal and state governments would halt food relief to the strikers and would not stand in the way of local growers if they tried to shut down the strikers' camps. A concerted federal- and state-sponsored back-to-work initiative was started immediately. Despite counseling from CAWIU leaders that striking workers should accept the seventy-five-cent wage, strikers voted overwhelmingly to remain on strike and seek an eighty-cent wage.

Faced with this intransigence, local growers and law enforcement authorities moved to break worker power by finally breaking up the Corcoran encampment. On October 24, some 3,000 armed growers marched on the camp. They were stopped by the timely arrival of the state chief of the highway patrol and a local sheriff who feared the bloodshed that would inevitably result. Two days later, Kings County sheriff Buckner announced his intention to close the camp, arguing that it was not necessary now that growers had accepted the fact-finding committee's compromise wage. Buckner gathered a force of officers and newly deputized local growers and townspeople, all heavily armed, outside the main camp gate to assure the 3:00 P.M. deadline for evacuating the camp was met. Instead of leaving, strikers, many armed, gathered on their side of the fence, ready to defend their turf. Labor commissioner Frank McDonald rushed to the scene in hopes of negotiating a settlement that would avert the pending battle. Buckner moved his deadline back to 4:00 P.M. to assure time for the Hearst Movietone News camera and crew to arrive to record the event, and during this time, McDonald was able to convince the sheriff to back down, at least for a day.[49]

For many workers, the standoff proved a Pyrrhic victory. Despite their clear willingness to fight, and despite their clear preference to remain on strike until an eighty-cent wage had been won, their own strike leadership determined there was little more to be gained by prolonging the strike and convinced workers to return to the fields on October 27 at seventy-five cents. Without the leadership's support for continuing the strike, workers reluctantly returned to the fields. Within days the strikers' camps were empty. In a fine irony, most of the growers' camps to which workers returned, neglected during the three weeks of the strike, were inferior in sanitation and housing to the ones they had created themselves.[50]

Seeing Struggle in the Landscape

There is something sublime about driving through the southern San Joaquin Valley on an early cold, overcast autumn morning. The browns and grays of the flat, low cotton fields, studded with a fluffy whiteness if they have not yet been picked, blend with the grays and whites of the foggy sky. There is no horizon, no perspective: the vanishing point is everywhere at once, and space has become flattened. Bands of subtle, muted, horizontal colors are broken only occasionally by solitary oaks and trees lined up as windbreaks. On a back road, with no traffic, the quiet is startling. The Valley can be extraordinarily beautiful at times like these, not majestic like the Sierras to the east, but more subtle—a sort of severe, angular aestheticism of modernism: low, sleek, efficient. A landscape, according to geographers Stephen Daniels and Denis Cosgrove, "may be represented in a variety of materials and on many surfaces—in paint on canvas, in writing on paper, in earth, stone, water, and vegetation on the ground." It is also made and represented with the blood of workers, murdered as they attempted to refigure the way they were forced to lead their lives within the landscapes of the state. Or, as Daniels has also noted, landscape is "an ideology, a sophisticated 'visual ideology' which obscures not only the forces and relations of production, but also more plebeian, less pictorial experiences of nature." On a fall morning, or even more, later in the winter, when the cotton harvesting in the San Joaquin Valley is complete, and when the sublime aesthetics of the place become irresistible, it is indeed hard to remember the "forces and relations of production," and that what we are looking at is not *simply* a picture. But it is too a picture of how the world is *supposed* to look; it is a representation of the "natural" relations obtaining on the land.[51]

In the southern San Joaquin Valley in 1933, that picture had been upended, ripped from its frame, ground back into the earth by the militancy and newfound power of the workers, coupled with the violent response of growers seeking to protect their property and their profits. The goal for the state quickly became one of righting the picture again, even if the frame and the contents themselves had to be altered. All this is difficult, if not impossible, to readily *see* as you gaze upon the landscape. Rather, the lie of the land hides these processes well, just as a commodity tells us little of the relations that went into its making. The "lie" that is the landscape fooled even as perceptive an analyst as Jean Baudrillard; there is no doubt of that. After driving through the San Joaquin Valley in search of America, as noted in Chapter 1, he could still claim there is no history on this side of the Atlantic. For him, I guess, struggles like the Corcoran cotton strike just don't count as history.

With the strike settled in 1933, the cotton was picked. Early mornings became quiet once more, as the horizons of fog and soil were broken only by lines of trees and not by the bodies of radical workers and their adversaries facing off across the huge divide that private property reinforces in the Central Valley. Landscape had been torn asunder by the militant actions of migratory workers no longer content (as if they ever had been) to accept the dictates of a powerful cabal of growers. But in the end, the landscape returned, looking like a picture—only now it was incredibly unsteady, jolted by radical workers who insisted on being their own subjects, rather than just the subject and object of the picturesque view.

But the story of this unsteady picture is not yet complete. For the croplands of California to become visible once more as a landscape, growers and the state would have to learn again to control the spaces of agricultural labor reproduction such that the bloody violence of battles like the Corcoran cotton strike would truly "fade into the distance faster and faster in the rear-view mirror of memory."[52]

7 / Reclaiming the Landscape: Learning to Control the Spaces of Revolt

If the cotton growing areas of the southern San Joaquin Valley can be eerily beautiful, then the reclaimed desert of the Imperial Valley presents a much more rough-hewn visage. From a desert rise, the fields look raggedy, fringed by greasewood and ocotillo. To the east of the Imperial Valley, vast fields of sand dunes, bisected by the All-American canal suggest just how tenuous the hold on this land may be. But as we saw in Chapter 4, no matter how rough or tenuous, carving farmland out of the scorching desert was seen by many as a "heroic," patriotic endeavor—the "master passion" of the "master race." It was also an endeavor made possible only by the most brutal repression of any vestiges of workers' rights. Indeed, battles in Imperial were all the more virulent precisely *because* the ideology of "mastering"—mastering both the desert and the people in it—was so strong, while the farming enterprise itself was still quite shaky, subject, as elsewhere, to whims of nature and the market.

During the Depression, the Imperial was hardly a settled landscape, at least in the terms in which we have been taught to think about rural areas. Sixty-seven percent of the cropland in the Valley was held in absentia in 1934; and not only was farm labor turnover high, but so was turnover of tenants. Tenant farmers were squeezed by landlords and worked hard to drive down wages. In 1933 wages were as low as ten cents per hour. In 1934 a federal commission investigating conditions in Imperial Valley (the Leonard Commission) "found filth, squalor, and entire absence of sanitation, and a crowding of human beings into totally inadequate tents or crude structures built of boards, weeds and anything that was found at hand." A slightly reinvigorated Division of Immigration and

Housing (DIH) affirmed the Leonard Commission's findings. Inspectors in February 1934, at the height of the lettuce season and just before the pea season, found no camps rated "good" (that is, lawful), 20 rated "fair" (violating the Camp Sanitation Act in at least one respect), and 42 that were "bad" (dangerous to the health of the occupants and the community). For the entire inspection season (lasting through June), DIH made first inspections of 302 camps. Only eight were "good." Of the remainder, 77 were "fair," and 217 were "bad." Reinspections were made in 203 camps, and DIH found that 20 had been made "good" (most of which had been "fair" in earlier inspections), 109 were improved to or remained "fair," and 12 were still "bad." 40 camps had closed for the season when inspectors sought to reinspect them, and 22 were simply abandoned at the threat of reinspection and possible criminal proceedings lodged against their operators.[1]

Civil Liberties, Uncivil Violence

The Cannery and Agricultural Workers Industrial Union (CAWIU) saw conditions such as these as fertile ground for widening its battle against agribusiness in California. Even toward the end of the battle in Corcoran, while the rank-and-file were urging a continuance of the strike, CAWIU was shifting resources to the Imperial Valley, gearing up for battles it saw as inevitible. Confident in the militancy of local and migrant workers in the Valley (this is where the activism had all begun in 1928 and 1930), however, CAWIU sent inexperienced organizers to Imperial, expecting that organization largely would take care of itself. And it did not count on Imperial growers learning quite as much from Corcoran as they did. Early on growers decided that nothing short of total violent repression would be necessary to ensure their crops would be harvested. Nonetheless, for even greater insurance, growers revived the hibernating Unión de Trabajadores del Valle Imperial as the "official" (company) union for the area in hopes of diverting some of the worker allegiance the radical union was quickly gaining among workers in the Valley. The Mexican consul, perhaps fearful of the influence of communists among the Mexican workers in the Imperial Valley, aided in the resurrection of La Unión. By the beginning of November, growers had informed La Unión that they would pay 22½ cents per hour for harvesting winter crops. There was no written agreement. When the lettuce harvest began, many growers failed to meet this wage and even the puppet La Unión protested. Workers staged a one-day strike on November 13, and growers agreed to meet with La Unión in late December to discuss grievances. In the meantime, CAWIU organizers succeeded in convincing many workers that it, not La Unión, better represented their interests. With CAWIU thus taking an active lead, workers demanded a raise to thirty-five cents at the meeting with growers. The growers refused, and CAWIU called a strike for the peak of the lettuce harvest, January 8, 1934.[2]

CAWIU organizers, perhaps belatedly, began their work in earnest, organizing numerous camp-based locals. On the day of the strike, some 3,000 workers responded immediately. Within a day, the number of strikers had doubled. The growers' response to the strike was quick and decisive. On January 9, organized growers violently dispersed strikers as they prepared to caravan to a meeting at Brawley. Tear gas, billy clubs, and drawn guns were all brought to bear, with the Brawley police chief averring that such tactics were necessary because the strikers had failed to obtain a parade permit. Three days later, a mass strike meeting was called at the strike center, Azteca Hall in Brawley. During the meeting, the hall was surrounded by an army of deputies and vigilantes, led by the Brawley police chief. Despite claiming that he was only there to serve warrants on the communist strike leaders, the police chief ordered all exits blocked and fired tear gas into the hall. In the panic that ensued, workers had to break all the windows in the hall to escape the noxious fumes. After workers had fled, the police raided the empty hall, smashing equipment and confiscating papers. The warrants were never served.[3]

Following the raid on Azteca Hall, demoralized lettuce pickers returned to work throughout the Valley, except in the immediate Brawley area, the original center of the strike. The Brawley police chief declared all strike meetings illegal and ruled that a congregation of two or more striking workers on the streets constituted unlawful assembly. No similar rules were promulgated for militant growers. Hoping to capitalize on the publicity generated by the violent attack on Azteca Hall, and hoping to bring increased attention to the abuse of civil liberties in the Valley, the American Civil Liberties Union (ACLU) came to the Valley to demand the protection of workers' rights. The ACLU called a defiant meeting for Azteca Hall on January 23 and demanded police protection. The ACLU succeeded in obtaining a federal court order restraining local officials from interfering in any way with the meeting. Even so, just before the start of the January 23 meeting, vigilantes abducted ACLU activist A. L. Wirin, who was to be the featured speaker (and who had earlier been instrumental in presenting the workers' case before the fact-finding commission in Corcoran). As state and local police looked on, Wirin was hauled out to the desert, beaten, robbed, and left shoeless for his eleven-mile walk back to town. The Azteca Hall meeting was canceled. When Wirin made it to Brawley, he was met by vigilante growers who threatened him with even worse abuse if he stayed in the Imperial Valley. He left. Federal mediators and the judiciary refused to act against local growers and authorities for their role in this outrage, arguing that the abduction of Wirin did not interfere with the scheduled meeting: it could have been held in his absence, they claimed. The strike ended with no gains made by CAWIU.[4]

Concerned about the negative publicity events such as Wirin's abduction were generating, and concerned that the federal Leonard Commission (whose membership included former California Commission of Immigration and Housing director Simon Lubin and former Department of Industrial Relations director Will French) was too sympathetic to militant workers, growers created an "official" committee headed by University of California's dean of the Agricultural College, C. B. Hutchison, to refute the Leonard Commission and expose the true roots of unrest in the Imperial Valley.[5] Even this decidedly progrower committee was forced to admit that the Wirin abduction deserved to be "unreservedly condemn[ed]." But, the committee quickly added, Wirin's kidnapping "must be judged in light of the entire situation." This entire situation was that the ACLU came to the Valley only to "create trouble and prevent the harvesting of the Valley's crop." By securing the injunction against local authorities, according to the Hutchison Committee, the ACLU was scheming to allow communists—CAWIU—"to meet under the protection of the American Civil Liberties Union." The granting of the injunction, the committee held, posed a grave danger to the "citizens" of the Valley, who feared that "the protection of the constituted authorities had been removed from the residents of the Valley and given to those whose ultimate objective was to overthrow the government." While the actions of the residents ought to be condemned, the committee suggested, they were certainly understandable: the residents and growers of the Valley were not faced with a legitimate work stoppage, but with an invasion by "outsiders" bent on destroying both their harvest and America. While overzealous, residents were simply being good patriots.[6]

"The use of violent strikebreaking tactics was common to most of the agricultural strikes in California during the early 1930s," California farm labor historian Cletus Daniel has noted,

> but nowhere did farm employers and local authorities bring so much enthusiasm to their strikebreaking activities or pursue a course of violence and terror as single-mindedly and purposefully as in the Imperial Valley. The vigilantism that flourished there in 1934 was not just a strikebreaking expedient, but the highest and most graphic expression of regional and class patriotism.[7]

The techniques used to crush the lettuce strike were hardly subtle. But they did provide the axis around which further debate about agribusiness in the Valley (and elsewhere in the state) revolved. These debates, of course, were directly concerned with the structure of the landscape. Was it possible to maintain the "heroic" landscape of the reclaimed desert and still allow for workers to possess any rights at all—or any dignity for that matter? The Leonard Commission put the matter this way in its report to the federal government on the lettuce strike:

> It is regrettable that men who have put heroic effort into the reclamation of desert wastes are threatened with the loss of their hard earned fortunes. It is deplorable that many workers are not able to earn sufficient wages to maintain even a primitive, or savage, standard of living, and consequently are forced upon charities. It is horrible that children are reared in an environment as pitiable as that which we saw in more than one locality. But worse than these is the harsh suppression of that which we in the United States claim as our birthright, the freedom to express our lawful opinions and legally to organize to better our lot and our fellow-men.[8]

Since most growers did not consider workers to be legitimate members of the local community, and since they were convinced most of their workers were not citizens, the Leonard Commission's concerns probably made little sense.

Rather growers' concerns were expressed by the Hutchison Committee, who claimed that the problems in the Valley were not due to repressive tactics on the part of growers, but were the result of foreign and outside agitators who insisted on using American rights and liberties for revolutionary, not legitimate, purposes. In a supplementary report on conditions to the Imperial Valley made to the nascent Associated Farmers of California, Inc., and later distributed by that organization, the Hutchison Committee criticized the Leonard Commission's report on a point-by-point basis. The Leonard Commission had made as its first recommendation:

> That Federal and State Governments exercise every power and authority to maintain in fact the rights of free speech, free press, and free assembly, and that men, whether citizens or aliens, shall not be harassed by permanent, temporary, amateur, or self-appointed officers of the law.

The Hutchison Committee retorted in its Supplementary Report:

> The Committee supports the rights of free speech and free assemblage, but it points out that it is time to make a distinction between free speech and unlicensed speech, and that any organization demanding the protection of the Constitution must be able to show clean hands and no connection with a movement to overthrow the Constitution or subvert these rights.

Free speech had to be licensed, controlled, and cleaned until it fit the needs and desires of the growers of the Valley. With the domination of nature that the production of the Imperial Valley agricultural landscape implied, growers also assumed that they had an inalienable right to control utterly the land and people they had conjured into existence. "Outside" criticism was not lightly tolerated.[9]

The Spring Pea Strike

Despite victory in the lettuce strike, growers did not lessen their vigilance. The spring pea harvest began almost on the heels of the lettuce harvest, and with appalling conditions the rule in the pea pickers' camps, a strike was all but certain. DIH was quite concerned with camp conditions in the pea growing areas, as it had been since the Commission first turned its attention to this agricultural region at the time of World War I; but even with a strike imminent, it made no move to prosecute any camp operators, arguing that "all camps were soon to close" (the pea season is quite short). To no one's surprise, pea pickers did indeed call a strike the second week of February. CAWIU had remained active in the Valley after the lettuce strike was crushed, and pea pickers were well organized. Some 3,500 to 4,000 workers immediately walked off the job. Growers responded just as they had in the lettuce pickers strike: with all the violence they could muster. The growers' first line of defense was to evict striking workers from their camps and to throw up fences and station guards to "protect" those who "chose" to work. Workers were "free" to work, growers proclaimed; the guards and fenced compounds only assured that agitators would be kept out and workers' freedoms would be protected.[10]

Two DIH inspectors rushed to Calipatria, the center of the pea strike. Finding "comparatively little picking was being done," the inspectors reported that many of the "idle families" had been forced to settle in a squatters' camp about ten miles from Calipatria. This camp grew quickly over the course of the first days of the strike, finally housing perhaps 2,000 residents in 225 tents and shelters. Two or three miles away "another large group of unemployed [that is, striking] workers were to be found." According to inspector Leo Mott, the second camp housed Mexican workers, while the first housed "American[s]."[11]

The growers, learning from Corcoran, feared both these encampments and moved to have them immediately shut down. With the cooperation of the DIH inspectors (who simultaneously refused to act against unlawful growers' camps), Dr. W. F. Fox, the county health officer, declared the two strikers' camps unsanitary and served abatement notices on the lessees of the land. The strategy worked. When the camps were forcibly dispersed, the strike fell into disarray. DIH inspector Mott described the event:

> Since the labor trouble started it is said to have been the general practice of the strikers to collect at a different point each day and start out with a parade of automobiles throughout the area and, wherever workers have been found in a

field, to harass and intimidate them. However, an emergency ordinance was passed Saturday by the Board of Supervisors to curb this play in a measure and while I haven't read the ordinance we are under the impression, from what we saw yesterday, at Wilkerson Camp [the second camp referred to above] that if it lacked any necessary features to prevent a parade that phase was taken care of on the ground by officials. At any rate, the parade started, but after the first car got under way the remainder of 40 or 50 were stopped and standing there late in the afternoon when we left. There was a general display of guns and clubs and, while the situation looked pretty tense, no serious trouble developed. During the afternoon, the sheriff's van drove up and took away a dozen or so of the leaders, and that was probably the climax of the Imperial Valley pea strike—last night the Sheriff searched the Young camp [the first strikers' camp] . . . for arms—it was then posted "No Trespassing" together with the other camping places—and was visited this morning by deputies and County Health Officials and occupants were given orders to move on. The leaderless strikers, with their backs against the desert, gave up and along about noon a general exodus was started—the pickers scattering to various fields and we noticed that many of them were flocking to the town of Calipatria. We look for the big camp to be entirely vacated unless unforeseen difficulties arise but, in view of the fact that the pickers have not gained anything there may be sporadic trouble until the crop is finally harvested two or three weeks hence.[12]

The following day, local deputies oversaw the final and complete evacuation of the Young camp. For reasons of sanitation, Mott burned all the grass and brush huts (and not a few of the meagre possessions of the inhabitants). Many of the families in the Young camp moved to another vacant patch of land, but deputies routed them from there as well. According to Inspector Fred Rugg, most of the workers in the pea harvest were parts of families and most of the workers had no choice but to return to work or else see their children starve. When the strikers' camps were broken, the pea strike was effectively over. As Mott wrote his supervisor, employing a phrase common to describe the movement of migratory workers: "All of the workers have flocked back into the fields." The imagery is not too far off. Reading reports of the battles in the Imperial Valley gives the impression that farmworkers were understood to be like crows or blackbirds in a cornfield, fleeing the scene when frightened (perhaps by gunfire) only to alight again where they thought they could.[13]

Even with the strike crushed, growers were concerned about the flock of migratory workers in their midst. They felt they could not allow even the most rudimentary expression of workers' rights in the Valley. Throughout the spring, whenever workers tried to meet, they found their gatherings violently dispersed. ACLU activists, union organizers, rank-and-file workers, and even federal labor commissioners all were subjected to harassment and often physical violence as growers tried to maintain their absolute control over labor conditions in the

Valley. Workers' attorneys were beaten as local police officers stood idly by; and judges advocated violence from the bench. As hearings before a U.S. Senate committee investigating abuses of the rights of workers (the La Follette Committee) made abundantly clear at the end of the decade, for all the patriotic rhetoric and citizen outrage, many of the acts of violence were well orchestrated by a cabal of large growers who dominated the politics and economy of the Valley. Their position was simple: violence paid in increased profits. The *Los Angeles Times,* ever willing to trumpet the growers' cause, placed blame for the constant violence in the Imperial on the workers and their organizations. Relations in the Valley had been "particularly cordial," according to the *Times.* But the "peaceful sky" of the bountiful desert had been marred by clouds of unrest created by "outside agitators" of whom not just the growers, but also the peaceful workers, were "quite fed up."[14]

Unsure that it had the power to implement the recommendations of its own Leonard Commission, which had called for federal assistance in effectively organizing workers, the Roosevelt administration sent a "conciliator" to the Valley to restore peaceful labor relations. The conciliator, former Washington, D.C., police chief Pelham Glassford, immediately sided with the growers and worked to assure that the spring melon harvest would proceed uninterrupted. He publicly endorsed a grower plan to "smash what remained of CAWIU in the region." CAWIU was controlled by communists, after all, and Glassford asserted that the union's "only objective was to create dissension, destroy private property and foment a strike." Glassford therefore lent his authority to the grower-created "Mexican Association of the Imperial Valley" (which even he called a company union) and suggested that growers engage in voluntary reform. But with their brutal methods and with their complete intransigence, growers were adept at turning even their allies against them, and Glassford soon was forced to dissociate himself from the agriculturalists of the Valley. They had all but invented the communist menace in their effort to assert complete dominance over the affairs of the Valley, Glassford admitted. The desires and needs of the workers were just. "It is my conviction," Glassford informed the Imperial County Board of Supervisors after he turned against the growers,

> that a group of growers have exploited a "communist" hysteria for the advancement of their own interests; that they have welcomed labor agitation, which they could brand as "Red," as a means of sustaining supremacy by mob rule, thereby preserving what is so essential to their conspiracy—*Cheap labor.*[15]

In the end, Glassford did little in the Valley as growers guaranteed their own harvest by threatening not just CAWIU, but the federal mediators as well. Indeed, as Cletus Daniel ruefully concludes, "Glassford and the federal government had willingly participated in or condoned nearly every union-busting activity for which the general [Glassford] so indignantly called employers to account after his strategy for voluntary reform had failed." And with the grower victory that violent intransigence brought over workers and the state alike, work and living conditions in the Valley sunk to new lows.[16]

Controlling Space, Controlling Workers

The Alameda Plan

Concerned that the tactics employed in Imperial and elsewhere around the state during the bitter strikes of 1933 and 1934 were ultimately self-defeating, Alameda County District Attorney Earl Warren sought to create a less violent, more rational system of labor control—a system that did not necessarily imply the defeat of the state as it had in Imperial. Like his colleagues elsewhere, Warren was convinced that the strikes around the state were caused by "outside" agitators and exacerbated by a great influx of migratory workers thrown into the fields by the economic crisis. Warren worked with DIH, local relief officials, and area growers to devise a plan to prevent unrest before it even began. Warren was concerned "because in the year 1933, the uprisings that took place from one end of the state to the other started in Alameda County."[17]

A first step in Warren's plan to prevent trouble before it started was to "break the continuity" between workers' struggles by using only local labor in the spring pea harvests. Formalizing their policies of 1933, Alameda County welfare authorities agreed for 1934 that all "able-bodied" workers would be released from relief at the beginning of the harvest, even if there was no chance that, as inexperienced fieldworkers, they could make a living wage. The Department of Industrial Relations approved this plan. Its director, Timothy Reardon, told growers through the press that "if local workers are given preference, agitators will have little chance of creating trouble." The use of the local unemployed was to be supplemented, in Warren's scheme, by a housing plan that both Warren and DIH felt would minimize the possibility of successful agitation. At Warren's urging, Alameda County supervisors passed an ordinance requiring all camp operators to secure a county permit, which would only be issued when the camp had been approved by DIH inspectors. For its part, DIH urged growers to move their camps off the main roads, and therefore away from where picketers could operate. Finally, Earl Warren sponsored an Alameda County ordinance that outlawed assembling, speaking, picketing, or playing musical instruments for the purpose of inducing people to quit work or boycott a shop. Parades and protest meetings were allowed only if a permit was obtained in advance. For a permit, applicants had to secure the written support of three "reputable residents of the county of Alameda," certifying the good moral character of the applicant. The applicant also had to provide proof of "a good character and a reputation for peace and quiet in the neighborhood in which he resides." The City of Oakland took the idea one step further and simply outlawed picketing and assembly.[18]

The plan "worked out successfully," boasted DIH chief Vincent Brown late in 1934, noting that there had been no strikes in Alameda that year. Earl Warren was likewise pleased with the success of his strategy, writing to DIH to express his gratitude for the hard work performed by inspector Milton Edwards, who was given authority by Warren to change the layout of camps even if it was against the wishes of their operators, and by C. A. Degnan, the Fresno DIH bureau director who had been called north to perform undercover work for Warren in the various camps of the county. Both Warren and DIH sought to replicate the plan throughout the state as the harvest progressed in 1934, achieving what they felt was a good degree of success. In public statements about the plan, Edward Brown and inspector James Iames suggested guarding the entrance to each labor camp "against encroachment by disturbers." For Brown, simple locational decisions could make all the difference between a peaceful harvest and one marred by unrest. Moving camps off main roads and protecting their integrity with armed guards allowed the "real workers" to continue working undisturbed regardless of the "strikers [who] were imported from other districts to give the appearance of a strike." Earl Warren agreed with Brown and for the 1935 season went as far as lending Deputy Sheriff Hugo Radbrick to growers to supervise camps and evict troublemakers as necessary.[19]

Many in the state government and among the more progressive factions of the growers' ranks called Warren "the best district attorney in the country" for his efforts; Simon Lubin hoped that Warren's plan "might set the pace for all the other counties"; and DIH chief Vincent Brown distinguished Warren as a district attorney "who happens to have a social view point"—all this because he had hit on a spatial solution for controlling the right of labor to organize. Perhaps this is where histories of Earl Warren's role in liberalizing civil liberties during his years as chief justice of the Supreme Court should begin.[20]

Land and Labor in Brentwood

The Alameda Plan spawned its most successful progeny a bit to the east, in the San Joaquin Delta town of Brentwood. Brentwood was the major town of a fruit growing region nestled between the eastern foothills of Mount Diablo and the reclaimed marshlands of the Delta. The region and the town were both dominated by the British firm Balfour-Guthrie Investment Company (BG). BG was a paragon of capitalist factory farming. It was a wholly owned subsidiary of Balfour-Guthrie Co. Ltd., which itself was controlled from London by Balfour, Williamson and Company, an international investment, importing, and insurance firm. The Balfour-Guthrie Investment Company was the farming branch of this far-flung enterprise, and its name was suggestive of what it was actually growing in the fields of Brentwood. As an important "farmer" in the state (it also owned land in Imperial Valley and elsewhere), BG was well connected to other large-scale agricultural concerns, including the Cal Pak Corporation (later Del Monte), H. P. Garin Company (which we met in the previous chapter), and the D. D. Watson Company, all of which farmed extensive acreage in and around Brentwood. The smaller growers of the region usually contracted with one of these larger firms for labor and marketing services. The four largest firms therefore wielded impressive political power within Brentwood and Contra Costa County.[21]

BG owned or controlled some 4,100 acres of crop and orchard land in the Brentwood area, of which 1,500 acres bore labor-intensive fruit crops. The Brentwood orchards normally employed about 2,000 workers during the month-long harvest season. To house the influx of temporary workers, BG built a series of labor camps, but it also relied on surplus labor from the nearby ditch-bank camps that invariably developed during the harvest season. BG's own camps were comparatively well appointed. In 1929, under the supervision of DIH, BG created a model labor camp that attracted a good deal of attention around the state. Both supporters and detractors of BG invariably called the BG camp a "concentration camp" both because BG contracted workers who gathered in it to other growers, and because of the fences erected around it. BG officials, members of the Associated Farmers and other farmer organizations, and DIH all saw the BG model camp as a good example of the beneficent regard with which corporate farmers held their employees. Even so, BG officials were clear that the camp was first and foremost part of a system of labor control: the construction of a model camp allowed BG greater surveillance over its workers. And it allowed for greater control over how employees spent what little money they earned. As one BG executive asserted, BG never provided charity to its workers. Rather, the seventy-five cabins, 460 tent platforms, running hot and cold water, and electricity were part of the temporary workers' pay.[22]

Workers were less sanguine about the motives for (and the conditions of) the camp on the BG property. In 1931, the *Sacramento Valley Labor Bulletin* received a number of complaints about the camp and opened an investigation.

The paper's investigators found that BG regularly advertised for a surplus of laborers during the harvest season, a tactic doubly unnecessary in a region with chronic seasonal unemployment. Rather than working the six to twelve months BG promised in its advertisements, most workers found work for no more than a few days. Moreover, BG specifically sought to import family laborers since families found it harder to leave in search of better opportunities than did single men. Many families in Brentwood, therefore, became captive labor in a market that demanded fluidity. Those housed in the "model camp" built to DIH specifications, according to the *Labor Bulletin*, found themselves placed in a "double stockade," with "no supervision other than to maintain quiet." If workers owed money to the company, and most did because rent and food costs tended to outstrip their pay from the overcrowded orchards, they were not allowed to remove their belongings from the camp. In essence, BG harvested its crops by indenturing labor. Armed with these discoveries, the *Labor Bulletin* asked DIH to intervene, and held off publishing the results of its investigation until DIH did. When DIH failed to respond, the *Labor Bulletin* ran the story, noting particularly that the various divisions of the Department of Industrial Relations (including DIH) had sought to shove responsibility for investigating and mitigating the conditions at the BG ranch on the others. For its part, BG justified its use of a "double stockade"—two eight-foot-high fences around the workers' camp variously guarded by a caretaker or a deputy lent by the Contra Costa County sheriff—by suggesting it protected the "high-class of people who live in this camp" from trespassers.[23]

By 1934 BG was asserting that it provided some of the best labor camp conditions in the state, and thus unrest such as that at Corcoran and Imperial would be impossible in Brentwood. If there was any unrest, then it could only be because people who were not "real" workers had come to town to stir up trouble. As was their practice, Brentwood farmers had induced a labor oversupply for their summer harvest in 1934. But this time, as the apricot harvest began on June 1, unemployed workers sought to make common cause with those employed in the orchards. Street corner and park meetings were organized and CAWIU, though weakened by its losses in Imperial, worked to transform the incipient revolt into a productive strike. CAWIU demanded increased wages and, more importantly, an eight-hour day, which would have had the effect of easing much of the local unemployment during the critical harvest period.[24]

Brentwood growers and shippers, along with the newly formed Associated Farmers, argued that the strike was not a strike at all, but rather an action by unemployed workers who camped along creeks and railroads. Those who "wanted to work" (and who therefore were housed in guarded and fenced company camps) had shown themselves to be content with their lot. As recalled by Philip Bancroft, the 1938 Republican senatorial candidate, vice president of the county Associated Farmers, local fruit grower, and son of famous California historian H. H. Bancroft:

> The situation that had been going on over there in Brentwood was outrageous, the way they [the farmers] were treated. For instance, in the strike out there it wasn't the men who were working that were striking, making the trouble, it was the men from outside who flooded in there looking for jobs, and there weren't any jobs for them. They were in an unfortunate position, and then these agitators came in and harangued them. Of course, they claimed that the farmers had been agitating to get a whole lot of people in there, more than they needed and all that, which was not true, because that's the kind of action that's apt to make trouble and the farmers weren't looking for trouble, they were just looking for people to harvest their crops. . . . We would seldom have to work to find laborers. There were a lot of them floating around at that time.[25]

Those that were working, Bancroft claimed, remained content, and appreciated the fence around the camp:

> Because [the BG camp] was surrounded by a substantial fence surmounted by plenty of barbed wire, with the entrance guarded day and night, agitators continually referred to it as a stockade, a cattle corral or a prison and its inhabitants as prisoners. Obviously the fence and the guard were there to keep the lawless element out, not to keep the contented workmen in.[26]

Despite the assertion that workers were content, and despite the support for that contentment the fence provided, local law enforcement officers and growers quickly resorted to violence to break the strike. On June 6, Contra Costa Sheriff R. R. Veale banned all picketing, and later that day, a posse of newly deputized farmers and townspeople, assisted by a California highway patrol officer, "herded" two hundred striking workers—women, men, and children— into a cattle corral by the Southern Pacific railroad tracks. Fifteen "agitators" were immediately arrested and the rest of the group was identified, questioned, and then formed into a caravan and escorted to the county line. In neighboring San Joaquin County, a group of "officers took up 'riding the herd' and drove the caravan through the county." The *San Francisco Examiner* reported that "further deportations of undesirables [were] scheduled" for the following day.[27]

The deportation did not break the strike, and CAWIU, now under the local leadership of Caroline Decker, made common cause with Julius Nathan, a Trotskyist organizer for the American Federation of Labor's (AFL's) fledgling cannery union in the region. This alliance proved so frightening to employers and establishment labor alike that Paul Scharrenberg, president of the California

Federation of Labor, quietly informed the Associated Farmers that the AFL would withdraw from efforts to organize cannery workers in the Bay Area. But in the meantime, the alliance allowed strikers to step up their pickets against the BG and D. D. Watson ranches. With picketing proving successful, BG executives and other local growers next solicited the help of Lodi agribusinessman and state Associated Farmers executive "Colonel" Walter Garrison to plan an escalation of violence against strikers. Garrison called a meeting at the Brentwood High School and allowed a representative of the Department of Industrial Relations to present the combined unions' demands. The growers dismissed these demands by claiming that "their own employees made no demands and were in nowise interested in or concerned with the unionization movement." Under Garrison's advice, C. B. Weeks, the manager of BG's Brentwood operations, swore out a complaint and had Nathan arrested. In the face of the withering attacks on their picket lines that ensued, strikers soon capitulated. And so ended not just the Brentwood strike of 1934, but also the last organized effort by CAWIU.[28]

The Brentwood Plan of 1935

Brutal repression had proved effective in 1934 in Brentwood, but following the lead of Earl Warren in Alameda County, more and more law enforcement officers and growers were questioning its long-term efficacy. The new sheriff in Contra Costa County, John Miller, was determined that there "will be no labor trouble in Brentwood" in 1935. He wanted to assure that violence on the part of growers would simply not be necessary to control labor. C. B. Weeks likewise hoped to avoid violence and stepped up his program of labor camp improvement. Along with other area growers, Weeks hired a respected public health nurse, Eva Barnes, at the tail end of the 1934 season, to inspect the camps and to "teach migratory workers something of the ideals, physical and mental, for which America stands." Barnes worked closely with DIH inspectors at both the BG and Watson camps. And to dispel any public fear that the camps were part of the cause of that year's unrest, Barnes publicly announced that the camps were "the best found inside the state or elsewhere." She was effusive in her praise:

> Of the various localities in which I have worked, outside of California as well, I think the Brentwood camps are the best. Camps are cleaned thoroughly every day, and there is a[n] excellent foreman in every place. Due to the co-operation on the part of the state housing and immigration department with the Balfour Guthrie Company, I believe their housing conditions are the best for this type of labor camp that I have ever seen. There is nursery and playground equipment for the

children with a fine woman in charge of each camp. It is the first that I have ever seen a nursery in a Mexican camp. I wish that more camps throughout the state would take not[e] of the one here.[29]

During the off-season, Sheriff Miller worked closely with Charles Weeks and D. Watson, of Watson farms, as well as with Bancroft and Garrison from the Associated Farmers, to design a foolproof method of labor control and surveillance. Miller's scheme revolved around the establishment of a centralized worker registry in Brentwood, staffed by the sheriff and his deputies, which would clear all area job applicants before they applied to particular farms and orchards. Miller also created a "'Diablo Valley Public Relations Committee' composed of five small ranchers selected by the sheriff, five large farmers selected by the farm organizations, and five merchants or laboring men selected by the ten farmers." In addition to doing public relations work before, during, and after the harvest, the committee established and published "an equitable wage scale, fair to all concerned." The wage scale, Miller claimed, was always "agreed upon to the satisfaction of the entire community." Finally, at the start of the harvest season, Miller moved his operations over Pacheco Pass from Martinez to Brentwood, so that the sheriff and his deputies would be on hand to greet workers as they arrived for work in the area, thereby assuring that all were properly registered.[30]

To register for work, each applicant filled out in triplicate a form that included the worker's name, address (including temporary addresses in the area), marital status, family status, physical description, nationality, union affiliation, automobile registration, citizenship status, and so forth. The worker was then given an employment registration card, which allowed him or her to apply for employment at any Brentwood farm. A greater portion of this card was given over to space for comments by the sheriff and ranchers: each was to fill out information regarding the worker's ability, the type of job performed, the adequacy of service the worker rendered to the employer, and the usefulness of the worker's family in assisting with the harvest. Whenever a farmer hired a worker, his or her registration number was reported to the sheriff, and the sheriff recorded all pertinent information regarding the worker. In subsequent years the registry could be referred to each time a worker applied for work.[31]

Miller was as proud of his plan as Earl Warren and DIH were of theirs. Asked by Senator Robert La Follette, Jr. (during an investigation of labor relations in California) if the plan had "produced industrial peace in Contra Costa County," Sheriff Miller replied: "It has sir, absolutely. We have no trouble in that area whatever. We haven't had a strike; we haven't pulled a trigger; and we have nothing but friendship with the workers." The reasons for this peace were obvious to Miller: they were a product of his own hard work at gaining control over all aspects of workers lives:

> The utilization of this method [of registration] gives me and my officers complete surveillance over every fruit worker in the district, and as the season progresses, we make a daily round of the fruit workers in the community, asking if they have registered and if they want work, advising them that it will be necessary to register; otherwise, they will not be needed in the community. You can see that at once we have complete control of the situation and can choose our workers from those who have had good past records, as at the expiration of the picking season, each farmer makes a report on his registration sheet showing at which type of work the worker is proficient, how much he was paid, and what type of work he produced.[32]

And complete control, Miller asserted, led to complete contentment for the workers. "You may be surprised to know," the sheriff wrote to those interested in duplicating his system, "that in the past several seasons, the fruit workers at Brentwood have actually been proud to possess a card of registration." But to assure this level of pride, Miller had to remain an activist sheriff. He spent weeks in Brentwood during the harvest, "never leaving night or day, in a sincere effort to meet each worker personally, giving him a hardy handclasp and a happy smile." Miller was sure to perform his job in "my working clothes," so workers would recognize him as one of their own, and he often paused in his rounds to pick "a little fruit with each worker and [again] give him a happy smile." When these techniques proved insufficient to establishing the level of control Miller desired, he was not adverse to bringing county prisoners to the orchards and fields of the county, complete with guards, to pick fruit at the "established rates" (but with the county taxpayers picking up the tab for room, board, and guards).[33]

In earlier publicity about his plan, Miller had called the "Diablo Valley Public Relations Committee" the "Brentwood Welfare Board," suggesting another aspect of his plan. In his first year as sheriff, Miller enlisted the aid of the State Emergency Relief Agency (SERA) and the state Social Services Department in forcing those on relief in the county to work in the orchards of Brentwood. Like Earl Warren, he thought this would help "break the continuity" formed by agitators among migratory workers. But again, he wanted to leave nothing to chance. He arranged during that first year for nightly entertainment for workers, with SERA providing an orchestra. These shows, Miller thought, would "keep the workers' minds turned in the right direction." The upheavals of 1933 and 1934 would not be repeated under his watch, Miller was "ready to tell the great state of California"—"Nothing will be overlooked to make the fruit workers a happy, contented, and peaceful lot." In 1936, the second year of his plan, instead of orchestras to amuse the workers, Miller contracted with the notoriously progrower U.S. Employment Service and the California State Employment Service to assist in the registration process, and to assure that enough workers were always on hand. Working with these agencies, Miller warned area growers that there were probable agitators among the workers and asked farm managers to blacklist any workers that either they or the sheriff suspected of inciting trouble or that had past records of union involvement. In addition to his "happy smiles," Miller deployed undercover deputies in the field to keep tabs on the conversations of suspected "agitators."[34]

Policing Space

To assure peace and contentment, Miller coupled surveillance over workers with tightened control over the public spaces of the town. With the cooperation of local growers, Miller effectively banned all free speech and assembly, even while allowing the seeming ability of workers to meet as they pleased. Miller "personally talked to" the registered workers, informing them that they were required to report to him any moves toward unionization, and any work by agitators of which they might have knowledge. The network of informants he hoped to establish would assure that any organizing was halted even before it began. Confident in his self-policing worker network, Miller granted "outside agitators" the "right to come in and talk to individuals, or . . . [to] hire a hall to speak to them." On the city streets or in local parks, however, these rights were highly attenuated:

> Where they get up on soap boxes and address a group from a street corner or in the open, the people of Brentwood take the position that these people are inciting a riot and disturbing the peace of the residents of the community; and so therefore they swear out a warrant on that basis.

However, with the warrant in hand, and aware of the propaganda advantages afforded to "agitators" if their meetings were broken up by the police, Miller moved cautiously. "It is upon serving the warrant and the method used that the peace officer either makes or breaks the case," he reasoned. Miller ordered his deputies to allow a speaker to finish before they made an arrest:

> If an arrest is made at the time that the soap box orator is in the midst of his oration, the peace officer immediately puts every last one of the hearers against him, and therefore, the peace officer blows the entire situation. We attack the matter in an entirely different way as follows: the resident swears out a warrant for disturbing the peace; our officers keep the soap box orator under surveillance during the time he makes the oration; we allow him to finish; we watch him carefully, and

when he gets alone somewhere away from the scene, we place him under arrest and take him to the County Jail. . . . [B]y employing [this method] we absolutely eliminate the belligerent attitude of the mob and in this way the psychology of the entire proceedings is to have the mob with you rather than against you. (That in a nut shell is the secret of our success at Brentwood more than anything else.)[35]

In practice, Miller and his deputies did not always wait for the orator to finish speaking before removing him or her from the county. Rather they did all they could to keep her or him off the soapbox in the first place. During the 1936 harvest, Miller intercepted Julius Nathan, the Trotskyist strike leader from 1934, and ordered him to leave the county "on the basis of saving his life," which Miller claimed had been threatened by angry growers and pickers (which is a rather curious way to punish those who threaten violence). When Nathan retreated to a friend's house in nearby Byron, Miller established around-the-clock surveillance of the house until Nathan "had peacefully left the district." The deputies' orders were to assure Nathan's safety "and to see that he did not enter Brentwood that night or the next day."[36]

Miller had been informed of Nathan's presence in the area by "Colonel" Garrison, who in his role as president of the Associated Farmers had provided Miller with photographs and license numbers for all of Nathan's entourage. The Associated Farmers had been involved in Brentwood since 1934, and its registry of workers was proving indispensable to sheriffs throughout the state. Many of the "known communists" working in the California fields were placed under constant surveillance by the Associated Farmers, the Bureau of Criminal Identification, various detective agencies, and vigilant sheriffs like Miller. For the average worker, however, surveillance was always more visceral than the rather abstract surveillance organized by these agencies. On the reverse side of the worker registration card developed by Miller, workers were required to sign a statement agreeing:

That the Employer has the right to discharge me at any time without cause or previous notice; that if I quit or am discharged for any reason whatsoever, I will remove myself, my family, and my belongings from the quarters furnished by Employer and from his land; that if I do not do so upon verbal demand by the employer, Employer shall have the right to remove my belongings from his land, using whatever means necessary to do so; provided, however, that the Employer shall not be obligated to remove them further than the nearest public highway.

BG went even further. A job at BG was bought with a contractual obligation to utterly bare one's life to the glare of the corporation. In order to work, and to live at the BG camp, a worker granted the "undersigned owner the right to search my cabin at any time he may see fit."[37]

With Sheriff Miller's hard work, peace returned to the fields of Brentwood beginning in 1935, and workers returned to their happy, contented lot. The Hutchison Committee in Imperial Valley had called for a licensing of speech and assembly rights, Earl Warren in Alameda had worked to assure that no protests occurred without his permission, and Sheriff Miller realized both these desires. And with the assistance of the reactionary Associated Farmers, Miller's and Warren's methods of surveillance and control over space was widened to encompass the state, as senate investigators found at the end of the decade. Such techniques provided what Cletus Daniel has aptly called a "passage to no man's land" for farmworkers, a fitting metaphor for the re-creation of a landscape in which workers were made so utterly visible to the structures of power that they could once again become invisible in the landscape.[38]

The Ordinary Landscape

As Raymond Williams pointed out two decades ago, countryside seen as landscape must appear unworked. But Sheriff Miller's efforts in Brentwood, as much as the vigilante tactics in Imperial, indicate just how much work is necessary to erase all signs of work, and all signs of the contentious reproduction of workers. As revolt threw into question the standard practices that provided the structure of the agricultural landscape at the beginning of the Depression, violent control, and less violent surveillance, provided tools to reestablish "peaceful" social relations in the second half of the 1930s. Both workers *and* the spaces through which they moved, toiled, slept, ate, organized, and recreated, had to be carefully policed so that peace could reign. The damned *still* made the beauty of California possible, but now they found ever more aspects of their lives fully opened to the eyes of power. In this sense, the fields of California were truly being modernized: as Matt Hannah has shown, modern power, organized through surveillance, is only possible when individuals can be accurately *placed*. And that was precisely the point of the registration plan Sheriff Miller devised.[39]

At the same time that Senator La Follette's Committee was investigating abuses of the rights of workers in California industry and agriculture, the Works Progress Administration's (WPA's) Federal Writers Project published its *California: Guide to the Golden State.* The authors of this volume, though well-attuned to the labor unrest that had marked the state, found little of interest in the Brentwood area. There was some colorful local history concerning Dr. John Marsh's disputes with his Mexican neighbors in the 1850s (disputes that ended only when the neighbors murdered Marsh), and the authors remarked on the "large fruit and nut orchards" that crowded the highways. Brentwood was exceptionally ordinary, not at all remarkable. But this too is testimony to the hard work of settling the disputes that make the landscape. The ordinary landscape of Brentwood was hardly simply a reflection of the "culture" that lived in it, as some cultural geographers would have us believe. Rather, its very form—and its very ordinariness—were the result not just of explosive moments like the 1934 strike with its mass deportations, but the grueling, painstaking work of learning to control the people and spaces of the agricultural districts so that the WPA writers would have nothing to see. All this work was necessary to get workers to stop resisting, really to disappear so that the landscape could materialize as an object, a settled, solid thing, ready to be described by the WPA for motorists who raced past on their way from the East Bay to Yosemite.[40]

Julius Nathan was more direct in his assessment of the causes and effects of unrest in Brentwood and elsewhere around the state—and how to end it:

> From 1913 to 1934 every [labor] outbreak has been caused by the same thing: low wages, unsanitary housing conditions, refusal of the employers to deal with labor, and an agitating group of some kind. . . . Agitators do not cause strikes, but as long as intolerable living and job conditions exist, as long as employers pay low wages and insist that they can afford to pay no more, you will have strikes. An agitating group will always spring up out of the people themselves.[41]

This, of course, was also Carleton Parker's diagnosis after Wheatland, and his solutions were remarkably similar to those proposed by Warren and Miller. In the more than two decades since Wheatland, there had been many changes in the composition of the farm labor force, but many of the struggles remained the same. And the problem facing growers dependent on the system of migrancy that had made California agriculture possible likewise remained the same: how can labor power be made readily available when (and only when) and where (and only where) it was necessary without simultaneously giving to workers any power at all to determine the conditions under which they labor? Migrant workers themselves continued to negotiate the answers to this question as they negotiated the chasm between their representation as "contented" and the brutal and brutalizing conditions in which they lived.

8 / Workers as Objects/Workers as Subjects: Re-making Landscape

The Federal Labor Camp Program

Jean Baudrillard was right about one thing. Mobility is everything to the state of California. Without migrant labor, the agricultural economy of the state would be impossible as it now exists. Nor would the agricultural valleys of the state look anything like they do. From Carleton Parker through Carey McWilliams when he became chief of the Division of Immigration and Housing in 1939, even the most progressive critics of California agriculture conceded the necessity of migratory labor. Any other system was simply unthinkable. "Throughout the foreseeable future," argued Harry Drobrish of the California Relief Administration (and later the New Deal Resettlement Administration), "it will be necessary that laborers shall migrate *to serve the crops* of California. The *nature* of crop plantings, which can be altered only slowly and within the limits of soil, water and climate, and of economic structure, *compels* labor mobility" (emphases added). And here we reach the crux of the matter. Even the most progressive elements of the state apparatus understood that workers *served crops,* not capitalist farming and farmers. The relations of the fields were largely *natural,* though they could be altered by positive state intervention and made more rational. The natural/economic structure of agriculture in California was largely immutable: attention had to be focused on finding more efficient, socially healthier ways for people to serve the crops. The answer for Drobrish, as it had been for Parker and Lubin, was an environmental one. The state needed to involve itself, he argued, in creating better, less oppressive labor camps.[1]

176

Drobrish found a ready ally for this renewed environmentalist program in the University of California at Berkeley's Paul Taylor. Following his investigation of the Corcoran cotton strike, Paul Taylor grew increasingly concerned with the role that migrant labor living conditions played in social upheaval. The system of private labor camps and ditch-bank settlements throughout the state little allowed for a healthy work force, much less one able to exercise even rudimentary rights. Accordingly, Drobrish and Taylor, working through the state director of rural relief in the California State Relief Administration, developed a plan for government-sponsored labor camps that would be both healthful and islands of relative safety for the rights of workers. Moreover, a government camp might forestall the development of massive striker encampments like those in Corcoran and Calipatria, which Drobrish and Taylor agreed *induced* violent responses on the part of outraged growers:

> Of course, camps do not make strikes, but they may become centers of activity. . . . In 1933, for example, the evicted cotton pickers congregated at a small private auto camp at Corcoran which suddenly expanded from almost nothing to four acres and a population of perhaps thirty-five hundred people. (The Alameda County camp ordinance . . . is around to prevent such a situation.) The strike leaders assumed control of the camp, fenced it with barbed wire, posted "Keep Out" signs and patrolled the fence with armed sentries. They organized the layout, and life of the camp, its sanitary facilities and its recreation program. The strike leaders organized defense committees, picketing activities, and almost continuous strike meetings. Local authorities hardly dared arrest anyone within the camp with or without a warrant. Strike leaders, as usual, were arrested only when they went outside the camp and were caught singly. A private camp operated in this fashion under complete strike control obviously was a conspicuous center of public attention during the strike.[2]

While Taylor admired the strikers in Corcoran, he saw strikers' encampments as an irrational response to an irrational situation.[3]

Drobrish and Taylor's plan for government camps began with the assumption that government camps could be centers of civil liberties in a landscape marked by an utter disregard for these liberties. But their larger scheme was to assure that the destruction of rights and liberties would no longer be *necessary* in the fields. "Good camps are conducive to better industrial relations," Drobrish argued in one planning document. Should a strike occur, however, camp administrators promised objectivity. As long as they were approved by the camp manager, strike activities would be allowed in the government camps. But here, the power to determine the course of the strike was removed from the strikers and placed in the hands of the camp administration. In this the government camp plan closely resembled Carleton Parker's prescription for avoiding violent confrontations in the fields of California: remove what little power workers possessed and vest it with a benevolent agent of the state who could more rationally determine workers' needs and desires.

At the Corcoran and Alameda strike encampments, strike leaders had used frequent meetings and entertainment to reinforce solidarity. In government camps, by contrast, the camp manager would determine appropriate times and places for strike meetings, and, by policy, strike meetings and picket organizing could only be conducted if they did not "disturb the peace and quiet of the camp." What is more, farmers were allowed to meet in the camps under the same conditions as striking residents. Unlike at strikers' camps, growers were to be given complete access to the spatial structures of worker power. By definition, then, the government camps developed by Taylor and Drobrish could not be free and safe havens for union activity in the same way that strikers' camps were. And that was exactly what the planners were hoping to accomplish: the camps were designed to "demonstrate to a large neglected laboring group that its government is interested in it despite some of the 'agitators' who with increasing success assert to the contrary." The camps would also "contribute . . . to better mutual understanding" between growers, town residents, and "the large submerged nomadic population which moves in and out among them."[4]

The rationale for the development of government camps in California is quite complex, and worth examining in detail. Drobrish and Taylor developed their plans from within the state rural relief apparatus, and oversaw its transfer to the federal Resettlement Administration, which was concerned particularly with providing aid to farmers uprooted by the ecological disaster and economic restructuring of the Dust Bowl. While certainly a response to Mexican and Filipino radicalism during the 1930s, government camps were even more a response to the changing composition of the migratory labor force. Beginning about the time of the 1933 upheaval, more and more *white* workers, thrown into the fields by the economic and environmental disasters of the decade, were entering the migratory labor stream. The increase in white migratory workers greatly concerned state agents and growers alike. The government camp program was designed specifically for white workers. "You know what we forgot," the owner of the land upon which the government camp at Arvin was built wrote to one of the planners. "A unit in the Kern County Migrant Camp for the colored folks. . . . The new man [the camp manager] said they couldn't put colored folks with the white people, which of course is true. We have lots of colored folks in Kern County."[5]

Early Dust Bowl migrants began arriving in California about the time of the 1933 upheaval, and some growers saw this new component of the migratory labor stream as quite dangerous to their interests. One cotton grower told Paul Taylor during the Corcoran strike:

> We chased this white trash from the south to Arizona and then from Arizona to California. Next time we're going to chase them into the Pacific Ocean. White trash, not "red agitators," are leading this strike. The white trash was never any good, never would work and now they are stopping the Mexicans from working. While they were in the South they said nothing but now that they've gotten rid of the wrinkles in their belly they've become "fat and sassy."[6]

In many, sometimes obvious, often quite subtle, ways, white workers scared California farmers. Even in the times of greatest Asian and Mexican labor supply, white laborers formed an important part of the total migratory labor stream in California. But as their numbers started to swell in the mid-1930s (after the Corcoran and Imperial strikes, many growers began a concerted Mexican repatriation and deportation movement), growers worried that white workers would not be as tractable as had been the racialized workers who dominated the labor supply for the past decade. George Clements of the Agricultural Department of the Los Angeles Chamber of Commerce, an important mouthpiece for grower concerns in the 1920s and 1930s, summed up growers' concerns about the changing racial composition of the labor force. Clements estimated in 1936 that 90 percent of the total labor in the fields of the state was now white (though this number is surely an exaggeration). Conveniently forgetting the radicalism of Hispanic workers in 1933 and 1934, Clements eulogized the departing Mexican workers: "Another feature in their favor was that they were adaptable labor in the agricultural field. They were impossible of unionizing: they were tractable labor." On the other hand, the "white transients are not tractable labor. Being American citizens, they are going to demand the so called American standards of living."[7]

The influx of migrants from states such as Oklahoma, Arkansas, Missouri, and Kansas grew rapidly between 1934 and 1937. The in-migration of destitute families overwhelmed the minimal social services provided in agricultural towns and the coastal cities. This new migration was incredibly visible. Migrants were white, and the population of the state found it much harder to ignore the Hoovervilles and squatter settlements that housed them. Malnourished and unkempt, Dust Bowl migrants forced an even greater visibility to the rural conditions of the state. Growers both rejoiced at the influx of desperate workers seeking any kind of work at all, and feared it. Perhaps the new migrants were *too* hungry. John Steinbeck theorized that Dust Bowl migrants quickly exposed the shaky legitimacy upon which many agricultural empires were founded:

Once California belonged to Mexico and its land to Mexicans; and a horde of tattered feverish Americans poured in. And such was their hunger for the land that they took the land. . . . They put up houses and barns, they turned the earth and planted crops. And these things were possession, and possession was owner-ship. . . . Then, with time, the squatters were no longer squatters, but owners. . . . And the hunger was gone from them. . . . And it came about that owners no longer worked on their farms. They farmed on paper . . . many of them had never seen the farms they owned.

And then the dispossessed were drawn west—from Kansas, Oklahoma, Texas, New Mexico. . . . They streamed over the mountains, hungry and restless— restless as ants, scurrying to find work to do—anything, any burden to bear, for food. . . .

They were hungry, and they were fierce. And they hoped to find a home and they found only hatred. Okies—the owners hated them because the owners knew they were soft and the Okies strong, that they were fed and the Okies hungry; and per-haps the owners heard from their grandfathers how easy it is to steal land from a soft man if you are fierce and hungry and armed.[8]

Hoovervilles sprang up around the state by the end of 1935. In Marysville, north of Sacramento, for example, investigators for the State Relief Administra-tion found "about two dozen shacks built of linoleum and cardboard cartons," and nearby another cluster of some thirty to forty rude shacks housing migrant families as well as single men. In Bakersfield, two large squatter settlements had been developed by mid-1935: Hooverville and Hollywood (which, of course, was the nicer of the two). Families in these shack-towns lived in shelters fash-ioned from discarded lumber, brush, tin, and canvas. Nearly two hundred fam-ilies lived in the two settlements, working in harvests whenever they could. Similar developments grew at the edges of nearly every city and town in the agricultural areas, and in vacant lots in San Francisco, Oakland, Los Angeles, and San Diego. Not only did new arrivals in the state find overwhelmed relief workers hostile to their presence, they also suffered constant police raids and visits from vigilante nightriders. And for the most part, the Division of Immigration and Housing (DIH) found itself powerless to mitigate conditions, because the encampments qualified as neither regular labor camps, nor official auto camps.[9]

As growers soon realized, many squatter settlements often became *commu-nities,* which threatened the historic "right" of growers to determine how their workers interacted with each other. "Keep those two squatting men apart; make them hate, fear, suspect each other. . . . For here 'I lost my land,' is changed. . . . 'We lost *our* land.' . . . This is the beginning—from 'I' to 'we.'" On the heels of the unrest of 1933 and 1934, the influx of angry, desperate migrants from the

Dust Bowl was both a blessing and a curse to California agribusiness. The surplus of labor created was to be celebrated, but issues of control immediately jumped to the surface. It was quite unclear, in 1935, how this new migration would be rationalized and put to productive *work*. One of the goals of the government camp program was precisely to provide a means of rationalization. Drobrish and Taylor hoped that the construction of camps would help show how "labor strife may be moderated and elevated from meetings of contending parties with guns, clubs and tar buckets, to a plane where discussion and conference are possible"; but for this to be so the government's camps would have to make this new labor supply safe to the entrenched interests of the farmers who had grown used to the seeming advantages of a highly racialized labor force.[10]

The institutional history of the government camp program tells us something about how its planners and managers understood it. The idea for government camps developed first in the California State Rural Rehabilitation Division, but the program was soon transferred to the United States Resettlement Administration (RSA), which elsewhere in the country sought to re*settle* uprooted farmers (and others displaced by the Depression) on farms, as small-scale, independent farmers. And in California, RSA did do some of that, at one point experimenting with highly creative efforts to establish communal, truly cooperative farming colonies in the midst of agribusiness. RSA also sought to support the development of small family farms in California. But most of its work was geared toward creating a series of government-run labor camps up and down the state. Resettling the landscape in the wake of the worker uprising really meant moving workers around in a safer (to both agribusiness and the workers) and more efficient (again to both) manner, given the current economic structure of the agricultural industry. In California, "resettlement" really meant "rational mobility."

The architects of the camp program argued that continued labor mobility was desirable, both for the economy and for the workers:

> A mobile element in the labor supply is not only necessary, but it is highly desirable, as every plan for "decasualization" recognizes. Were each locality in California to supply all its peak labor needs, the labor market would be so drenched with laborers that their standard of living would fall below its present distress level.[11]

Again, they simply took the present structure of the farming economy in California for granted, something that neither the Industrial Workers of the World (IWW) or the Cannery and Agricultural Workers Industrial Union (CAWIU), the two organizations that garnered the greatest support from farmworkers, ever did. When government camp operators argued that they wanted to show migratory workers that "the government is interested in" them, then they did so, as Cletus Daniel has pointed out, within "the Roosevelt Administration's essentially conservative approach to the problems of agricultural labor in the state." In a governmental reshuffle, the camp program was later assumed by the Farm Security Administration (FSA), and again the name is evocative. In essence, as government camps assumed some of the cost of reproducing mobile labor power in the fields, they provided a subsidy to the growers of the state. The security provided by FSA was as much to industrialized farmers as it was to destitute farmworkers. Perhaps not purposefully, but certainly in effect, government camps helped secure the future of industrialized farming.[12]

By the end of the decade, RSA/FSA had constructed or authorized twelve permanent migratory labor camps, three mobile labor camps (in which the sanitary facilities, management offices, and so forth moved from site to site), twelve permanent labor home sites (including the two cooperative farming enterprises), and numerous health clinics and relief-granting offices. And it certainly was the case that the government camps *were* an improvement over the existing conditions in most private and squatter camps, that individual rights and notions of democracy *were* jealously guarded and developed within the camps, and that the government camp program *was* largely successful and quite popular with white migratory workers and even many farmers. Some of the camps eventually served as centers of union activity, and many migratory workers were able to use them as a base to regain lost dignity and to break out of the vicious crop-following life. Yet these improvements were purchased at a price, and at times they seemed almost incidental.[13]

The Better the Cage

"Housing is the principle thing to me," Frank Palomares once remarked. "The better the cage, the longer the bird will survive and he will live with a certain degree of content." The analogy is not too far off from how most growers seemed to apprehend their workers: they were animals, often quite useful, but also prone to wildness. If they could be tamed and put to productive use, not only they, and not only the growers, but the whole state would benefit. Similarly, Harry Drobrish argued that "the social political hazard of not building good camps is greater than of building them." Housing is the thing, and a gilded cage paid rich dividends. It also paid dividends to the visual image of California "the beautiful." As one of its primary aims, the camp program was designed to "demonstrate a way to clean up the human debris which now litters the highways and fields in the richest and most fertile valleys of the state." The camps were designed to help "relieve the most *visible* symptoms of [worker] powerlessness" (emphasis added), in Cletus Daniel's words.[14]

This aestheticization of migratory workers and their "cages" was interestingly combined with an anthropological sensibility by Tom Collins, the most prominent RSA/FSA camp manager. Collins's job was to open each camp, establish its internal government, stabilize the everyday management, and turn it over to other managers before he moved on to the next camp to be built. Collins sent voluminous reports back to his supervisors, and these reports, detailing the everyday life of "Okie" campers, became an important source for the pictures John Steinbeck painted of government camps. In fact, Collins provided the model for the beneficent camp manager in *The Grapes of Wrath*.[15]

Like an anthropologist in the colonies seeking to understand the "natives" in order to better lift them toward "civilization," Collins began with intensive fieldwork. With his assistants, Collins established himself at a squatter camp in Marysville and worked to win over the residents. To do this, Collins and his crew constructed a small playground for children in the midst of the camp. But rather than introduce the children to it, the government crew retreated and watched from afar until the children discovered it themselves and began to play on it. When the children were comfortable with the new playground, Collins and his crew returned and used the children as a bridge to their parents, allowing the kids to convince their parents that Collins could be trusted. When the parents' trust was earned, Collins and crew quickly rebuilt the camp as a model government camp:

> Now, an amazing thing happened, the morning of the fourth day, as a result of our success with the playground experiment. We stood by as broken down cars, trailers, trucks, men with packs on their backs deserted the camp. We thought the whole population was moving out on us, a second exodus of the Egyptians. . . . Tramps, bindle stiffs, pan handlers, loafers, realizing at last that the camp was to be supervised and administered for the migratory workers, had made a hasty retreat to the four winds. From that moment and to the present time we have not had a loafer or a drone at the camp. This proved most conclusively that the Resettlement Administration Camps will be given the "go by" by that class which will not work and which prefers to remain as aloof as possible from the conventions of a well regulated and orderly community.

With the "loafers" on the run, with the exodus of "Egyptians" complete, a tame and orderly, and quite directed, community was established:

> With the independent spirit of the migrants and their abhorrence for dependence, and the cooperation they so willingly gave us, we shall help them to help themselves. And, in helping them to raise themselves to a higher level of living stan-

dards, they will make available to the farmers of the State of California CON-TENTED, CLEAN and WILLING workers. [Original emphasis][16]

Growers were not easily convinced of the worth of these camps, nor of their ability to adequately control the labor housed in them. Charles Weeks, manager of the Brentwood Balfour-Guthrie operations, worried that public manage-ment of the camps usurped necessary grower power over workers. "My opinion [is] a result of experience I have had with this class," he explained at the dedi-cation of the Marysville government camp. "I predict that the better class . . . will not be found in this camp and you will find yourself beset with the scum and the rabid. . . . They won't work; never did work; can't make them work, dirty, insanitary. . . . That is my opinion of what will result in these camps even with the best management. They are public camps." At private camps, on the other hand, "we can pick or choose who comes in."[17]

Weeks's concerns were echoed a few months later in the Bakersfield area, where Collins had moved to establish and manage the government camp at Arvin (which was the camp Steinbeck portrayed in *The Grapes of Wrath*). Grow-ers met during February 1936 in Bakersfield under the rubric of the Kern County Tax Enclave to discuss the new camp. Frank Palomares invited Collins to meet with growers to hear their concerns. At the meeting, both Palomares and a powerful local grower named Frick (who owned land adjacent to the camp) charged that "communistic activities" were being fostered at the govern-ment camps, and the conclave passed a motion opposing the continuation of the camp program. In response, Collins invited the growers to come with him right then and inspect the camp. "The camp was thoroughly inspected [by the growers]," Collins wrote in his weekly report. "We had no chance to phone the camp in advance." But Collins was not worried; he saw the camps as their own best propaganda (Figure 12). The growers, Collins reported, saw for themselves that the "Okies" were more or less flourishing in the new settlement, and in such settings, "agitators" had little to work with. The camps were proving their worth, Collins felt, by diminishing the *need* for radical agitation. They were indeed "better cages," and the growers returned from their visit at least a little less hostile to the camp program.[18]

Collins was proud of the civilizing influence his camps had on white migra-tory workers. Describing a photo of campers voting in a camp election, he wrote:

We might title this picture, "The Repatriation of American Exiles," men and women cast out of society to make their homes on carpets of rubbish and debris against a background of filth and an atmosphere of stench. Knocking around from one hog wallow to another they have been the forgotten men and women of

Figure 12. The Kern County Farm Security Administration Camp soon after it opened. Dorothea Lange's photograph shows the community garden plots in the foreground and one of the sanitary units in the middle. The sanitary units included women's and men's laundries, showers, and toilets. The tents are on wooden platforms. This camp served as the model of the government camp in *The Grapes of Wrath*. (Courtesy, Bancroft Library.)

the State of California[.] American citizens exiled to the distant corners by the growers in an effort (so it seems) to create in California a class of peons, uncouth, uncared for . . . cowed and without ambition to fight the battle for their existence.

Men and women of the Resettlement Administration camps now hold up their heads. They go among the citizens of the county, clean of body, and cleanly dressed. *They are humans once again.* The camp is their home and they are justly proud. The self governing community of which they are a part compensates, to a degree, for the lack of essentials required for proper living and which their meager earnings prohibit them procuring. [Emphasis added][19]

Camp administrators saw the "repatriation" of migratory workers, and the safeguarding of democracy within the camps, as one of their great victories. Camp residents created their own elected committees to oversee everything from maintenance and janitorial work to entertainment. They elected camp delegates who together established rules of conduct for the camp. Camp residents also created "visiting committees" to welcome new arrivals and to help with whatever welfare needs a family might have.

But the limits to democracy were tightly drawn. All residents were required to register with the United States Employment Service (which frequently shared intelligence with the union-busting Associated Farmers), and the camp manager retained veto power over any decisions camp delegates made. Importantly, issues of camp finance were never democratically decided. They remained the province of the camp manager and the RSA/FSA administrators. Like a Band-Aid on the hemorrhaging wounds of class war in the California fields, democracy in the camps was hardly adequate. In his reportage on migratory labor in California, Steinbeck enthused over the democratic possibilities inherent in the government camps. But his comments read more like a eulogy for actually existing democracy in America than a celebration of truly democratic possibilities: "As experiments in natural and democratic self-government," he wrote, "these camps are unique in the United States."[20]

Within a few years, in fact, the formal trappings of democracy in the camps declined. By 1940, voter turnout at camp elections was slim, many of the libertarian rules of behavior in the camp had been rescinded, and most workers had little interest in either serving on camp councils or submitting to their (often arbitrary) rules regarding behavior and social mores. Historian Walter Stein attributes the decline of "democracy" in the camps to the independent "nature" of "Okie" culture. The stark isolation of farm life on the plains, and the "rugged individualism" that life demanded, according to Stein, ill prepared Dust Bowl migrants for the demands required of a collectivity. The "we" Steinbeck saw being born through a common experience of oppression, Stein suggests, was not strong enough to overcome their "natural" individualism.[21]

A more reasonable conclusion on the decline of "democracy" in the camps, however, and one that Stein notes in passing, is that the limited "democracy" allowed migratory workers through the government camp program was essentially meaningless in the context of the constant disempowerment migratory workers faced everywhere else. Lack of control over the most basic aspects of their existence—the ability to eat regularly, for example—was not made palatable by the ability to choose camp unit delegates. The limited democracy of the camps provided no means for workers to challenge and transform the system that put them in the camps. As we have seen, the camps were designed for quite the opposite purpose. "Democracy" in the RSA/FSA camps functioned much as it does in American high schools: as a paternalistic educative palliative given to win consent from people who possess little formal access to effective power and control, but who seemingly can become "irrational" and threatening to existing power structures at any time. If strikers' camps in 1933 and 1934 became bases for *expanding* worker power and control, the government camps of the latter part of the Depression served rather to ghettoize and control worker power.[22]

Even so, democracy and a degree of control over their own lives were important to camp residents, and they were strongly resisted by growers. The Associated Farmers worked continually to close the camps, or to get their management transferred out of the federal government and into friendlier county governments. In a classic scene, Steinbeck has Tom Joad learn of an Associated Farmers (Steinbeck called the organization the "Farmers' Association") plot to create a fight at the weekly camp dance. The Associated Farmers hoped to use the brawl as a pretext for "a bunch of deputies [to] go in and clean the camp." Tom was perplexed. "Why for God's sake? Those folks ain't bothering nobody." Tom's informant replied, "I'll tell you why. . . . Those folks in the camp are getting used to being treated like humans. When they go back to the squatters' camps they will be hard to handle." And the dictates of the farm economy in California demanded that they *would* go back to the squatter settlements as they scoured the state looking for work. As Ma Joad retorted to Pa when they were forced to leave the Weed Patch (Arvin) camp because there was no local work, and Pa did not want to lose the "hot water an' toilets" he had grown accustomed to: "Well, we can't eat no toilets." "CONTENTED, CLEAN and WILLING," the workers of the camps may have been. But they were still starving, and no amount of "democracy" or dignified living would change that fact.[23]

Migratory labor camps, however, were built not just to better house migratory laborers. They were state interventions in the landscape, designed in part to show the people—workers, farmers, urban and suburban citizens—of the state what labor relations in the fields *could* be. They were pictures of what a saner, more efficient agricultural system would look like. Indeed, for the original architects of the camp program, the camps were designed as an explicit critique of grower practices:

> Since camps will be occupied by laborers who are employed or who are seeking employment, industrial conflicts involving them may raise peculiar problems. This is particularly true since observance of constitutional rights within the camps is to be expected, yet outside the camps the repressive ordinances of counties will undoubtedly be given full force by local peace officers.

If farmworkers were given a controlled space within which to exercise their rights, the camp program suggested, growers would soon find they had little to fear. Violence by workers and growers and the destruction of workers' rights, camp designers assumed, was *incidental,* not *instrumental,* to the labor relations of the state. For this theory to be borne out, literally to be *shown* to be true, however, the migratory camps had to become open houses, *displaying* the now tamed migratory workers to the curious public. Camp managers arranged nearly constant field trips to the government camps in the first years of their operation. Boy Scouts came to visit, as did Associated Farmers, Chambers of Commerce, high school social studies classes, and all manner of interested local residents. Camp life became something like a diorama, a snapshot of the "natural history" and environment of the migrant worker. Workers, stripped once again of their radical subjectivity, became objects to be viewed.[24]

If this pictorial sensibility perforce guided much of the development of the camp program, alternative voices were still heard around the state. A writer for *The Worker*, commenting on the numerous studies that assumed an environmental solution to the problem of migratory labor in California, reminded his readers: "In the opinion of the writer, there are more fundamental causes, deeply embedded in the economic structure of the capitalist mode of production, which are responsible and unless these are eliminated strikes are unavoidable." The camp program proved a great, if contested, advance in the housing and living conditions of many workers, but it certainly did not (and could not) address the structuring relations of the agricultural economy. For many white workers, the government camps provided an oasis of sanity and sanitary conditions— both precious commodities in the tumultuous fields of the state. But the hold on sanity in the face of grower intransigence was tenuous and always discontinuous. "Well for Christ's sake," Tom Joad beseeched the night watchman at the Weed Patch camp, "Why ain't they more places like this?" "You'll have to find that out for yourself," the watchman replied.[25]

The Associated Farmers and the Control of Space

One reason, as Tom soon found, was that the Associated Farmers (AF) saw the camps as a direct threat to the ability of farmers to control social relations in the fields. The Associated Farmers had been formed in March of 1934, and almost immediately became an important force in the labor relations of the state. The AF consisted of both county-based "locals" and a statewide umbrella organization. While many small farmers were members (and there is evidence of strong-arm tactics used by AF functionaries and allies in agribusiness to garner their membership), the activities of the state AF were directed by large farming and industrial concerns. Most of the financing for the AF came from urban-based transportation, utility, manufacturing, and energy industries bent on destroying any form of unionism in the state, urban or rural. The AF organized vigilante activities in most agricultural strikes in the state between the one in Brentwood in 1934 and World War II. It also conducted much of the investigative work that made possible the arrest of most of the CAWIU leadership (including Caroline Decker and Pat Chambers) on criminal syndicalism charges in 1935. By 1936, the AF was coordinating a series of local antipicketing initiatives similar to those developed by Earl Warren in Alameda. And, by 1938, the AF was an important force in the electoral politics of the state, providing grassroots support for Philip Bancroft in his senatorial campaign, fighting against Upton Sinclair's populist End Poverty in California (EPIC) gubernatorial battle, and sponsoring a statewide antipicketing initiative.[26]

The Associated Farmers vigorously opposed the federal labor camp program, seeking especially to have all supply camps placed under "community" (i.e., farmers') control. While one of the goals of the RSA/FSA program was certainly to provide a benevolent means for creating contented and willing labor—Carleton Parker's "new man" at last!—the AF feared that supervision was not close and visceral enough. It wanted to control every movement, every action, indeed, every thought of the migratory workers of the state. Most workers, the AF reasoned in a timeworn manner, wanted to work for whatever the farmers were willing to pay. The only hindrance to their fulfilling this desire was the constant hectoring by agitators bent on overthrowing not just the farm economy but the American government as well. Besides opposing federal camps, therefore, the AF also worked to control all the spaces of the towns, cities, and fields of the state such that "agitators" would have no room to agitate.

One of the AF's favorite weapons in this war over space was the antipicketing ordinances it sponsored around the state. The Sonoma County antipicketing ordinance was rather typical of the Associated Farmers' efforts in this regard. Passed in 1937 during a strike, and directly sponsored by the Associated Farmers, this ordinance made it illegal "for any person to watch, beset, or picket" any place where another person is employed "for the purpose of inducing any such employee by compulsion, threats, coercion, intimidation, or any act of violence, or by putting employee in fear, to quit his or her employment." The same restriction applied to attempting to encourage or discourage someone from patronizing a business. Likewise, whether to encourage striking or boycotting, it was illegal to congregate "with one or more persons" on public streets or private property. Derogatory comments spoken loudly enough to be heard by any other person were outlawed, as was the organizing of caravans and parades as a means of representing an economic cause. Finally, it was illegal to block any street, drive, walkway, doorway, or other passage "so as to annoy or molest persons passing along or over the same."[27]

The need for such a stringent bill was obvious to the Sonoma County commissioners. Though they claimed that "Nothing herein contained should be construed to prohibit or abridge the right of lawful or peaceful picketing . . . if not accompanied by violence," the commissioners knew that peaceful picketing was impossible (and indeed, U.S. Supreme Court decisions on this point largely supported them):

> The ordinance is hereby declared to be an urgency measure and necessary for the immediate preservation of the public peace, health and safety, for the reason that there threatens to exist in the County of Sonoma a serious situation involving the interference of persons not directly or indirectly interested therein in the conduct of lawful enterprises; the purpose of such persons being to agitate and disturb the peace of the people of the County . . . by inciting and prolonging disputes between employers and employees . . . ; that unless the prevention of people congregating upon the streets and highways and other public places for the purpose of unlawfully interfering with lawful business is discontinued, such practice will tend to attract criminal, vicious, and undesirable characters and to cause great disorder and many breaches of the peace and quiet of the County of Sonoma, and constitute a menace to life, limb, and property.[28]

The intent is quite clear: to make the use of the streets for fighting against the wishes of the economic powers of the area impossible.

In 1921, writing for the Supreme Court, Chief Justice William Howard Taft had argued in *American Steel Foundries v. Tri-City Central Trades Council* that picketing was inevitably violent and thus the state had the right (in fact the duty) to regulate it. There was still room for persuasive speech, Taft argued, but only if it was highly regulated and controlled. Since picketing "cannot be peaceable," as Taft put it, he sought to replace picketing with "missionaries" stationed at the entrance to struck businesses. The behavior of these missionaries should be tightly controlled:

> We think the strikers and their sympathizers engaged in the economic struggle should be limited to one representative for each point of ingress and egress in the plant or place of business and that all others should be enjoined from congregating or loitering at the plant or in the neighboring streets by which access is had to the plant, that such representatives should have the right of observation, communication and persuasion but with special admonition that their communication, arguments and appeals shall not be abusive, libelous, or threatening, and that they shall not approach individuals together but singly, and shall not in their single efforts at communication or persuasion obstruct an unwilling listener by importunate following or dogging his steps.[29]

A decade and a half later, in response to the partial success farmworkers had in controlling public space during the 1933 and 1934 revolts, the Associated Farmers attempted to write Taft's spatial proscription for labor-capital struggle into the California State Constitution by sponsorship of Proposition 1, a strike-limiting amendment.

Proposition 1 limited the right to strike to issues of wages and conditions (strikes for a closed shop, union recognition, and so forth were specifically outlawed), and the activities of strikers were carefully proscribed. Pickets, limited to "one at each entrance," had to remain at least twenty-five feet apart at all times, and could only patrol on foot. Picketers were allowed to wear a single armband and carry one banner (two feet by three feet) that announced that a strike was on. No other words, pictures, or designs were permitted. Offensive language was banned. Attorneys for the Associated Farmers explicitly referred to Taft's *American Steel Foundries* decision to explain the validity of the amendment. They argued that Taft's decision established a clear precedent in which the *only* permissible picketing was a single peaceful missionary. Such restrictions, as the authors of the proposition well knew, would make striking and picketing an extensive agricultural field all but impossible.[30]

The shape of the landscape is clearly a question of power, and the goal of the AF was to tilt the field of power in their interest. Growers knew that the reproduction of labor power was a continual struggle, and that to the degree they could control the form that struggle took—by controlling both actions and spaces—they could make over the landscape in their own image. David Harvey has argued that "improvements in the quality of labor power . . . through a host of intangible means which affect the discipline, the work ethic, respect for authority, consciousness, and the like can have a salutary effect on surplus value production." But the efforts of the Associated Farmers in deploying pick-axes and ballot initiatives show that the opposite is also the case: beating down the rights of labor can *also* have a "salutary effect on surplus value production." The control of space—as in the antipicketing initiative's restriction on the use of public space—and the control of people—as in the initiative's restrictions on how strikers may behave—were seen quite clearly by the AF as a means of protecting their material interests. And, as the landscape (the look of the land, its historical development, its representation as a "natural" outcome of people working on the land) both embodies and represents the relations of power at any moment, battles such as those over Proposition 1 could be decisive. In fact, the AF lost this particular battle, in an election marked by a liberal groundswell that led to the election of California's "Little New Deal" government headed by Culbert L. Olson. But it certainly did not lose the war.[31]

Olson's administration was quite sympathetic to the plight of agricultural workers in the state. The new governor appointed Carey McWilliams, even then at work on his important *Factories in the Field,* to the directorship of the

Division of Immigration and Housing. (He was fired four years later as one of Governor Earl Warren's first official acts.) Within the bureaucratic framework he had inherited, McWilliams sought to make DIH once again an effective voice within the government for agricultural reform, earning along the way a great deal of enmity from the Associated Farmers, which labeled him "California's Agricultural Pest Number One" and worked diligently for his removal from DIH. Like Marx before him, McWilliams had a great deal of admiration for the efficiency of modern large-scale capitalist enterprise. But also like Marx before him, he argued that the unjust foundations of modern capitalism had to be transcended if those efficiencies were to serve all people, and not just the privileged few. Nowhere was this clearer than in the agricultural fields of California, McWilliams maintained. He argued that the presence of the federal government in the fields of California, even though forced by the appalling violence of organized farmers, coupled with the almost continuous unionizing drives of the 1930s, signaled the "end of a cycle" and a "trend toward stabilization." With federal involvement, the historic patterns of irrational mobility were finally giving way to an ordered agricultural production system. But the camps and other stabilization programs in the state were only a start, and especially after his appointment to DIH, McWilliams understood that there was an incredibly long way to go before the agricultural fields could ever be "democratic."[32]

Like Steinbeck, McWilliams understood California growers to be motivated by fear and guilt. The growers in the state, McWilliams explained some years later,

> are not unaware of the inconvenience and misery, the hardship and suffering, which is implicit in the system itself. But they sense, even if they will not willingly admit, that a readjustment of this system would involve a readjustment of the entire agricultural economy. Hence they are driven to defend the system and its consequences much as slave-owners were driven to defend chattel slavery. Suggestions for the improvement of labor camps are brushed aside with stories about farmworkers who urinate in kitchen sinks, cut holes in the floor for toilets, and chop up the partitions for kindling wood. . . . I can testify from bitter personal experience [as DIH chief] that for every suggestion [for camp improvement] they have a time honored rationalization; for every criticism a hoary and preposterous fable.

The growers had much to fear in the system they so violently supported, McWilliams went on to report:

> There are many phases of California agriculture that will not bear public scrutiny, such as certain phony marketing agreements, the lush subsidies . . . the rigging of market prices and so forth. . . . Many California growers live in mortal fear of any

interruption in the careful schedule of labor operations upon which they may have gambled a fortune.[33]

But the sheer scale of California agriculture might quite possibly become its own reward. "The abolition [of the present] system involves at most merely a change in ownership," McWilliams concluded *Factories in the Field* (in a passage that quickly drew the ire of his opponents):

> The collective principle is there; large units of operation have been established, only they are being exploited by private interests for their own ends. California agriculture is a magnificent achievement: in its scope, efficiency, organization and amazing abundance. The great farm valleys of California, rescued from sagebrush and desert, are easily among the richest agricultural regions in the world. The anachronistic system of owenership by which they are at present controlled must be changed before the valleys can come into their own.[34]

Steinbeck likewise envisioned a radical transformation of the countryside, as the final scene in *The Grapes of Wrath* hints. Yet authors as well as activists trying to reap justice rather than violence in the fields often failed to realize how profound the transformations would have to be. Not just ownership, not just economic structures, but the very spaces and spatial practices of agricultural labor reproduction that undergird that ownership and economic structure would have to be remade if an agricultural revolution were to take hold. Class struggle in the California fields was truly a spatial struggle, a struggle over of the shape of the land. The experiment with federal camps—which both McWilliams and Steinbeck heralded as great advancements—led in just the opposite direction: workers remained quite marginalized because the camp program *supported* existing spatial arrangements. Because they were white, the migrants of the Dust Bowl era attracted a good deal more interest, curiosity, and sympathy than had many farmworkers before them. But growers little cared about the "race" of their workers as long as they were cheap, temporary, and powerless. The federal camps did little to redress imbalances of power.

And the Associated Farmers worked diligently during the second half of the 1930s to assure that organized, large-scale farmers gained, rather than lost, power. The writings of McWilliams and Steinbeck provided rallying points for farmer organizations, and, despite setbacks in the 1938 elections, the Associated Farmers remained a potent organization in California agricultural labor relations, continually seeking to expand control over the spaces and the lives of the labor force. The Associated Farmers clearly understood the importance of controlling the spaces of agricultural production and reproduction. And it fought vigorously to maintain and expand that control.

The American Apotheosis Revisited

If one image of the American Apotheosis is the abundant, verdant productivity the Joads spied from the top of Tehachapi Pass, another is California as a land of the most efficient, modern agricultural production on the planet. Even as farmworkers were disrupting harvests all over the state in 1933, California enacted a state water plan that virtually demanded the continuation of industrialized, large-scale agriculture to make the capital expenditure on such a grandiose scheme worthwhile. But, in turn, for this industrialized agriculture to be maintained, so did armies of migratory workers still need to be produced for the benefit of "the crops." Irrigation on the scale proposed in the state water plan and realized in the Central Valley Project (Shasta Dam was begun in 1938) implied a further intensification of the agricultural landscape—one even more technologized and capital intensive. Militant migrant workers posed a clear threat to the grandiose schemes of California's water engineers and growers alike. With the increased attention to migratory workers forced by the uprisings of 1933 and the entrance of larger numbers of white migratory workers soon thereafter, Donald Worster has argued, "it became rather difficult for a liberal government in Washington to give subsidized, unrestricted water to groups like the reactionary Associated Farmers, to underwrite their labor policies and their concentration of wealth. At least somebody would have to do some homework first." Perhaps, then, modern, large-scale efficiency demands not the violent, bodily control the Associated Farmers sought to exercise over the migratory workers of the state, but the sort of modern, decentralized, spatialized systems of social control Foucault described: anonymous, "capillary," based on the discipline that fear of observation brings. Perhaps it demands the type of control expressed in Miller's Brentwood Plan or Drobrish and Taylor's migratory labor camps.[35]

But the struggles between growers and workers in California, from Wheatland on through to Brentwood (and beyond to some quite violent strikes in Marysville, Madera, and Salinas later in the decade) show that controlling the work of labor reproduction is truly a historical and geographical process, and growers were less interested in the normative concerns expressed by Worster than in simply using whatever means were available to maintain power over "their" laborers. The Associated Farmers, like the California Commission of Immigration and Housing, RSA/FSA, and Earl Warren, certainly understood the importance of modern, spatial solutions to the "problem" of subversive mobility. But AF knew these solutions were even *more* effective when they were supplemented by the outright control that murder, jail, and "riding herd" provided. And the AF knew, also, that it *could* get away with the direct exercise of violence even if those in Washington did their homework.

The history of the California landscape is the history, on one side, of finding ways to control the movement of labor, and, on the other, of finding the means to make that mobility subversive. Between these two sides, there is a long history of state interventions—messy attempts to both adjudicate struggles and protect landed interests. And beyond all that, there remained the need, on the part of both individual growers and the farming economy as a whole, to constantly produce and reproduce a labor *over*supply, without which California agriculture would fail. In the words of one analyst in the 1920s, "California agriculture was declared *by nature* to be such as to demand a permanent supply of itinerant laborers."[36]

With the war economy heating up by 1941, and with white agricultural workers beginning to be absorbed into the growing military-based industrial economy of the state, growers grew alarmed once again at the prospect of a labor "shortage." A federal government now more concerned with supplying the needs of the war machine than with investigating whether such labor was actually needed or not, acquiesced in 1942 to a grower-sponsored plan (the Bracero Program) to repeat the strategy of World War I and import contract workers from Mexico. Created the same year Senator La Follette released his committee's scathing analysis of the agriculture economy in California, the Bracero Program was a boon to farmers. It outlasted the war, surviving until 1964, when a renewed farmworker militancy helped make government involvement in the pauperization of agricultural labor once again less politically tenable. The Bracero Program reenacted the same issues that had governed California industrialized agriculture throughout the first half of the twentieth century: how can a "sufficient" labor supply be made available when and where it was needed, and in such a manner that it was incapable of threatening the economic and political interests of powerful growers? The Bracero Program was a peculiarly "premodern" form of labor control, predicated as it was on the careful control of individual, contractual laborers, often carefully guarded in fields and camps. But it was a form of labor control that growers argued was absolutely essential to their highly modern form of industrial agriculture.[37]

With the near-absolute control that the Bracero Program provided, coupled with declining public interest in the plight of agricultural workers as the war developed, growers were able once again to reinvest in California *as* a landscape, as a place in which work became invisible to all but the most penetrating gaze. This landscape remained an unsteady image, however, at once solid, changeable, and vulnerable—little more than a mirage. The Joads, like so many others, had come to California in pursuit of just this mirage. "But I like to think how nice it's gonna be, maybe, in California. Never cold. An' fruit ever'place, an' people just bein' in the nicest places, little white houses in among the orange trees," Ma Joad daydreamed before the family left Oklahoma. Granpa was even more direct in his evocation of the California Dream (precisely the dream celebrated by California historian Kevin Starr with his claims that California grew by its development of Virgilian and biblical, though still libertine, imagery). "An' by God," Granpa declared before the Joads left Oklahoma, "they's grapes out there, just a-hangin' over inta the road. Know what I'm a-gonna do? I'm gonna pick me a wash tub full of grapes, an' I'm gonna set in 'em, an' scrooge aroun', an let the juice run down my pants." Tom remained cautious, and Steinbeck uses that caution to make a telling reference for his knowing readers. "Tom said, 'Don't roust your faith bird-high an' you won't do no crawlin' with the worms.' 'I know that' right. That's Scripture, ain't it?' [Ma replied]. 'I guess so,' said Tom. 'I never could keep Scripture straight sence I read a book name' *The Winning of Barbara Worth.*'"[38]

The landscape itself quickly disabuses the Joads of their dreams, and their struggle fades to invisibility. Both *The Grapes of Wrath* and *Factories in the Field* were published in 1939, and they both created a huge uproar among growers around the state. More than a call to arms, they were rather a culmination of the struggles that marked the 1930s. Yet farmworkers' struggles never entirely disappear; they just take new forms, responding to changing historical-geographical conditions. Mobility retained—and retains—its subversive potential: "I'll be ever'where—wherever you look. Wherever they's a fight so hungry people can eat, I'll be there. Wherever they's a cop beatin' up a guy, I'll be there. . . . An' when our folks eat the stuff they raise an' live in the houses they build—why, I'll be there." But Tom Joad found himself in a different world from that of Blackie Ford, Herman Suhr, and the IWW in 1913, when they too sought to be "everywhere." Now Tom had to negotiate a landscape "littered" with attempts to settle the turbulent social relations of the fields. Model camps, labor spies, technical improvements to toilets, concrete housing that can be "hosed down" after a Mexican family has lived there, antipicketing ordinances, striker encampments—all of these are components in the mix that produce and reproduce the view that the Joads saw as they looked down from Tehachapi Pass. But, most importantly, as long as the subversive potential of IWW and CAWIU activists, or even more, of the hundreds of thousands of ordinary workers like Tom Joad who daily trudged from one field to another in search of work existed—as long as it *still* exists—growers and the state were, are, and will be forced to respond, ever seeking to neutralize subversion such that workers always remain the objects they are meant to be, that workers remain *only* embodied labor power, and not a power unto themselves. This was clearly the message of the response by growers and the state to Wheatland, and so too was it the response to the upheavals of the 1930s.[39]

Subversion and the vigilance it calls up: that is what made the structure discovered by Paul Taylor and Clark Kerr when the fault slipped at Corcoran. That is what made Parker's "balking" environment. That is what truly *makes* the California landscape.

Conclusion / The Lie of the Land

The temptation at this point is *not* to conclude, not to provide a look down (and back) from the top of the hill, not to succumb to the seductions of landscape. Rather, the temptation is to leave the impression of an unceasing history of struggle. Whether from the vantage of 1942 where I ended the narrative, or from the present vantage of more than fifty years later when we know so well the continuing history of agricultural labor in California—the renewed organizing efforts in the 1950s (and the further consolidation of land and wealth), the rise of the United Farmworkers (UFW) in the 1960s (and the reinvestment in vigilante violence by growers), the eclipse of the UFW in the 1970s and 1980s (and yet another round of corporate consolidation that saw, for example, agricultural production taking on the characteristics of a "footloose" industry)—one lesson of the California landscape is that it is rarely stable. It seems somehow satisfying, and perhaps politically better, therefore, not to let the landscape—the lie of the land—rematerialize as a totality. Not looking back and seeking to provide an overarching explanation would put me in good stead with those scholars who have become increasingly suspicious of what Michael Curry has called the "architectonic impulse," the desire to create and explain overarching systems of social activity. The goal for these scholars is instead to focus on the local, the contingent, the partial. The goal is precisely *not* to "sum up."[1]

But the failure to develop a "way of seeing" the history and geography before us, and the failure even to attempt to *explain* it (a failure now hailed as a virtue by proponents of academic postmodernism) is just as problematic. If nothing else, succumbing to this desire not to see the historical and theoretical landscape before us means, to a degree and quite literally, that all the struggles in the fields of California were for nothing. They *mean* nothing. They remain invisible. We are left with just contingent history, a noble struggle perhaps, but one doomed in the end to be insignificant (except, maybe, to those engaged in it right at that moment). The lie of the land has done its work. For, even if we, as those with power to represent landscapes, fail to do so, that does not imply that others, with a great deal more power—spokespersons for the old Associated Farmers or its newer offspring like the Western Growers Association, for example—will also fail to make representations in their own interests. The landscape will be defined by someone. The only questions are who claims a voice in doing so, and how that voice is amplified and transmitted in all manner of discourses, popular, academic, or on the ground. The landscape will be materialized—in fact, and in representation. The architectonic impulse certainly should *not* be resisted by those of us who want to write oppositional landscape histories. We need to show, as I have attempted to do, precisely how it is that the landscape is formed and made known, and, certainly, how it functions as a system of social control and opportunity within capitalist economies.

If the Joads were to stand again, after all their journeys and struggles, at the top of Tehachapi Pass, they would realize the one truism of America: America as dream and image, America as landscape *view,* does not—cannot—match the reality of America as place and experience, as material landscape. The history of the making of the California landscape has shown that there is an important disconnection between representations of a landscape and its material reality. But the Joads would also realize that the landscape is indeed continually reconnected to its representation; it is re*formed.* This reformation is a continuous and quite costly process, and it is a necessary one, as everyone from Carleton Parker and Blackie Ford to Sheriff Miller and Julius Nathan understood. The severing of landscape representation from its material referent (so that it may be reattached in a new and more advantageous manner) is *essential* and *necessary* to the functioning of the political economy. In the same manner, it is essential to oppositional activity. The making of landscape in this sense is, as we have seen, a lot of work.

From Wheatland on through to the development of federal migrant labor camps, the lie of the land in agricultural California—the small and the massive farms, and the labor camps and squatter settlements that served them—was formed and reformed through the continual give-and-take of struggle over the social and spatial relations of agricultural labor reproduction. Creating a morphology, defining limits and edges in Latour's terms, is clearly a historical process, one that can only be stabilized when opposition is neutralized. Given what we have now seen of the construction of the California landscape, Carey McWilliams's argument (noted in the Introduction) that militancy has been essential to any gains made by migratory workers is less the political intervention—a call to arms—than it may have seemed, and more an obvious statement of fact. *Only* by being militant can workers keep themselves from becoming fully natural, dissolved into the landscape. Only by being militant, that is, can workers give lie to the land as powerful actors have tried to structure it for them. And only by resisting this militancy, therefore, have the state and agribusiness continually assured the reproduction of agricultural labor power.

Not only do migratory workers in agricultural California have to continually fight just to survive—to find shelter and food and money enough to maintain themselves and their families—they also have to continually fight their own aestheticization, their dissolution, in the landscape. The geographer James Parsons, as we saw in Chapter 1, felt that the type of history I have told is unnecessary for understanding and appreciating the beauty of the Central Valley landscape. At best, farmworkers were simply colorful additions to the spectacle of massive geographical space itself. For all that it perpetuates a useful myth of worker invisibility or irrelevancy, Parson's celebration of the agricultural landscapes of California marks a relatively new departure in the depiction of landscape. Only recently have the agricultural regions of the state materialized as places of aesthetic enjoyment or appreciation. Learning to see agricultural California in aesthetic terms is a project just begun. So long in the shadow of the spectacular seaside and mountain scenery, and the northern and southern cities that hem it in on all sides, the agricultural landscape has frequently been ignored in aesthetic depictions of the state. "The [Central] Valley has been a difficult subject for artists in the past," Heath Schenker writes in his extended review of the coffee-table book, *The Great Central Valley: California's Heartland*:

> As an example of the "other" landscape, i.e., by its "ugliness," it has helped define what is beautiful. . . . Because it did not fit the traditional European notions of landscape beauty that were perpetuated in American art for two centuries the Central Valley became an invisible landscape. Popular perceptions reflected the artists' difficulties, and the Valley remained a blank space in the center of the Golden State. However, the art world changes. In the new cultural climate of the late twentieth century, artists are suddenly interested in representing conflicts and contradictions in the contemporary landscape. Although the Valley's landscape has changed little, the artists' perceptions have shifted; the Central Valley has become an attractive subject *because* of the difficulties it presents.[2]

The old invisibility of the California agricultural landscape has been indispensable to its ability to work, to function as a productive landscape. Focused as California has been on the "natural" (i.e., nonhuman) or, conversely, on the cosmopolitan good life outlined by Kevin Starr, the actual California landscape has been allowed to go on in obscurity *except* when farmworkers have demanded that it be seen and taken seriously for what it is: a place of ruthless, relentless exploitation (and, indeed, a place of beauty), a place quintessentially modern both in its architecture (that functionality of purpose that Starr ascribes to packing sheds) and in its experiments with social control.

The Great Central Valley: California's Heartland is an impressive achievement, combining as it does the new work of photographers Stephen Johnson and Robert Dawson and the prose of Gerald Haslam with the social documentary photography of Dorothea Lange and the historical photographs of Carleton Watkins and Frank Day Robinson. In the pictures and text, the Central Valley emerges as an impressively complex conglomeration of regions, rural and urban, sublime and horrible, relentlessly modern and comfortably provincial, impressively productive and discouragingly polluted. Better than anywhere else—at least in print—we can now *see* the agricultural landscapes of the state.

But knowing the continuing history of struggle that has made these landscapes, *The Great Central Valley* leaves one uneasy. In the photographs, it is all so *beautiful* (even the frightening photograph of the ecological disaster that is the Kesterson National Wildlife Refuge). In the new photographs of Johnson and Dawson, there are few pictures of workers and the processes of work, though there are some included by Robinson and Lange from the 1920s and 1930s. Work in the Valley is almost fully historicized—only its products become visible, and they mostly as shimmering images. Workers fade in the rearview mirror of history, the easier to forget who *made* this landscape—and just as importantly under what conditions they did their work.[3]

Toward the end of *The Great Central Valley* is a stunning, eerily beautiful photograph by Stephen Johnson entitled "Asparagus Planters near Tracy, 1983." The picture is almost pure white. Fog fills the frame, leaving only a small band of dark earth visible in the foreground. Barely discernible through the haze, mere shadows threatening to dissolve altogether, are two stooped figures digging with their hands in the plowed field. It is impossible to tell who they are: Male or female? What ethnicity? Migrant workers or locals? Are they alone or are there more of them? How did they get there? If nothing else, I hope *The Lie of the Land* has provided a counterpoint to that image. I hope I have shown, if not exactly who the workers were at any given time, then at least the conditions under which they worked, and, just as importantly, their role in transforming those conditions. I hope I have shown how quite beautiful images like this one were made, and that, though it is not at all comfortable to do so, it is important to understand that this image cannot be separated from the image of the "anonymous English boy" dead at Wheatland; from the fact of employers claiming the "right" to search belongings, to evict, and to deport; or, indeed, from the progressive attempts to settle once and for all the social relations of agricultural labor reproduction by investing in spatial strategies of comfort and control. The production of the beautiful that is now being celebrated in the agricultural valleys in California was (and remains) itself a quite ugly process. So, more than anything, I hope that by connecting landscape to the facts of its production, by stressing the importance of these ugly processes, I have provided a way of seeing that helps make sure those asparagus planters do not indeed simply dissolve into the foggy landscape they made.

Notes

Introduction / Migratory Workers and the California Landscape, 1913–1942

1. Carey McWilliams, *California: The Great Exception* (Santa Barbara: Peregrine Smith, 1976 ed.), xiii.

2. Kenneth Olwig, "Sexual Cosmology: Nation and Landscape at the Conceptual Interstices of Nature and Culture; or What Does Landscape Really Mean?" in Barbara Bender (ed.), *Landscape: Politics and Perspectives* (Oxford: Berg, 1993), 307–43, quotations from 307–8, 339–40; W. J. T. Mitchell, "Imperial Landscape," in W. J. T. Mitchell (ed.), *Landscape and Power* (Chicago: University of Chicago Press, 1994), 5–34, quotation from 5; Stephen Daniels and Denis Cosgrove, "Iconography and Landscape," in Denis Cosgrove and Stephen Daniels (eds.), *The Iconography of Landscape: Essays on the Symbolic Representation, Design and Use of Past Environments* (Cambridge: Cambridge University Press, 1988), 1–11.

3. Edward Soja, *Postmodern Geographies: The Reassertion of Space in Critical Social Theory* (London: Verso, 1989); Henri Lefebvre, *The Production of Space* (Oxford: Basil Blackwell, 1991, trans. Donald Nicholson-Smith).

4. Denis Cosgrove, *Social Formation and Symbolic Landscape* (London: Croom Helm, 1984).

5. Lefebvre, *Production of Space*, 44.

6. W. J. T. Mitchell, "Introduction," in W. J. T. Mitchell, *Power and Landscape* (Chicago: University of Chicago Press, 1994), 1–4; Elizabeth Helsinger, "Turner and the Representation of England," in ibid., 103–25.

7. Raymond Williams, *The Country and the City* (New York: Oxford University Press, 1973), 32–34; Neil Smith, *Uneven Development: Nature, Capital, and the Production of Space* (Oxford: Basil Blackwell, 1990, 2nd ed.), chapter 2.

8. Carl Sauer, "The Morphology of Landscape," in John Leighly (ed.), *Land and*

203

Life: A Selection from the Writings of Carl Ortwin Sauer (Berkeley: University of California Press, 1963, essay originally published 1925); Karl Marx, *Capital,* Volume I (New York: International Publishers, 1987 ed.), 40.

9. Marx, *Capital,* Volume I, 173–74. The language is dated, but the argument is valid; indeed, I would want to rewrite this quotation in the plural to better stress the social character of labor.

10. Daniels and Cosgrove, "Iconography and Landscape."

11. McWilliams, *California: The Great Exception,* xiii; John Steinbeck, *East of Eden* (Viking, 1952); *The Grapes of Wrath* (New York: Viking, 1939); David Wyatt, *The Fall into Eden: Landscape and Imagination in California* (Cambridge: Cambridge University Press, 1986); Joan Didion, *Slouching Towards Bethlehem* (New York: Farrar, Straus and Giroux, 1961).

12. The records of CCIH (Department of Industrial Relations, Division of Immigration and Housing, *Records,* Bancroft Library, University of California, Berkeley) are an immense trove of information not just on labor relations in agriculture (and mining, lumbering, and construction), but also on urban housing for new immigrants, social relations between immigrants and host societies, immigrant education (including "Americanization" programs) and Progressive ideology. To my knowledge, I am the first to have undertaken a thorough examination of these records (with the exception of Samuel Wood, who had access to them before they were archived for his dissertation on the Commission's institutional history). There is plenty of work yet to be done in these archives.

13. Carey McWilliams, *Factories in the Field* (Santa Barbara: Peregrine Smith, 1971 ed.), 153.

14. Neil Smith poses this question in *Uneven Development,* xiii, but it is clearly exactly the question continually asked and just as continually (if always provisionally) answered by agribusiness and state agents alike in their struggles with labor.

1 / California: The Beautiful and the Damned

1. John Steinbeck, *The Grapes of Wrath* (New York: Viking, 1939), 250–51.

2. On the historical structuring of landscape views, see John Barrell, *The Dark Side of Landscape: The Rural Poor in English Painting, 1730–1840* (Cambridge: Cambridge University Press, 1980); John Berger, *Ways of Seeing* (London: Penguin, 1972); Ann Bermingham, *Landscape and Ideology: The English Rustic Tradition, 1740–1860* (London: Thames and Hudson, 1987); Denis Cosgrove, *Social Formation and Symbolic Landscape* (London: Croom Helm, 1984); and "Prospect, Perspective, and the Evolution of the Landscape Idea," *Transactions of the Institute of British Geographers* 10 (1985): 45–62; Denis Cosgrove and Stephen Daniels (eds.), *The Iconography of Landscape: Essays on the Symbolic Representation, Design and Use of Past Environments* (Cambridge: Cambridge University Press, 1988); W. J. T. Mitchell (ed.), *Landscape and Power* (Chicago: University of Chicago Press, 1994); Simon Pugh (ed.), *Reading Landscape: Country—City—Capital* (Manchester: Manchester University Press, 1990). On the ideals embedded in images of the countryside, see Michael Bunce, *The Countryside Ideal: Anglo-American Images of Landscape* (London and New York: Routledge, 1994); Raymond Williams, *The Country and the City* (New York: Oxford University Press, 1973).

3. Kevin Starr, *Americans and the California Dream, 1850–1915* (New York: Oxford University Press, 1973); *Inventing the Dream: California through the Progressive Era* (New York: Oxford University Press, 1985); *Material Dreams: Southern California through the 1920s* (New York: Oxford University Press, 1990).

4. Steinbeck, *Grapes,* 265, 270.

5. George Henderson, "John Steinbeck's Spatial Imagination in *The Grapes of Wrath:* A Critical Essay," *California History* 68 (Winter 1989/90): 211–33.

6. Walter Stein, *California and the Dust Bowl Migration* (Westport, CT: Greenwood Press, 1973), 201–12. Steinbeck's contemporary, Carey McWilliams, was likewise pilloried by defenders of California agriculture for his publication of *Factories in the Field* (Santa Barbara: Peregrine Smith, 1971 ed., originally published 1939). See Testimony of Roy Pike, United States Senate, Subcommittee of the Committee on Education and Labor (the La Follette Committee), Hearings on S. Res. 266, *Violations of Free Speech and the Rights of Labor,* 75 parts (Washington, DC: Government Printing Office, 1936–1940), Part 48, 17865–17895 (hereafter "LFC *Hearings*").

7. The iww's irony, of course, refers to F. Scott Fitzgerald's *The Beautiful and the Damned* (New York: Charles Scribner and Sons, 1922); Agnes Benedict, "The Barefoot Boy," *Survey* 58 (1927): 89–90.

8. For an excellent review of dystopian fiction, itself presented as part of a dystopian (but still stunningly accurate) social history, see Mike Davis, *City of Quartz: Excavating the Future in Los Angeles* (London: Verso, 1990), chapter 1; James Parsons, "A Geographer Looks at the San Joaquin Valley," *Geographical Review* 76 (1986): 371–89, quotation from 387.

9. Parsons, "A Geographer Looks," 375, 376, 387; Parsons actually invokes the image of "capitalism gone rampant" only to criticize those he feels dwell too much on the negative side of California agrarian development.

10. William Preston, *Vanishing Landscapes: Land and Life in the Tulare Basin* (Berkeley: University of California Press, 1981), 173, 198; see Cletus Daniel, *Bitter Harvest: A History of California Farmworkers, 1870–1941* (Ithaca: Cornell University Press, 1981 and Berkeley: University of California Press, 1982); Carey McWilliams, *Factories in the Field* and *Ill Fares the Land: Migrants and Migratory Labor in the United States* (Boston: Little Brown and Co., 1942); Ellen Liebman, *California Farmland: A History of Large Agricultural Landholdings* (Totowa, NJ: Rowman and Allenheld, 1983); Varden Fuller, "The Supply of Agricultural Labor as a Factor in the Evolution of Farm Organization in California," LFC *Hearings*, Part 54, Exhibit 8762–A, 19777–19898.

11. Kevin Starr, *Americans and the California Dream.*

12. Starr, *Inventing the Dream,* 128, 134; on the creation of land monopolies, see Liebman, *California Landholdings;* Varden Fuller, "The Supply of Agricultural Labor."

13. Frederick Mills's diaries are quoted in Gregory Woirol, "Rustling Oranges in Lindsay," *California History* 62 (Summer 1983): 82–97, quotations from 86–87, 92.

14. Starr, *Inventing the Dream,* 143–44.

15. See Williams, *The Country and the City.*

16. Jean Baudrillard, *America* (London: Verso, 1988), quotations from 64–66, 6–7, 79–80, 72.

17. Baudrillard, *America,* 64; Starr, *Americans and the California Dream.*

18. David Wyatt, *The Fall into Eden: Landscape and Imagination in California* (Cambridge: Cambridge University Press, 1986), 108.

19. Wyatt, *Fall into Eden,* xvii, 206; see also Carey McWilliams, *Factories in the Field;* and *California: The Great Exception* (Santa Barbara: Peregrine Smith, 1971 ed.). Timothy Mitchell has suggested that grasping the world as a picture is a condition of western forms of knowing; see, "The World-as-Exhibition," *Comparative Studies in Society and History,* 31 (1989): 217–36.

20. Starr, *Americans and the California Dream,* especially chapters 12 and 13.

21. Wyatt, *Fall into Eden,* 209; Entrikin argues, conversely, that Sauer was quintessentially antimodernist; J. Nicholas Entrikin, "Carl O. Sauer, Philosopher in Spite of Himself," *Geographical Review* 74 (1984): 387–408.

22. Carl Sauer, "The Morphology of Landscape," in John Leighly (ed.), *Land and Life: A Selection from the Writings of Carl Ortwin Sauer* (Berkeley: University of California Press, 1963, essay originally published 1925), 343, 326.

23. Sauer, "Morphology," 316; Sauer, "Foreword to Historical Geography," in John Leighly (ed.), *Land and Life,* 351–79, quotation from 358; see also Denis Cosgrove, *Social Formation and Symbolic Landscape.*

24. James Duncan, *The City as Text: The Politics of Landscape Interpretation in the Kandyan Kingdom* (Cambridge: Cambridge University Press, 1990), 3; see also Duncan, "The Superorganic in American Cultural Geography," *Annals of the Association of American Geographers* 70 (1980): 181–98; Peter Jackson, *Maps of Meaning: An Introduction to Cultural Geography* (London: Unwin Hyman, 1989), chapter 1; Cosgrove, *Social Formation,* chapter 1. The most developed superorganic approach is to be found in Wilbur Zelinsky, *The Cultural Geography of the United States* (Englewood Cliffs, NJ: Prentice-Hall, 1973). See also my critique of geographers' use of the concept of culture in "There's No Such Thing as Culture," *Transactions of the Institute of British Geography,* 20 (1995): 102–16. For an exceptionally clear example of landscape studies—studies certainly influenced by Sauer and his students—that assume all the key terms to be transparent, see Peirce Lewis, "Axioms for Reading the Landscape: Some Guides to the American Scene," in Donald Meinig (ed.), *Interpretations of Ordinary Landscapes: Geographical Essays* (New York: Oxford University Press, 1979), 11–32. For a critique of the gendered nature of the last assumption in this paragraph see Gillian Rose, *Geography and Feminism* (Minneapolis: University of Minnesota Press, 1993). Arguing about the significance of Sauer and his students is something of a growth industry; see in addition to the above citations, Entrikin, "Carl O. Sauer;" Martin Kenzer (ed.), *Carl O. Sauer: A Tribute* (Corvallis: Oregon State University Press for Association of Pacific Coast Geographers); Marie Price and Martin Lewis, "The Reinvention of Cultural Geography," *Annals of the Association of American Geographers* 83 (1993): 1–17 (see also the commentary by Cosgrove, Duncan, and Jackson in the September issue of the same volume of the *Annals*); Michael Solot, "Carl Sauer and Cultural Evolution," *Annals of the Association of American Geographers* 76 (1986): 508–20; Michael Williams, "'The Apple of My Eye': Carl Sauer and Historical Geography," *Journal of Historical Geography* 9 (1983): 1–28.

25. Stephen Daniels and Denis Cosgrove, "Iconography and Landscape," in Cosgrove and Daniels (eds.), *The Iconography of Landscape,* 1; Cosgrove, *Social Formation;* and "Prospect, Perspective and the Evolution of the Landscape Idea;" see also, James Duncan and Nancy Duncan, "(Re)Reading the Landscape," *Environment and Planning D: Society and Space* 6 (1988): 117–26; A. Baker and G. Biger, *Ideology and Landscape in Historical Perspective* (Cambridge: Cambridge University Press, 1992); the phrase "way of seeing"

is from John Berger, *Ways of Seeing*. Berger has been a major influence on geographers studying landscape as ideology. The idea that landscapes appear "unworked" is most well developed in Raymond Williams, *The Country and the City*; Barrell, *Dark Side of Landscape;* and Lewis, "Axioms," 12.

26. Cosgrove, *Social Formation;* Daniels, "Marxism, Culture, and the Duplicity of Landscape," in R. Peet and N. Thrift (eds.), *New Models in Geography, Volume II* (London: Unwin Hyman, 1989), 196-220.

27. Cosgrove's more recent work, which I interpret as something of a departure from his earlier concern critiquing the ideological construction and function of landscape and more toward a celebration of differing "visions" may be found in *The Palladian Landscape: Geographical Change and Its Cultural Representations in Sixteenth-Century Italy* (University Park: Pennsylvania State University Press, 1993); "Contested Global Visions: *One World, Whole Earth,* and the Apollo Space Photographs," *Annals of the Association of American Geographers* 84 (1994): 270–94; "Environmental Thought and Action: Pre-Modern and Post-Modern," *Transactions of the Institute of British Geographers* 15 (1990): 344–58; "Landscapes and Myths, Gods and Humans," in B. Bender (ed.), *Landscape: Politics and Perspectives* (Oxford: Berg, 1993), 281–306; "Geography Is Everywhere: Culture and Symbolism in Human Landscapes," in D. Gregory and R. Walford (eds.), *Horizons in Human Geography* (London: Macmillan, 1989); see also Stephen Daniels and Denis Cosgrove, "Spectacle and Text: Landscape Metaphors in Cultural Geography," in J. Duncan and D. Ley (eds.), *Place/Culture/Representation* (London: Routledge, 1993), 57–77. His discussion of landscape as an outsider's way of knowing is in "Prospect, Perspective," 49; Jackson, *Maps of Meaning*, 177; see also Donald Meinig, "The Beholding Eye," in Meinig (ed.), *The Interpretation of Ordinary Landscapes,* 33–48; Rose, *Feminism and Geography,* 89–101.

28. Trevor Barnes and James Duncan, "Introduction: Writing Worlds," in T. Barnes and J. Duncan (eds.), *Writing Worlds: Discourse Text and Metaphor in the Representation of Landscapes* (London: Routledge, 1992), 1–17.

29. Cosgrove, *Social Formation,* 16.

30. James Duncan begins to make this point in "After the Civil War: Reconstructing Cultural Geography as Heterotopia," in K. Foote, P. Hugill, K. Mathewson, and J. Smith (eds.), *Re-Reading Cultural Geography* (Austin: University of Texas Press), 401–8.

31. Henri Lefebvre, *The Production of Space,* trans. David Nicholson-Smith (Oxford: Blackwell Publishers), 143.

32. Kenneth Olwig, "Sexual Cosmology: Nation and Landscape at the Conceptual Interstices of Nature and Culture; or, What Does Landscape Really Mean?" in Barbara Bender (ed.), *Landscape: Politics and Perspectives* (Oxford: Berg, 1993), 307–43, quotation from 311.

33. Sharon Zukin, *Landscapes of Power: From Detroit to Disneyland* (Berkeley: University of California Press, 1991), 16, 19; many of my ideas here will be recognized as an adaptation of Lefebvre, *The Production of Space*; see also, Kay Anderson, "The Idea of Chinatown: The Power of Place and Institutional Practice in the Making of a Racial Category," *Annals of the Association of American Geographers* 77 (1987): 580–98; Cosgrove, *Social Formation*; Simon Pugh, "Introduction: Stepping Out into the Open," in Simon Pugh, (ed.), *Reading Landscape: Country-City-Capital* (Manchester: Manchester University Press, 1990), 1–6.

34. W. J. T. Mitchell, "Introduction," in W. J. T. Mitchell (ed.), *Landscape and Power* (Chicago: University of Chicago Press, 1994), 1–4, quotation from 1–2; Zukin, *Landscapes of Power*, 16.

35. These ideas and the discussion of Bruno Latour that follows is adapted from my paper, "Landscape and Surplus Value: The Making of the Ordinary in Brentwood, California," *Environment and Planning D: Society and Space* 12 (1994): 7–30.

36. Bruno Latour, *Science in Action: How to Follow Scientists and Engineers through Society* (Cambridge, MA: MIT Press, 1987), 88, 87, 92, 93, 94; see also Latour, *The Pasteurization of France* (Cambridge, MA: Harvard University Press, 1988); Neil Smith, *Uneven Development: Nature, Capital, and the Production of Space* (Oxford: Blackwell Publishers, 1990, 2nd ed.).

37. Latour, "Ethnography of 'High-Tech': About the Aramis Case." Paper presented to the Center for the Critical Analysis of Contemporary Culture, Rutgers University, 4 February 1992; in the case of the system analyzed by Latour, the form never did stabilize completely, and the system never became reality.

38. Latour borrows the term "quasi-object" from Michel Callon, "Some Elements of a Sociology of Translation: Domestication of the Scallops and the Fishermen of St. Brieux Bay," in J. Law (ed.), *Power, Action, Belief: A New Sociology of Knowledge?* Keele Sociological Review Monograph 32 (Andover, Hants: Routledge, Chapman and Hall, 1986), 196–229, and "Society in the Making: The Study of Technology as a Tool for Sociological Analysis," in W. Bijker, T. Hughes, and T. Pinch (eds.), *New Developments in the Social Studies of Technology* (Cambridge, MA: MIT Press, 1987), 83–106.

39. Smith, *Uneven Development;* David Harvey, *The Limits to Capital* (Oxford: Basil Blackwell, 1982).

40. David Harvey, *The Urbanization of Capital* (Baltimore: Johns Hopkins University Press), 133; Harvey, *Limits to Capital;* see also Zukin, *Landscapes of Power,* chapter 1.

41. Karl Marx, *Capital,* Volume I (New York: International Publishers, 1987 ed.), 537, 168; for a development of this point within feminist geography, see Liz Bondi and Linda Peake, "Gender and the City: Urban Politics Revisited," in Jo Little, Linda Peake, and Pat Richardson (eds.), *Women in Cities: Gender and the Urban Environment* (New York: New York University Press, 1988), 21–40; and Linda McDowell, "Towards an Understanding of the Gender Division of Urban Space," *Environment and Planning D: Society and Space* 1 (1983), 59–72; see also Doreen Massey's essays, collected as *Space, Power, and Gender* (Minneapolis: University of Minnesota Press, 1994); for a review of the literature in geography on this point, see Susan Hanson, "Geography and Feminism: Worlds in Collision?" *Annals of the Association of American Geographers* 82 (1992): 559–86. An excellent example of showing how production and reproduction cannot be divorced is American Social History Project, *Who Built America? Working People and the Nation's Economy, Politics, Culture, and Society* (New York: Pantheon, Volume I: 1989; Volume II: 1992).

2 / Labor and Landscape: The Wheatland Riot and Progressive State Intervention

1. The flier is reprinted in Carleton Parker, *The Casual Laborer and Other Essays* (New York: Harcourt, Brace and Howe, 1920), 179. Most accounts of the events of

Wheatland follow Carleton Parker's two official reports: "A Report to His Excellency Hiram W. Johnson, Governor of California, by the Commission of Immigration and Housing of California on the Causes and All Matters Pertaining to the So-Called Wheatland Hop Fields Riot and Recommendation [sic] as a Solution to the Problems Disclosed," in Parker, *Casual Laborer,* 171–99; and "Report on an Inquiry into the Social and Economic Causes that Led to the Wheatland Hop-Field Riot of August 3, 1913," in United States Senate, Subcommittee of the Committee on Education and Labor (the La Follette Committee), Hearings on S. Res. 266, *Violations of Free Speech and the Rights of Labor,* 75 parts (Washington, DC: Government Printing Office, 1936–1940), Part 54, Exhibit 8768, 20069–20073, "country vacation" quotation from 20069 (hereafter "LFC Hearings"). The events are fictionalized (quite inaccurately) in Wallace Stegner, *Joe Hill: A Biographical Novel* (Lincoln: University of Nebraska Press, 1950, originally published as *The Preacher and the Slave*). Other accounts of Wheatland can be found in California Commission of Immigration and Housing, *First Annual Report* (Sacramento: State Printing Office, 1915); Cletus Daniel, "In Defense of the Wheatland Wobblies: A Critical Analysis of the IWW in California," *Labor History* 19 (1978): 485–509; and *Bitter Harvest: A History of California Farmworkers, 1870–1941* (Ithaca: Cornell University Press, 1981 and Berkeley: University of California Press, 1982); Melvyn Dubofsky, *We Shall Be All: A History of the Industrial Workers of the World* (Urbana: University of Illinois Press, 1988, 2nd ed.); Philip Foner, *The History of the Labor Movement in the United States, Volume IV: The Industrial Workers of the World, 1905–1917* (New York: International Publishers, 1965); Stuart Jamieson, *Labor Unionism in American Agriculture* (New York, Arno Press, 1976, reprint); Carey McWilliams, *Factories in the Field* (Santa Barbara: Peregrine Smith, 1971 ed.); Don Mitchell, "Fixing in Place: Progressive Science and Landscapes of Repression in California," *Historical Geography* 23 (1993): 44–61; and "State Intervention in Landscape Production: The Wheatland Riot and the California Commission of Immigration and Housing," *Antipode* 25 (1993): 91–113; Samuel Wood, "The California Commission of Immigration and Housing: A Study of Administrative Organization and the Growth of Function," unpublished Ph.D. dissertation, University of California, Berkeley, 1942.

    2. Parker, *Casual Laborer,* 179, 181–82; see also Parker "Report," 20070.

    3. Parker, *Casual Laborer,* 174; information on toilets and water is from 181–85. In his report to the U.S. Commission on Industrial Relations ("Report"), Parker toned down his language but still managed, without letting the Dursts off the hook, to blame the workers for a good percentage of the appalling conditions.

    4. Parker, *Casual Laborer,* 185; "Report," 20071.

    5. Daniel, *Bitter Harvest,* 89; Parker to Scharrenberg, June 6, 1914, Department of Industrial Relations, Division of Immigration and Housing Records, Bancroft Library, University of California, Berkeley (hereafter DIR Records), Carton 1, "General Correspondence"; Durst to Lubin, June 9, 1914, Simon Lubin Papers, Bancroft Library, University of California, Berkeley, Box 2.

    6. Daniel, "In Defense;" Parker, *Casual Laborer,* 192.

    7. Parker, "Report," 20072; McWilliams, *Factories in the Field,* 161; Daniel, *Bitter Harvest,* 90; Parker, *Casual Laborer,* 192.

    8. American Social History Project, *Who Built America? Working People and the*

Nation's Economy, Politics, Culture, and Society (New York: Pantheon, Volume I: 1989; Volume II: 1992) provides a quite accessible introduction to the labor history of the United States.

9. McWilliams, *Factories in the Field,* 162; Parker, *Casual Laborer,* 172, 89.

10. McWilliams, *Factories in the Field,* 161–62; Daniel, "In Defense"; Testimony of A. B. McKenzie, United States Commission on Industrial Relations, *Final Report and Testimony, Volume V,* 64th Congress, 1st Session, Senate Document 415 (1916): 4994–4999; Bancroft Library, University of California, Berkeley, holds two large scrapbooks (available on microfilm) of newspaper clippings detailing the events at Wheatland and the panic that ensued.

11. Parker, *Casual Laborer,* 88.

12. See the discussion in Daniel's *Bitter Harvest,* Chapter 1.

13. "The pattern" is shorthand used to describe California agricultural relationships in a number of historical studies; see Wood, "The California State Commission;" Varden Fuller, "The Supply of Agricultural Labor as a Factor in the Evolution of Farm Organization in California," in LFC *Hearings,* Part 54, Exhibit 8726–A 19777–19898; Ellen Liebman, *California Farmland: A History of Large Agricultural Landholdings* (Totowa, NJ: Rowman and Allenheld, 1983); California State Relief Administration, *Migratory Labor in California* (San Francisco: Mimeo, 1936); Paul Taylor and Tom Vassey, "Historical Background of California Farm Labor," *Rural Sociology* 1 (1936): 282–85; Marx is quoted in McWilliams, *Factories in the Field,* 56; on the "more so" status of California, see Carey McWilliams, "Introduction," in Carey McWilliams (ed.), *The California Revolution* (New York: Grossman Publishers, 1968), 5.

14. This is one of the main themes of Parker's *Casual Laborer.*

15. CCIH, *Advisory Pamphlet on Camp Sanitation and Housing* (Sacramento: State Printing Office, 1914), 5; Parker, *Casual Laborer,* 197, 198.

16. A biography of Lubin is included in Wood, "California State Commission," 82–93; CCIH, *First Annual Report,* 7; see the series of letters in Simon Lubin Papers, Box 4, "Outgoing letters, Aug-Oct, 1912;" Lubin to Blaustein, 23 August 1912; Simon Lubin Papers, Box 4, "Outgoing letters, Aug-Oct, 1912;" Wood, "California State Commission," 92; Johnson to Lubin, 20 August 1912 in Wood, "California State Commission," 93.

17. Wood, "California State Commission," 97.

18. See Wood, "California State Commission," 108–9; CCIH, *First Annual Report,* 7–8.

19. CCIH, *First Annual Report,* 8, 15.

20. Lubin to Whom it May Concern, n.d. (December 1913), DIR Records, Carton 1, "General Correspondence, 1913." Parker ran the offices of CCIH, but Lubin assumed the position of "executive officer," setting the terms of policy, largely by means of extensive correspondence and personal communication with the executive secretary. Parker resigned from the Commission after only a year, in part because of disagreements with other commissioners, but he was enormously influential in establishing the course that the Commission would take in its work on agricultural landscapes. Biographical information on Parker, who was quite fascinating, may be found in Cornelia Parker, *An American Idyll: The Life of Carleton Parker* (Boston: Atlantic Monthly Press, 1919). The nascent CCIH was pleased with the dual assignment because it could reap the

respectability that the well-established U.S. Commission offered. Parker to Weinstock, 10 January 1914; Lubin to Gibson, 12 January 1914, Simon Lubin Papers, Box 4, "Outgoing Letters, 1914—January to March;" Parker, *Casual Laborer*, 88.

21. This was a general goal of the California Progressive movement, which generally distrusted the working classes. See George Mowry, *The California Progressives* (Berkeley: University of California Press, 1951).

22. Parker, "Report," 20072.

23. Lubin to Parker, 2 February 1914, Simon Lubin Papers, Box 4, "Outgoing Letters, 1914—January to March"; Parker, "Report," 20072.

24. Parker to Lubin, 31 December 1913, DIR Records, Carton 1, "General Correspondence, 1913"; see also "A Brief Report of the Commission of Immigration and Housing of California to the Honorable Hiram W. Johnson, Governor of California, July 10, 1914," 9–10; copy in Simon Lubin Papers, Carton 1. The agents hired by Parker were a rather remarkable bunch. Paul Brissenden later authored the first comprehensive history of the IWW: *The IWW: A Study of American Syndicalism* (New York: Columbia University Press, 1919); Paul Elliel became an economics professor at Stanford University and a publicist for the antiunion Industrial Association of San Francisco during the 1934 General Strike; and Frederick Mills became a well-regarded professor of economics at Columbia University.

25. I am making this conflation on purpose: as we will see, Parker's discussion of what constitutes the "environment" echoes last chapter's discussion of what constitutes, in materiality and image, "the landscape."

26. Parker, *Casual Laborer*, 28.

27. Ibid., 88.

28. For similar analyses of the problem of migratory labor, see, for example, Alice Solenberger, *One Thousand Homeless Men* (New York: Survey Associates, Inc., 1911); Nels Anderson, *The Hobo* (Chicago: University of Chicago Press, 1923). On Yerkes, see Donna Haraway, "A Pilot Program for Human Engineering: Robert Yerkes and the Yale Laboratories of Primate Biology, 1924–1942," in her *Primate Visions: Gender, Race and Nature in the World of Modern Science* (New York: Routledge, 1989), 59–83; on Goddard see Stephen Jay Gould, *The Mismeasure of Man* (New York: W. W. Norton, 1981). On Progressive scientific relationships between eugenics, industrial relations, sanitary housing, and feeblemindedness, see also, Gould, "Bound by the Great Chain," in his *The Flamingo's Smile: Reflections on Natural History* (New York: W. W. Norton, 1985); Arthur Lovejoy, *The Great Chain of Being* (Cambridge, MA: Harvard University Press, 1936); Mark H. Haller, *Eugenics: Hereditarian Attitudes in American Thought* (New Brunswick: Rutgers University Press, 1984); Morris Knowles, *Industrial Housing* (New York: McGraw-Hill, 1920).

29. Parker, *Casual Laborer*, 96, 30–32, 35–37. Parker used "tendencies" and "instinct" interchangeably. He claimed that his list of tendencies (which is longer than what I have included here) was the summation of the latest advances in experimental psychology, Darwinian evolutionism, and behavioralist psychology. The letters reprinted in Cornelia Parker's, *An American Idyll* testify that Parker's ideas were well received by the eastern scientific establishment. See also Gould's discussion of the scientific context within which theories of racial difference as evolutionary "distance" were developed in "Bound by the Great Chain."

30. Parker, *Casual Laborer,* 33–34.

31. Ibid., 46–48, 89.

32. Haraway, "Teddy Bear Patriarchy: Taxidermy in the Garden of Eden, New York City, 1908–1936," in her *Primate Visions,* 26–58, quotation from 55; Parker, *Casual Laborer,* 197–99, 48.

33. Parker, *Casual Laborer,* 95, 49.

34. Parker, *Casual Laborer,* 49; his findings were supported by Solenberger, *One Thousand Homeless Men* and Anderson, *The Hobo;* and later by E. Southerland and H. Locke, *Twenty Thousand Homeless Men* (New York: Lippencott, 1936). On Progressive paternalism see Stuart Brandes, *American Welfare Capitalism, 1880–1940* (Chicago: University of Chicago Press, 1976).

35. Parker discusses the role of the "militant minority" throughout the essays in *Casual Laborer.*

36. Parker, *Casual Laborer,* 51–52.

37. CCIH discussed worker fulfillment in the introduction to its *Advisory Pamphlet on Camp Sanitation* (Sacramento: State Printing Office, 1914); discussion of bad conditions and strikes is found on page 7 of the same pamphlet; the key discussion of spatial strategies of discipline is, of course, Michel Foucault, *Discipline and Punish* (New York: Vintage, 1979); Foucault's emphasis, at least in this work, on "total institutions" such as prisons and workhouses limits its usefulness, except as a study of "ideal types"; see Felix Driver, "Power, Space, and the Body: A Critical Assessment of Foucault's *Discipline and Punish,*" *Environment and Planning D: Society and Space* 3 (1985): 425–46. In the much messier world of unruly migratory laborers, strategies of surveillance and discipline, as we will see, were baroquely complex.

38. CCIH, *Advisory Pamphlet,* 7–12; CCIH, *Second Annual Report,* 13; "Camp Department: Arrests and Convictions for Violation of the Camp Sanitation Act," DIR Records, Carton 10.

39. CCIH, *Second Annual Report,* 15; Wood, "California State Commission."

40. CCIH, *Second Annual Report;* Parker to Gibson 7 July and 18 July 1914; Parker to Lubin, 23 July 1914; Bell to McBride, 18 August and 4 October 1915, all in DIR Records, Carton 1; Bell to Lubin, 28 April, 30 April, and 2 May 1914, Simon Lubin Papers, Box 1; CCIH, *Advisory Pamphlet.*

41. CCIH, *Second Annual Report,* 20.

42. Ibid.

43. CCIH, *Fifth Annual Report,* 25, 26.

44. Lubin to Horst, 14 February and 14 March 1914; Horst to Commission, 12 February 1914; Lubin to Rowell 14 February 1914; all in Simon Lubin Papers, Carton 1, "Outgoing Letters 1914—January to March."

45. IWW Flier, copy in Simon Lubin Papers, Box 3.

46. IWW Sticker, copy in Simon Lubin Papers, Box 3. Actually, CCIH was even stricter on this last point; it recommended one toilet for every ten persons in camp and one for every forty in the fields; CCIH, *Advisory Pamphlet,* 28.

47. Parker to Lubin, 7 July 1914, Simon Lubin Papers, Box 3; Parker to Scharrenberg, 6 June 1914, DIR Records, Carton 1, "General Correspondence;" Durst to Lubin 9 June 1914, Simon Lubin Papers, Box 2.

48. A. Johnson to Parker, 27 March 1914; Durst to Lubin, 23 June and 28 June

1914; Simon Lubin Papers, Box 2; Bell to Lubin 6 May 1914, Simon Lubin Papers, Box 1; Parker to Lubin, 27 March 1914, Box 3; CCIH, *First Annual Report*; *Second Annual Report*; *Fifth Annual Report*; *Annual Report* (for 1922); see also Lubin's resignation statement, Lubin to Richardson, 2 November 1923, DIR Records, Carton 63; Bell to Lubin 28 April 1914; CCIH, "A Brief Report," 11, both in Simon Lubin Papers, Carton 1; Bell to Lubin, n.d., DIR Records, Carton 1, "General Correspondence, 1914."

49. Stephen Daniels, "Marxism, Culture, and the Duplicity of Landscape," in Richard Peet and Nigel Thrift (eds.), *New Models in Geography, Volume II* (London: Unwin Hyman, 1989), 196–220; see also Driver, "Power, Space, and the Body"; Matthew Hannah, "Space and Social Control in the Administration of the Oglala Lakota ("Sioux"), 1871–1879," *Journal of Historical Geography* 19 (1993): 412–32; David Matless, "An Occasion for Geography: Landscape Representation, and Foucault's Corpus," *Environment and Planning D: Society and Space* 10 (1992): 41–56; C. Philo, "Foucault's Geography," *Environment and Planning D: Society and Space* 10 (1992): 137–62.

50. On "the power to define" see Kay Anderson, "The Idea of Chinatown: The Power of Place and Institutional Practice in the Making of a Racial Category," *Annals of the Association of American Geographers* 77 (1987): 580–98; Edward Said, *Orientalism* (New York: Vintage, 1978); John Western, *Outcast Capetown* (Minneapolis: University of Minnesota Press, 1981).

3 / Subversive Mobility and the Re-formation of Landscape

1. Kelly's Army was an organization of several thousand unemployed transient workers that demanded relief in San Francisco and marched on Sacramento, where eight hundred or so special deputies raided their encampment and violently drove them out of the city. For accounts of the panic caused by the problem of migratory labor at various times in U.S. history, see Eric Monkonnen (ed.), *Walking to Work: Tramps in America, 1870–1935* (Lincoln: University of Nebraska Press, 1984), especially the chapters by P. F. Clemment, "The Transformation of the Wandering Poor in Nineteenth–Century Philadelphia," 56–86; and Michael Davis, "Forced to Tramp: The Perspective of the Labor Press, 1870–1900," 141–70.

2. My point in this book is not to explore the history of agricultural development in the nineteenth century. Excellent accounts are available in Cletus Daniel, *Bitter Harvest: A History of California Farmworkers, 1870–1941* (Ithaca: Cornell University Press, 1981 and Berkeley: University of California Press, 1982); Varden Fuller, "The Supply of Agricultural Labor as a Factor in the Evolution of Farm Organization in California," United States Senate, Subcommittee of the Committee on Education and Labor (the La Follette Committee), Hearings on S. Res. 266, *Violations of Free Speech and the Rights of Labor*, 75 parts (Washington, DC: Government Printing Office, 1936–1940), Part 54, Exhibit 8762-A, 19777–19898 (hereafter LFC *Hearings*); Carey McWilliams, *Factories in the Field* (Santa Barbara: Peregrine Smith, 1971 ed.).

3. Paul Taylor and Tom Vassey, "Historical Background of California Farm Labor," *Rural Sociology* 1 (1936): 282–85; Fuller, "The Supply of Agricultural Labor," 19779; CCIH, *Second Annual Report* (Sacramento: State Printing Office, 1916), 391–92; on

gendered and ethnic divisions of labor and working conditions in canneries, see Vicky Ruiz, *Cannery Women, Cannery Lives: Mexican Women, Unionization, and the California Food Processing Industry, 1930–1950* (Albuquerque: University of New Mexico Press, 1987).

4. Liebman, *California Farmland: A History of Large Agricultural Landholdings* (Totowa, NJ: Rowman and Allenheld, 1983), 55; Fuller, "The Supply of Agricultural Labor."

5. Quoted in McWilliams, *Factories in the Field*, 25.

6. McWilliams, *California: The Great Exception* (Santa Barbara: Peregrine Smith, 1976 ed.), 169.

7. Cletus Daniel, *Bitter Harvest*, 64.

8. Matthew Hannah, "Space and Social Control in the Administration of the Oglala Lakota ("Sioux"), 1871–1879," *Journal of Historical Geography* 19 (1993): 412–32. Hannah's work is the best development in geography of Foucault's concern with power and visibility as it pertains to depersonalized, "modern" forms of social control. See Michel Foucault, *Discipline and Punish* (New York: Vintage, 1979); and the essays and interviews collected in C. Gordon (ed.), *Power/Knowledge: Selected Interviews and Other Writings* (New York: Pantheon, 1980).

9. Surveys of migratory workers in the first decades of the twentieth century were often confined to male workers. Carleton Parker's 1915 survey of male migratory workers disclosed that 48 percent were native born; 76 percent were unmarried, and another 7.1 percent were separated from their wives; 47 percent were under thirty years old and 33 percent were between thirty and forty. Fifty-two percent were classified as "unskilled" in spite of the fact that many agricultural tasks were highly skilled; Carleton Parker, *The Casual Laborer and other Essays* (New York: Harcourt, Brace and Howe, 1920), 72–73.

10. Parker, *Casual Laborer*, 73; On domestic spying at this time see William Preston, *Aliens and Dissenters: Federal Suppression of Radicals, 1903–1933* (New York: Harper Torchbooks, 1963); more specifically on the military's role in domestic espionage see Joan Jensen, *Army Surveillance in America, 1775–1980* (New Haven: Yale University Press).

11. Military Intelligence Division, U.S. Army, Military Intelligence Reports: Surveillance of Radicals in the United States, 1917–1941 (Ann Arbor: University Microfilms, 1988), Reel 2 (hereafter MID Reports).

12. For a historical discussion of conditions faced by migratory workers during the nineteenth and early twentieth centuries, see the papers in Monkonnen (ed.), *Walking to Work*. Wallace Stegner's fictionalized descriptions in *Joe Hill: A Biographical Novel* (Lincoln: University of Nebraska Press, 1950) are evocative of the role that IWW union halls played in migratory workers' lives at this time. Good general studies of the IWW that describe the "culture" of migratory workers are Paul Brissenden's early *The IWW: A Study in American Syndicalism* (New York: Columbia University Press, 1919); Philip Foner, *History of the Labor Movement in the United States, Volume IV: The Industrial Workers of the World, 1905–1917* (New York: International Publishers, 1965); Melvyn Dubofsky, *We Shall Be All: A History of the Industrial Workers of the World* (Urbana: University of Illinois Press, 1988, 2nd ed.); Joseph Conlin, *Bread and Roses Too: Studies of the Wobblies* (Westport, CT: Greenwood Press, 1970); Salvatore Salerno, *Red November, Black November* (Albany: State University of New York Press, 1989); and the official his-

tory, Fred Thompson and Patrick Murfin, *The IWW: Its First Seventy Years, 1905–1975* (Chicago: IWW, 1975).

13. Foner, *Industrial Workers of the World*, 151; Robert Tyler, "Rebels of the Woods and Fields: A Study of the IWW in the Pacific Northwest," Ph.D. dissertation, University of Oregon, 1953, 19–20; quoted in Foner, *Industrial Workers of the World*, 151; Parker, *Casual Laborer*, 10.

14. Quoted in Carleton Parker, "The IWW," *Atlantic Monthly* V (November 1917), 651–62.

15. Arno Dorsch, "What the IWW Is," *World's Work* 26 (n.d.): 402–20; the preamble to the IWW constitution has been reprinted in numerous places (including the histories listed in note 12); but the most interesting place it can be found is on the inside cover of the IWW's "Little Red Song Book": *Songs We Never Forget* (Chicago: IWW, 1990, 35th ed.).

16. The contention that the IWW played a central role in the restructuring of industrial capitalism in the western United States is supported in both Foner, *Industrial Workers of the World*; Dubofsky, *We Shall Be All*; and especially, Salerno, *Red November*; Henri Lefebvre, *The Production of Space,* trans. Donald Nicholson-Smith (Oxford: Basil Blackwell, 1991), 383.

17. Parker, "The IWW."

18. David Harvey, *The Condition of Postmodernity* (Oxford: Basil Blackwell, 1989), 234–35; The MID Records, Reel 2, make this point about the role mobility played in connecting struggles by showing how much arrested workers knew of actions by other workers all across the western United States. For a theoretical account of the importance of subversive mobility to political action, see Neil Smith, "Contours of a Spatialized Politics: Homeless Vehicles and the Production of Geographical Scale," *Social Text* 33 (1992): 55–81.

19. A sense of the moral economy of the migratory workers my be gleaned from the glossary of hobo, lumberjack, and mining terms collected in Joyce Kornblugh (ed.), *Rebel Voices: An IWW Anthology* (Ann Arbor: University of Michigan Press, 1964), 405–8.

20. Philip Foner, *Fellow Workers and Friends: Free Speech Fights as Told by Participants* (Westport, CT: Greenwood Press, 1981); Dubofsky, *We Shall Be All*, 184–86; Foner, *Industrial Workers of the World*, 185–89; see also Don Mitchell, "Political Violence, Order, and the Legal Construction of Public Space," unpublished paper, Department of Geography, University of Colorado.

21. Histories of the various free speech fights may be found in Foner, *Fellow Workers and Friends.*

22. Quoted in Foner, *Industrial Workers of the World*, 185; Little was murdered by hired thugs during a strike of miners in Butte, Montana, a few years later.

23. Dubofsky, *We Shall Be All*, 173.

24. Don Mitchell, "Locational Conflict from the Underside: Free Speech, People's Park, and the Politics of Homelessness in Berkeley, California," *Political Geography* 11, (1992): 152–69; "The End of Public Space? People's Park, Definitions of the Public, and Democracy," *Annals of the Association of American Geographers* 85 (1995): 108–33; and "Political Violence, Order, and the Legal Construction of Public Space."

25. Foner, *Industrial Workers of the World*, 189; Testimony of George Speed, U.S. Commission on Industrial Relations, *Final Report and Testimony,* Volume V; see also Daniel, *Bitter Harvest.*

26. Frank Hamilton, "A Screed and a Suggestion," *Solidarity* (November 21, 1914): 2–3; quoted in Dubofsky, *We Shall Be All*, 314.

27. Dubofsky, *We Shall Be All*, 315–16.

28. Stuart Jamieson, *Labor Unionism in American Agriculture* (New York: Arno Press, 1967 reprint), 64.

29. MID Records, Reel 2, records taken in Sacramento, January, 1918.

30. Dubofsky, *We Shall Be All*, 293.

31. Quoted in Gregory Woirol, "Observing the IWW in California, May-July 1914," *Labor History* 25 (1984): 437–47.

32. Testimony of George Speed, U.S. Commission on Industrial Relations, *Final Report and Testimony*, Volume V, 4941. Both Parker and Bell affirmed this claim in their testimony before the Commission on Industrial Relations, but even more elegant testimony resides in the reports filed by CCIH's undercover operatives in the California fields. These reports may be found in DIR Records, Carton 1, as well as in the Simon Lubin Papers.

33. Quoted in Foner, *Industrial Workers of the World*, 275.

34. Preston, *Aliens and Dissenters*, 58–49; Foner, *Industrial Workers of the World*, 274; Lambert to Ford 18 June, 1915, quoted in Foner, *Industrial Workers of the World*, 274.

35. Bell to Lubin, 12 August 1915, DIR Records, Carton 1, "General Correspondence, 1915"; Lambert to Ford, 6 June 1915, quoted in Preston, *Aliens and Dissenters*, 59.

36. IWW debates on sabotage are examined in Foner, *Industrial Workers of the World*, chapter 6; and Dubofsky, *We Shall Be All*, 34–36, 160–64; the advice for farmworkers is quoted in Daniel, "In Defense of the Wheatland Wobblies: A Critical Analysis of the IWW in California," *Labor History* 19 (1978): 485–509; quotation from 501; *Solidarity* (October 3, 1914).

37. Bell to Lubin, 30 September 1915, DIR Records, Carton 1, "General Correspondence, 1915"; Lubin to Field, 4 October 1915, Simon Lubin Papers, Box 5, "1915 May-Dec."; Bell to McBride, 4 October 1915; Bell to Lubin, 5 October 1915, DIR Records, Carton 1, "General Correspondence, 1915."

38. "Reported by M. A. Brady, investigator, Commission of Immigration and Housing, August 31st, 1915," Simon Lubin Papers, Carton 1.

39. Bell to Lubin, 12 August, 3 September, 19 September, 29 September (two letters), 1915; Bell to McBride, 4 October 1915, DIR Records, Carton 1, "General Correspondence, 1915"; "Report by M. A. Brady."

40. Foner, *Industrial Workers of the World*, 277–78; Preston, *Aliens and Dissenters*, 59–60; Scharrenberg is quoted in Daniel, "In Defense of the Wheatland Wobblies," 504.

41. Daniel, "In Defense of the Wheatland Wobblies," 500; on the beginnings of the sabotage program see, Wood, "The California State Commission," and Gregory Woirol, "Observing the IWWs in California, May–June, 1914," *Labor History* 25 (1983): 437–47; and "Men on the Road: Early Twentieth Century Surveys of Itinerant Labor in California," *California History* 69: 192–205.

42. Samuel Wood, "The California State Commission of Immigration and Housing: A Study of Administrative Organization and Growth of Function," Ph.D. dissertation, University of California, Berkeley, 1942, 263; see also Preston, *Aliens and Dissenters*, 58.

43. Bell to Lubin 17 October and 20 October 1914; Scharrenberg to Bell 20 March 1914, DIR Records, Carton 1, "General Correspondence, 1914"; see also the correspon-

dence between Thompson and Bell and Thompson and Lubin in the Simon Lubin Papers, Carton 1; Wood, "The California State Commission," 264–65; on Thompson, see Bruce Nelson, "J. Vance Thompson, Industrial Workers of the World, and the Mood of Syndicalism, 1914–1921," *Labor Heritage* 2 (October, 1990): 44–65. Both in his capacity as a commissioner of CCIH and as president of the California Federation of Labor, Paul Scharrenberg objected to Parker's use of "university boys" as Commission agents, and lobbied for their replacement with the likes of Thompson; Scharrenberg was also instrumental in getting Parker removed from the Commission in favor of George Bell, who was far less sympathetic to the IWW. CCIH frequently hired private detective agencies to supplement their own espionage staff. As these agencies profited by great conspiracies, great conspiracies were often found; see Wood, "The California State Commission."

44. "Vance" to Bell, 26 March 1917, Simon Lubin Papers, Carton 1; Thompson to Bell, 24 May 1917, Simon Lubin Papers, Box 3; and Cohn to Bell, n.d., Simon Lubin Papers, Box 2.

45. Jamieson, *Labor Unionism,* 65; MID Reports, Reel 2, Evidence against Sacramento Defendants; Preston, *Aliens and Dissenters,* 132. For records of the depth of anti-German sentiment in California see MID Report, Reels 1 and 2; see also Preston's discussion in *Aliens and Dissenters*; For IWW president "Big Bill" Haywood's response to the anti-German hysteria see "What Haywood Says of the IWW," *The Survey* 38 (August 11, 1917): 429–30. Thompson speaks of the IWW and the enemy in Thompson to Bell, 18 June 1917, Simon Lubin Papers, Box 1; see also Nelson, "J. Vance Thompson," 54.

46. Bell to Lubin, 18 June 1917, Simon Lubin Papers, Box 1; Wood, "The California State Commission," 267–69; Preston, *Aliens and Dissenters,* 134–37; Nelson, "J. Vance Thompson," 54.

47. Wood, "The California State Commission," 268 and fn. 31; Nelson, "J. Vance Thompson," 54.

48. *San Francisco Examiner* 26 July 1917; Boyle to Lubin 10 July 1917; Boyle to Lubin, 10 July 1917; Campbell to Lubin, 11 July 1917; all in Simon Lubin Papers, Box 3; Lubin to Campbell 6 July and 11 July 1917; Lubin to Lister, 16 July 1917; all in Simon Lubin Papers, Box 5; and see the series of coded telegrams between Lubin and Bell, 14 July to 25 July 1917, Simon Lubin Papers, Box 1; Lubin to Bell, 16 July 1917; Simon Lubin Papers, Box 5; Wood, "The California State Commission," 269–70.

49. Bell to Covington 1 September 1917, Simon Lubin Papers, Box 1; Wood "The California State Commission," 269–70.

50. Lubin to Bell, 21 July 1917, Simon Lubin Papers, Box 5.

51. Thompson to Bell, 23 July 1917, Simon Lubin Papers, Carton 1.

52. "Brief Summary of the Concrete Recommendations as to Cooperation Between the Federal Government and the Commission," Simon Lubin Papers, Carton 1.

53. See Chapter 4.

54. See Preston, *Aliens and Dissenters;* Wood, "The California State Commission." The arrests of radicals at this time extended well beyond the IWW to include prominent socialists (such as Eugene Debs) and nearly all other recognizable leaders of radicalism in the United States.

55. Carey McWilliams, *Factories in the Field,* 170–71; Wood, "The California State Commission," 271; see also Simon Lubin, "Can the Radicals Capture the Farms of California," speech before the Commonwealth Club, 23 March 1934, in LFC *Hearings,*

Part 68, Exhibit 11431, 24967–24873; Nelson, "J. Vance Thompson"; Dubofsky, *We Shall Be All;* Preston, *Aliens and Dissenters.*

56. Quoted in McWilliams, *Factories in the Field,* 172.

57. Quoted in the *San Francisco Examiner,* 8 May 1918.

58. Elizabeth Helsinger, "Turner and the Representation of England," in W. J. T. Mitchell (ed.), *Landscape and Power* (Chicago: University of Chicago Press, 1994), 103–26, quotations from 106, 105; records of the arrests and raids along with reports of vigilante actions are in the MID Records Reels 1 and 2.

59. McWilliams, *Factories in the Field;* Varden Fuller, "The Supply of Agricultural Labor."

60. Parker, *Casual Laborer,* 85, 86; The letters in the file "General Correspondence 1917" in the DIR Records, Carton 1, and in the Simon Lubin Papers are eloquent on this last point. See especially, Bell to Gibson, 27 November 1917; "MW" to Lubin, 19 July 1917; and the series of letters between Bell, Lubin, and the various governors of the western states who eventually cooperated with CCIH in its program of labor repression.

61. Lefebvre, *Production of Space,* 354.

62. Gerry Kearns, "Historical Geography," *Progress in Human Geography* 16 (1992): 406–13, quotation from 408.

4 / Marked Bodies: Patriotism, Race, and Landscape

1. *San Francisco Examiner,* 15 July 1917; collected in Federal Writers Project (FWP; Works Progress Administration) Papers, Bancroft Library, University of California, Berkeley, Carton 11, "Camps 1917–20."

2. Carey McWilliams, *Factories in the Field* (Santa Barbara: Peregrine Smith, 1971 ed.), 173–74; California Agricultural Experiment Station, *Report,* 1917–1918, quoted in FWP, *Child Labor in California Agriculture,* Monograph 1 (1938).

3. *San Jose Mercury Herald,* 13 May 1917; collected in FWP Papers, Carton 11, "Camps 1917–20."

4. *San Jose Mercury Herald,* 13 May 1917. The inadequacy of state labor bureaus had already been noted by Wobbly organizer George Speed in his remarks before the U.S. Industrial Relations Commission; see United States Commission on Industrial Relations, *Final Report and Testimony,* Volume V (Washington: Government Printing Office, 1916); CCIH agent Frederick Mills found the Sacramento Bureau to be corrupt, inefficient, and unable to compete with private agencies; Mills to Lubin, 3 July 1914; Department of Industrial Relations, Division of Immigration and Housing Records, Bancroft Library, University of California, Berkeley (hereafter DIR Records), Carton 1, "General Correspondence," 1914.

5. *San Jose Mercury Herald,* 13 May 1917.

6. FWP, *Labor in the California Peach Crop,* Monograph 7 (1938): 54–55; McWilliams, *Factories in the Field,* 176–79

7. FWP, *Labor in the California Peach Crop,* 54–55; McWilliams, *Factories in the Field,* 179.

8. FWP, *Child Labor in California Agriculture;* FWP, *Labor in the California Peach Crop,* 54; McWilliams, *Factories in the Field,* 176.

9. Varden Fuller, "The Supply of Agricultural Labor as a Factor in the Evolution of Farm Organization in California," United States Senate, Subcommittee of the Committee on Education and Labor (the La Follette Committee), Hearings on S. Res. 266, *Violations of Free Speech and the Rights of Labor,* 75 parts (Washington, DC: Government Printing Office, 1936–1940), Part 54, Exhibit 8762–A, 19777–19898, quotations from 19848–19849 (hereafter LFC *Hearings*); *Pacific Rural Press* quoted in McWilliams, *Factories in the Field,* 181. Tied to the land, California agriculture demanded circulating labor to make the continued circulation of capital possible; on the circulation of capital see David Harvey, *The Limits to Capital* (Baltimore: Johns Hopkins University Press, 1982). Since 1964 (the end of the Bracero Program), vertically integrated agricultural concerns have found a partial solution to this problem by mobilizing their farming operations rather than labor. Many concerns now own or lease land throughout the state (and elsewhere, including northern Mexico) and switch the location of production depending on labor and commodity market conditions, climatic factors, and differential state and local regulations. Agriculture too has become footloose; see Margaret FitzSimmons, "The New Industrial Agriculture: The Regional Integration of Specialty Crop Production," *Economic Geography* 62 (1986): 334–53; W. H. Friedland, A. E. Barton, and R. J. Thomas, *Manufacturing Green Gold* (Cambridge: Cambridge University Press, 1981); for the case of the Midwest, see Brian Page and Richard Walker, "From Settlement to Fordism: The Agro-Industrial Revolution in the American Midwest," *Economic Geography* 67 (1991): 281–353.

10. *San Francisco Examiner,* 5 May 1917, collected in FWP Papers, Carton 11, "Labor Camps, 1917–1920"; the University of California labor economist is quoted in McWilliams, *Factories in the Field,* 174.

11. "Proceedings of the 60th Convention of Fruit Growers and Farmers," *Monthly Bulletin,* California Department of Agriculture, XVIII (2), 115, quoted in FWP, *Oriental and Mexican Labor Unions and Strikes in California Agriculture,* Monograph 9 (1938), section on Mexican unions and strikes, 3; Richardson to Lubin, 31 July 1917, DIR Records, Carton 1, "General Correspondence, 1917; " Denis Nodín Valdés, *Al Norte: Agricultural Workers in the Great Lakes Region, 1917–1970* (Austin: University of Texas Press, 1991), 8.

12. Unmarked newspaper clipping, DIR Records, Carton 1, "General Correspondence, 1917."

13. Richardson to Lubin, 31 July and 7 August, 1917, DIR Records, Carton 1, "General Correspondence, 1917."

14. Unmarked newspaper clipping and Bell to Richardson, 20 September 1917, both in DIR Records, Carton 1, "General Correspondence, 1917."

15. Professor quoted in McWilliams, *Factories in the Field,* 180; Richardson to Bell, 20 September 1917, DIR Records, Carton 1, "General Correspondence, 1917."

16. These contradictions were best personified by Frank Palomares's, CCIH's Spanish-speaking agent. Palomares's job during and after the war was to head off incipient revolts among Mexican workers (a task he performed admirably by all accounts), and to convince workers that the employers, not unions or "agitators," were their best friends. Palomares frequently visited the "concentration camps" established to house imported labor, both to inspect sanitary conditions and to remind workers that they were being held behind fences for their own good. Palomares eventually became the labor agent

and chief recruiter for the giant Spreckles Sugar Company. By 1926 he had moved on to the large-grower-controlled San Joaquin Valley Labor Bureau, which we will encounter in the next chapter. Bell to Gibson 19 November and 27 November, 1917, DIR Records, Carton 1, "General Correspondence, 1917"; Hanna to Waterhouse (Spreckles Sugar Company), 11 February, and Houser to Palomares, 14 February, 1919, DIR Records, Carton 48, "F. J. Palomares"; Waterhouse to Bell, 14 May, and Bernatch to Cunningham, 27 August, 1918, DIR Records, Carton 63, "Letters of Approval—Palomares"; CCIH, *Fifth Annual Report* (Sacramento: State Printing Office, 1919), 24–25.

17. "Report from Memory of Events Connected with the Importation of Mexican Labor by the Sugar Interests of California during the Year 1918," (probably by J. R. Murrison), DIR Records, Carton 6, "Correspondence in Re Camps."

18. See the letters cited in note 16.

19. Agriculturalists and most others at the time made no distinction between "Mexicans," "Mexican Americans," and other Hispanic groups, except in the case of longtime members of the Californio elite who could trace connections to the Spanish and Mexican eras. For agriculturalists it was particularly convenient to claim that all Latinos were Mexicans, and therefore neither citizens nor equal to "Americans."

20. All quotations from Carey McWilliams, *North from Mexico: The Spanish-Speaking People of the United States* (Westport, CT: Greenwood Press, 1968 ed.), 190; figures from 174. CCIH kept records of the nationality of residents of inspected labor camps between its inception and 1940 with the exception of the war years. These records are not an entirely accurate indication of the nationality of all farmworkers, and they probably undercount nonwhite groups who stayed in camps less frequently. Nonetheless, they do give some indication of the relative strength of "Mexican" workers at different times. They accounted for between 11 and 15 percent of all camp residents in the years 1914 and 1915, falling to 7 percent in 1916. In 1922 they constituted 7.5 percent of the camp population, though by the following year the number was approaching 15 percent. With the passage of the 1924 Immigration Act restricting immigration from Europe and Asia, the Hispanic population in inspected camps rose to 25.5 percent of the total in 1926. The pre-World War II camp Hispanic proportion peaked in 1929 at 31.3 percent and again in 1933–34 with 32.5 percent. By 1935–36, the percentage of Mexican workers fell to 22 percent and remained around 20 percent at the beginning of the Bracero program in 1942 (during the 1930s DIH tallied camp population biannually rather than annually). "Report of Carey McWilliams, Chief, State Division of Immigration and Housing," LFC *Hearings,* Part 59, Exhibit 9371, 21887–21913; see also Edward A. Brown, "Labor Camp Sanitation and Housing in California: A History of Progress from 1913–1922," DIR Records, Carton 19, "Immigration."

21. On the history of racism against Asians in California see Roger Daniels, *The Politics of Prejudice: The Anti-Japanese Movement in California and the Struggle for Japanese Exclusion* (Berkeley: University of California Press, 1962); Alexander Saxton, *The Indispensable Enemy: Labor and the Anti-Chinese Movement in California* (Berkeley: University of California Press, 1971); see also Sucheng Chan, *This Bitter Sweet Soil: The Chinese in California Agriculture, 1860–1910* (Berkeley: University of California Press, 1986); a good early work on anti-Latino racism is McWilliams, *North from Mexico*. Kay Anderson's "Cultural Hegemony and the Race-Definition Process in Chinatown, Vancouver: 1880–1980," *Environment and Planning D: Society and Space* 6 (1988):

127–49 is particularly effective in exploring the relationships between landscape and race; see also her *Vancouver's Chinatown* (Montreal: McGill-Queens University Press, 1991). Tracts on the social construction of race that have been influential in geography include Stephen Jay Gould, *The Mismeasure of Man* (New York: W. W. Norton, 1981); R. Lewontin, S. Rose, L. Kamin, *Not in Our Genes: Biology, Ideology, and Human Nature* (New York: Pantheon, 1984); Robert Miles, *Racism and Migrant Labour* (London: Routledge and Kegan Paul, 1982); Nancy Stepan, *The Idea of Race in Science: Great Britain, 1800–1960* (London: Macmillan, 1982). Important geographical examinations of the construction of race include, Peter Jackson and Jan Penrose (eds.), *Constructions of Race, Place and Nation* (Minneapolis: University of Minnesota Press, 1993); Peter Jackson (ed.), *Race and Racism: Essays in Social Geography* (London: Allen and Unwin, 1987).

22. Miles, *Racism and Migrant Labour, 146.*

23. William Cronon, *Changes in the Land: Indians, Colonists, and the Ecology of New England* (New York: Hill and Wang, 1983), 6.

24. Kay Anderson, "The Idea of Chinatown: The Power of Place and Institutional Practice in the Making of a Racial Category," *Annals of the Association of American Geographers* 77 (1987): 580–98; quotation from 584; Anderson, "Cultural Hegemony," 131; Antonio Gramsci, *Selections from the Prison Notebooks* (New York: International Publishers; London: Lawrence and Wishart, 1971; ed. and trans. Geoffrey Nowell Smith and Quentin Hoare).

25. Growers frequently argued that white workers would not do the labor required on farms, and thus racialized labor was a "necessary evil," but since white workers never slipped below 45 percent of the total labor camp population during the period between Wheatland and World War II, explanation for agribusiness' preference for nonwhite workers has to be found elsewhere. "Report of Carey McWilliams"; Brown, "Labor Camp Sanitation and Housing in California"; Cletus Daniel, *Bitter Harvest: A History of Farmworkers in California, 1872–1941* (Ithaca: Cornell University Press, 1981 and Berkeley: University of California Press, 1982), 64.

26. On the relationship between the labor movement and the anti-Chinese movement, see Ira Cross, *History of the Labor Movement in California* (Berkeley: University of California Press, 1935); Daniels, *Politics of Prejudice;* Saxton, *Indispensable Enemy;* Lucie Cheng and Edna Bonacich (eds.), *Labor Immigration under Capitalism: Asian Workers in the United States before World War II* (Berkeley: University of California Press, 1984). Henry George is quoted in Daniels, *Politics of Prejudice,* 69.

27. Quotations from Saxton, *Indispensable Enemy,* 100–103; George discusses Mill in, among others, *Progress and Poverty* (New York: Robert Schellenback, 1971 ed.).

28. Saxton, *Indispensable Enemy,* in this white unionists possessed an important "power to define" that had distinct impacts on the shape of the California landscape. On rural Chinatowns, see Christopher Yip, "A Time for Bitter Strength: the Chinese in Locke, California," *Landscape* 22(2) (1979): 3–13.

29. Chan, *This Bitter Sweet Soil,* 403.

30. Yip, "A Time for Bitter Strength"; see also the data on tenantry and farm-ownership patterns derived from the 1910 census for Contra Costa, Solano, Sacramento, and San Joaquin counties in DIR Records, Carton 40, "Land—Agricultural Occupations

and Values." Toward the end of the nineteenth century, Japanese workers, small owners, and tenants, also ostracized from mainstream society, became important in the Delta.

31. Yip, "A Time for Bitter Strength." Locke remained an intact Chinese town through most of the twentieth century, and has now become a fairly popular tourist attraction. For a fuller discussion of Anglo constructions of "Chineseness," see Anderson, *Vancouver's Chinatown.*

32. Chan, *This Bitter Sweet Soil;* Daniel, *Bitter Harvest;* Daniels, *Politics of Prejudice;* Fuller, "The Supply of Agricultural Labor"; McWilliams, *Factories in the Field;* Frank Van Nuys, "A Progressive Confronts the Race Question: Chester Rowell, the California Alien Land Act of 1913, and the Contradictions of Early Twentieth-Century Racial Thought," *California History* 73 (Spring 1994): 2–13.

33. Regardless of their ethnic or religious affiliation, Indians in California were invariably called "Hindus" or "Hindoos." CCIH, "Power of Aliens to Hold Land in California," 27 May 1915, DIR Records, Carton 40, "Land, Aliens." Sucheta Mazumdar, "Punjabi Agricultural Workers in California, 1905–1945," in Lucie Cheng and Edna Bonacich (eds.), *Labor Immigration under Capitalism,* 549–78, quotations from 558; see also G. R. Hess, "The Forgotten Asian American: The East Indian Community in the United States," *Pacific Historical Review* 43 (1974): 576–96.

34. Brown to Iames, 15 December 1926, DIR Records, Carton 10, "James G. Iames"; Webb to Kearney, 12 July 1926, DIR Records, Carton 10, "Requests for Information"; CCIH *Annual Report* (for 1926) (Sacramento: State Printing Office, 1927).

35. E. A. Brown, "Notes for Yearly Report 'Agricultural Camps,'" DIR Records, Carton 53, "E. A. Brown"; Kearney to McGilton, 16 July 1926, DIR Records, Carton 10, "James G. Iames"; Brown to Edwards, 27 October 1926, DIR Records, Carton 36, "Milton E. Edwards—Inspector."

36. Brown to Johnson, 8 August 1919, DIR Records, Carton 48, "Edward A. Brown"; Edward A. Brown, "Japanese Housing," in State Board of Control, *California and the Oriental* (Sacramento: State Printing Office, 1920), 122. As late as 1939, Division of Immigration and Housing chief Carey McWilliams could report that showers or baths for white workers in California labor camps were a rarity; see "Report of Carey McWilliams, Chief, Division of Immigration and Housing," in LFC *Hearings,* Part 59, Exhibit 9371, 21887–21919; Brown, "Japanese Housing," 122; FWP, *History of Living Conditions Among Migratory Workers in California,* Monograph 17 (1938), 60; see also the photographs of white labor camps in CCIH, *Second Annual Report* (Sacramento: State Printing Office, 1916).

37. Iames to Brown, 13 December 1926, DIR Records, Carton 10, "James G. Iames"; CCIH, *Annual Report* (for 1924) (Sacramento: California State Printing Office, 1925), 14.

38. CCIH, *Annual Report* (for 1924), 14. Four years later CCIH was still trying to "Americanize" the Delta. Iames to Brown, 14 May 1928; Brown to McAllister, 15 May 1928; McAllister to Brown, 16 May 1928; all in DIR Records, Carton 8, "Edward A. Brown, Director"; the 1928 campaign was publicized in the *Sacramento Bee,* 16 May 1928.

39. Hemphill to Brown, 2 February 1922, DIR Records, Carton 19, "Letters Regarding Camp Sanitation."

40. Dr. Charles L. Bennett, *Housing for Field Employees* (n.p., n.d.), copy in DIR Records, Carton 59, "Housing for Field Employees." All quotations in this and the next four paragraphs are from this pamphlet.

41. This, of course, is precisely the theory that guided CCIH in its interventions in the labor landscape; it is also the standard ideology of company towns. See S. Buder, *Pullman: An Experiment in Industrial Order and Community Planning, 1880–1930* (New York: Oxford University Press, 1967); Morris Knowles, *Industrial Housing* (New York: McGraw-Hill, 1920); Jack Reynolds, *The Great Paternalist: Titus Salt and the Growth of Nineteenth-Century Bradford* (New York: St. Martin's Press, 1983).

42. Clements is quoted in Daniels, *Bitter Harvest,* 106; "Labor Camp Inspection Work," DIR Records, Carton 36, "Camp Statistics and Reports."

43. Rugg to Brown, 17 November 1923, DIR Records, Carton 12, "Fred J. Rugg." For a glimpse at the general tenor of the nativism of the 1920s (which has strong similarity to current times) see John Higham's classic, *Strangers in the Land: Patterns of American Nativism, 1860–1925* (New York: Atheneum, 1973); and William Preston, *Aliens and Dissenters: Federal Suppression of Radicals, 1903–1933* (New York: Harper Torchbooks, 1963).

44. CCIH, *Annual Report* (for 1926), 8, 10. This section of the annual report was written by Vincent S. Brown, who later became (a quite ineffectual) chief of the reorganized Division of Immigration and Housing. Brown had little experience in the fields of California. His expertise was in office management and complaint adjudication rather than migratory labor issues; see "Notes about Complaint Department," DIR Records, Carton 50, "Vincent S. Brown."

45. See the next chapter.

46. Hanna to Lee, 24 February 1926. On the response of Mexican-Americans to Hanna's position, see for example, Anonymous to Hanna, 3 March 1926, both in DIR Records, Carton 50, "Mexican Data." Of course these arguments have resurfaced in California in the 1990s with surprisingly little change in rhetoric. The passage of Initiative 187, which restricted rights of immigrants *and their citizen children* and the reelection of Pete Wilson as governor of California in November 1994 show the degree to which such arguments find receptive audiences.

47. FWP, *Labor in the California Cotton Fields,* Monograph 6 (1938), 51; see the fliers produced by the Associated Labor Bureau of the Imperial Valley in DIR Records, Carton 50, "Mexican Data."

48. CCIH, *Annual Report* (for 1926), 17.

49. Brown to Kearney, 23 August 1926, DIR Records, Carton 10, "Edward A. Brown."

50. Frank J. DeAndreis, "Report for December 1932," DIR Records, Carton 71, "Frank J. DeAndreis."

51. CCIH, *Annual Report* (for 1926), 17.

52. Rugg to Brown, 25 May 1926, DIR Records, Carton 10, "Fred J. Rugg"; "Camp Department Arrests and Convictions . . . ," DIR Records, Carton 10, "Arrests and Convictions"; Brown to Rugg, 1 June 1926, DIR Records, "Fred J. Rugg."

53. Rugg to Brown, 19 May and 20 May, 1926; Brown to Rugg, 24 May 1926 and 1 June 1926, all in DIR Records, Carton 10, "Fred J. Rugg."

54. Rugg to Brown, 25 May 1926; 1 June 1926; 26 June 1926; DIR Records, Carton 10, "Fred J. Rugg."

55. Daniel, *Bitter Harvest,* 108; Donald Worster, *Rivers of Empire: Water, Aridity, and the Growth of the Amercian West* (New York: Pantheon, 1985), 198.

56. Harold Bell Wright, *The Winning of Barbara Worth* (New York: A. L. Burt Co.,

1911), 508; quoted in George Henderson, "Romancing the Sand: Constructions of Capital and Nature in Arid America" *Ecumene* 1 (1994): 236–55, quotation from 248.

57. On this point see the CCIH report on the 1928 strike in the Imperial Valley in DIR Records, Carton 53, "Division of Industrial Accidents"; see also Paul Taylor, *Mexican Labor in the United States,* Volume I (New York: Arno Press, 1970, reprint); Liebman, *California Farmlands,* Daniel, *Bitter Harvest;* Worster, *Rivers of Empire;* Henderson, "Romancing the Sand."

5 / The Political Economy of Landscape and the Return of Radicalism

1. David Harvey, *The Limits to Capital* (Oxford: Basil Blackwell, 1982 and Baltimore: Johns Hopkins University Press, 1982), chapters 12 and 13; Neil Smith, *Uneven Development: Nature, Capital and the Production of Space* (Oxford: Basil Blackwell, 1990, 2nd ed.), chapter 4, especially 129; on the control of labor during deflation, see Varden Fuller, "The Supply of Agricultural Labor as a Factor in the Evolution of Farm Organization in California," United States Senate, Subcommittee of the Committee on Education and Labor (the La Follette Committee), Hearings on S. Res. 266, *Violations of Free Speech and the Rights of Labor,* 75 parts (Washington, DC: Government Printing Office, 1936–1940), Part 54, Exhibit 8762–A, 19777–19898 (hereafter LFC *Hearings*).

2. David Harvey, *The Urbanization of Capital* (Oxford: Basil Blackwell, 1989), 81; *The Limits to Capital,* 233; *The Condition of Postmodernity* (Oxford: Basil Blackwell, 1989), 83.

3. See the discussion of Filipino farm workers in Ronald Takaki, *Strangers from a Different Shore: A History of Asian Americans* (New York: Penguin, 1989), chapter 9.

4. Ellen Liebman, *California Farmlands: A History of Large Agricultural Landholdings* (Boston: Rowman and Allenheld, 1983), 91; United States Senate Subcommittee of the Committee on Education and Labor (the La Follette Committee), *Violations of Free Speech and the Rights of Labor, Report of the Committee on Education and Labor, Pursuant to S. Res. 266* (hereafter LFC *Report*). Report 1150, parts 1–4, 77th Congress (Washington, DC: Government Printing Office, 1942) and Report 398, parts 4 and 5, 78th Congress (Washington, DC: Government Printing Office, 1944). Part III: "The Disadvantaged Status of Labor in California's Industrialized Agriculture," 277–96; Gluth to Brown, 6 October 1928, Department of Industrial Relations, Division of Immigration and Housing Records, Bancroft Library, University of California, Berkeley (hereafter DIR Records), Carton 8, "John L. Gluth."

5. S. I. Merrill & Sons to Immigration and Housing, 11 September 1925, DIR Records, Carton 64, "Anton Scar, Chief Camp Inspector."

6. Liebman, *California Farmlands,* 97; LFC *Report,* Part III, 264.

7. LFC *Report,* Part III, section 3 and 268–97; Part IV, 414–26; Clarke A. Chambers, *California Farm Organizations* (Berkeley: University of California Press, 1952), 29; see also C. C. Teague, *Fifty Years a Rancher* (Self Published, n.d.); Carey McWilliams, *Factories in the Field* (Santa Barbara: Peregrine Smith, 1971 ed.), 186–87. McWilliams suggests that membership in cooperative associations was not always voluntary; incidents of violent persuasion to force compliance and membership (and thus control over

prices and markets) were not rare. Charles Teague's self-published *Fifty Years a Rancher* provides an enlightening, inside, story of the development of Sunkist and Diamond.

8. LFC *Report,* Part IV, 496–521; McWilliams, *Factories in the Field,* 190–93.

9. "Palomares Report," DIR Records, Carton 24, "Edward A. Brown."

10. CCIH, *Annual Report* (for 1922) cited in FWP, *Labor in the California Cotton Fields* (Monograph 6); Fuller, "The Supply of Agricultural Labor," Appendix A, Tables 24, 26–A, 42; U.S. Bureau of the Census, *Fifteenth Census of the United States: 1930, Census of Agriculture, Large Scale Farming in the United States, 1929,* 21.

11. Fuller, "The Supply of Agricultural Labor," 19779, appendix A, tables 24 and 42; William Preston, *Vanishing Landscapes: Land and Life in the Tulare Lake Basin* (Berkeley: University of California Press, 1981), 202–3; Paul Taylor and Tom Vassey, "Historical Background of California Farm Labor," *Rural Sociology* 1 (1936): 282–85.

12. Brown to Kearney, 22 April 1926, DIR Records, Carton 10, "Edward A. Brown."

13. When labor was much more militant during the 1930s, Brown's suggestion was finally acted upon. See chapter 8.

14. CCIH, *Annual Report* (for 1924) (Sacramento: State Printing Office, 1925), 18–19; LFC *Hearings,* "Report of Carey McWilliams, Chief, Division of Immigration and Housing," Part 59, Exhibit 9371, 21887–21919; Samuel Wood, "The California State Commission of Immigration and Housing: A Study of Administrative Organization and the Growth of Function," Ph.D. dissertation, University of California, Berkeley, 1942.

15. First quotation from Fuller, "The Supply of Agricultural Labor," 19869; second from McWilliams, *Factories in the Field,* 197.

16. Anon., "The Beggar on Wheels," *Industrial Pioneer* 3 (January 1926): 29.

17. CCIH, *Annual Report* (for 1924), 25.

18. "Itinerary for Inspector Edwards," DIR Records, Carton 33, "Itinerary of Camp Inspectors"; Iames to Brown, 22 August 1927; DIR Records, Carton 6, "James G. Iames—Inspector"; Brown to [Various Growers], 5 August 1922, DIR Records, Carton 6, "List of Hops Growers"; "1927—Camp Violation Record—Sacramento District," DIR Records, Carton 8, "James G. Iames."

19. Hewlett to Brown, 6 August 1927, DIR Records, Carton 6, "Correspondence in Re Camp."

20. Gluth to Brown, 10 September 1927; Brown to Gluth, 12 September 1927, DIR Records, Carton 6, "John L. Gluth."

21. See the correspondence in DIR Records, Carton 48, "IWW"; Scanlon to Lubin, 23 May 1923; Brown to Scanlon, 23 January 1923, DIR Records, Carton 12, "Letters M–Z"; Brown to Quinn, 23 March 1923, DIR Records, Carton 12, "Edward A. Brown, 1923"; Brown to Rugg, 27 October 1924, DIR Records, Carton 36, "Fred J. Rugg—Inspector"; "Report on IWW Situation," DIR Records, Carton 36, "Camp Statistics"; Kearney to Iames, 21 August 1926; Iames to Brown, 21 August 1926, DIR Records, Carton 10, "James G. Iames"; CCIH, *Annual Report* (for 1924), 25.

22. *San Francisco Examiner,* 25 August 1918. Fickert had a rather interesting career, including involvement in bombing the governor's mansion as a means of framing Sacramento IWWS. Federal investigators were never able to connect any arrested Wobblies to the bombing (in which Governor Stephens was not injured), and they had to settle instead for less spectacular charges of espionage and antidraft agitation; Lubin to Masden, 1 July 1918, DIR Records, Carton 1, "General Correspondence, 1918"; Wood,

"The California State Commission of Immigration and Housing"; Preston, *Aliens and Dissenters*.

23. Wood, "The California State Commission of Immigration and Housing, 122–23, 131–32.

24. Ibid., 130–38, quotations from 134, 137; see also Robert Burke, *Olson's New Deal for California* (Berkeley: University of California Press, 1953).

25. Carey McWilliams interview, in "Earl Warren: Visions and Episodes," Earl Warren Oral History Project, Regional Cultural History Project, Bancroft Library, University of California, 23; my assessment of the relative impotence of CCIH relies on the analysis of Wood, "The California State Commission."

26. Kearney to Inspectors, 14 April 1928, DIR Records, Carton 8, "Memoranda to Camp Inspectors."

27. For histories of this strike see Cletus Daniel, *Bitter Harvest: A History of California Farmworkers, 1870–1941* (Ithaca: Cornell University Press, 1981 and Berkeley: University of California Press, 1982), 108–9; Taylor, *Mexican Labor*, 45–54; Charles Wollenberg, "Huelga, 1928 Style: The Imperial Valley Canteloupe Workers' Strike," *Pacific Historical Review*, 38 (1969): 45–58; unmarked newspaper clipping, 10 May 1928a, DIR Records, Carton 61, "Imperial Valley Data—1928–29–30."

28. Unmarked newspaper clippings, 10 May 1928a, 10 May 1928b, DIR Records, Carton 61, "Imperial Valley Data—1928–29–30"; Degnan to Kearney, 12 May 1928, DIR Records, Carton 53, "C. A. Degnan—Fresno"; Taylor, *Mexican Labor*, 50; the growers' circular is quoted in Taylor, *Mexican Labor*, 49; Daniel, *Bitter Harvest*, 108.

29. Degnan to Kearney, 21 May 1928, DIR Records, Carton 53, "C. A. Degnan—Fresno"; Rugg to Brown, 23 May, 26 May, 25 June, 1928, Carton 8, "Fred J. Rugg."

30. Rugg to Brown, 25 June, 20 November, 3 December, 14 December, 18 December, 1928 and 9 June 1929; Brown to Rugg, 15 December 1928, DIR Records, Carton 8, "Fred J. Rugg"; Brown to Kearney, 11 January 1929, DIR Records, Carton 53, "Edward A. Brown"; Gluth to Degnan, 25 January 1929, Degnan to Kearney, 4 February 1929, DIR Records, Carton 53, "C. A. Degnan—Fresno"; "Report," DIR Records, Carton 53, "Division of Industrial Accidents."

31. My account here relies on Daniel, *Bitter Harvest*, 111–18; histories of the communist unions, their role in California and their relationship to the American labor movement may be found in Daniel, *Bitter Harvest*, 110–11; Stuart Jamieson, *Labor Unionism in American Agriculture* (New York: Arno Press, 1976, reprint), 19–21; Linda Majka and Theo Majka, *Farmworkers, Agribusiness, and the State* (Philadelphia: Temple University Press, 1982), 68.

32. On the domestic U.S. politics of the Philippines' independence, see Ronald Takaki, *Strangers from a Different Shore: A History of Asian Americans* (New York: Penguin, 1989), 331–32.

33. Daniel, *Bitter Harvest*, 120–21.

34. Rugg to Brown, 16 May 1930, DIR Records, Carton 86, "Fred J. Rugg"; "Report of the Division of Housing and Sanitation," 17 September 1930, and 21 October 1930; "Department of Industrial Relations Monthly Report: September," 28 September 1930, DIR Records, Carton 86, "Reports."

35. "October Report" (1930), DIR Records, Carton 86, "Edward A. Brown"; "Report for W. J. French," DIR Records, Carton 53, "Division of Industrial Accidents and Safety."

By the time descriptions of conditions made it to French's monthly report to the Governor's Council, all references to substandard conditions had been eliminated. See Edwards to Brown, 1 October 1930, DIR Records, Carton 61, "M. E. Edwards"; Iames to Brown, 14 October 1930, DIR Records, Carton 61, "J. G. Iames"; Brown to Gluth, 6 November 1930, DIR Records, Carton 61, "John L. Gluth"; DeAndreis to Kearney, 8 March 1930, DIR Records, Carton 86, "Frank J. DeAndreis"; Wiggins to Kearney, 1 October 1931, "L. B. Wiggins, Camp Inspector."

36. Barnes to Dr. A. Brown, 22 September 1930, DIR Records, Carton 61, "General Correspondence, A-M." See the comments by Dr. Lee Stone, LFC *Hearings*, "Conference on Housing Migratory Agricultural Laborers," 13 December 1934, Part 62, Exhibit 9577–A, 22547–22550.

37. Gluth to Division of Housing and Sanitation, 28 August 1930; Gluth to Brown, 29 August 1930, DIR Records, Carton 61, "John L. Gluth."

6 / The Disintegration of Landscape: The Workers' Revolt of 1933

1. Elizabeth Helsinger, "Turner and the Representation of England," in W. J. T. Mitchell (ed.), *Landscape and Power* (Chicago: University of Chicago Press, 1994), 107; see also John Barrell, *The Dark Side of Landscape: The Poor in English Painting, 1730–1840* (Cambridge: Cambridge University Press, 1980).

2. Henri Lefebvre, *The Production of Space* (Oxford: Basil Blackwell, 1991, trans. Donald Nicholson-Smith), 34; Paul Taylor and Clark Kerr, "Documentary History of the Strike of the Cotton Pickers in California, 1933," in United States Senate, Subcommittee of the Committee on Education and Labor (the La Follette Committee), Hearings on S. Res. 266, *Violations of Free Speech and the Rights of Labor*, 75 parts (Washington, DC: Government Printing Office, 1936–1940), Part 54, Exhibit 8764, 19945–20036 (hereafter LFC *Hearings*).

3. Ronald Takaki, *Strangers from a Different Shore: A History of Asian Americans* (New York: Penguin, 1987), chapter 9, provides an excellent account of the reception of Filipinos in California, their struggle to make a home there, and their militancy in the fields in face of an exceptionally violent (even by California standards) racist reaction to their presence. See also Carey McWilliams, *Factories in the Field* (Santa Barbara: Peregrine Smith, 1971 ed.), 137–43; *San Joaquin Valley Press,* 7 October 1926 and *San Francisco News,* 7 October 1926, both collected in Department of Industrial Relations, Division of Immigration and Housing Records, Bancroft Library, University of California, Berkeley (hereafter DIR Records), Carton 10, "Camp Clippings"; and "Report on the Filipino Situation, Exeter, California" (November 1929), DIR Records, Carton 53, "C. A. Degnan—Fresno"; Edwards to Brown, 10 December 1932, DIR Records, Carton 69, "1932 M. E. Edwards."

4. United States Senate Subcommittee of the Committee on Education and Labor (the La Follette Committee), *Violations of Free Speech and the Rights of Labor, Report of the Committee on Education and Labor, Pursuant to S. Res. 266* (hereafter LFC *Report*). Report 1150, parts 1–4, 77th Congress (Washington, DC: Government Printing Office, 1942) and Report 398, parts 4 and 5, 78th Congress (Washington, DC: Government Printing Office, 1944). Part III, 265–66; for a general account of agricultural

228 / Notes to Chapter 6

economies and practices in the Salinas Valley during different periods, see Margaret
FitzSimmons, "Consequences of Agricultural Industrialization: Environmental and
Social Change in the Salinas Valley, 1945–1978," Ph.D. dissertation, University of
California, Los Angeles, 1983.

5. Fortier to Edwards, 14 March 1933; Brown to Fortier, 16 March 1933; Edwards
to V. Brown, 18 March 1933; Edwards to E. Brown, 18 March 1933; Report of E. Brown,
31 March 1933, all in DIR Records, Carton 85, "1933 General Correspondence."

6. *San Francisco Chronicle,* 6 September, 7 September, 6 November, 1934; Howard
DeWitt, "The Filipino Labor Union: The Salinas Strike of 1934," *Amerasia* 5 (2) (1978):
15; Stuart Jamieson, *Labor Unionism in American Agriculture* (New York: Arno Press,
1976 reprint), 129–30; Carey McWilliams, *Factories in the Field,* 133.

7. "California Farm Wage Rate Data," LFC *Hearings,* Part 62, Exhibit 9575,
22525; and Part 48 Exhibit 8128, 17887; California State Relief Administration,
Migratory Labor in California—1936 (Sacramento: Mimeo, 1936); Cletus Daniel, *Bitter
Harvest: A History of California Farmworkers, 1870–1941* (Ithaca: Cornell University
Press, 1981 and Berkeley: University of California Press, 1982), 141.

8. Daniel, *Bitter Harvest,* 144–66; Jamieson, *Labor Unionism,* 17, 86–105; the as-
sumption that labor militancy was a white phenomenon is clearly expressed in Ellen
Liebman, *California Farmlands: A History of Large Agricultural Landholdings* (Boston:
Rowman and Allenheld, 1983); Linda C. Majka and Theo Majka, *Farmworkers,
Agribusiness and the State* (Philadelphia: Temple University Press, 1982). Sucheng Chan,
This Bitter Sweet Soil: The Chinese in California Agriculture, 1860–1910 (Berkeley: University of California Press, 1986), criticizes most of the standard histories of California
farmworkers for writing nonwhites out of the picture, though she surely is mistaken
when she accuses McWilliams, Fuller, Taylor, and other early historians of California
farm labor of blaming Asians and Mexicans for causing their own oppression. Rather
these authors all show quite clearly how nonwhite workers continually struggled against
the conditions within which they worked.

9. Buck to Bell, 1 May 1918, DIR Records, Carton 63, "Letters of Approval:
Palomares"; Daniel, *Bitter Harvest,* 136–40.

10. Daniel, *Bitter Harvest,* 136–40; Orrick Johns, *Times of Our Lives,* quoted in
McWilliams, *Factories in the Field,* 215–17.

11. Daniel, *Bitter Harvest,* 144; Jamieson, *Labor Unionism,* 89; McWilliams, *Factories
in the Field,* 215–17.

12. Daniel, *Bitter Harvest,* 144; *Oakland Tribune,* 13 April 1934; statement of
Vincent Brown, Conference on Housing Migratory Agricultural Workers, December
1934, in LFC *Hearings,* Part 62, Exhibit 9577–A, 22551; see also the Statement of
Conover, ibid., 22544–22545; Federal Writers Project, *Labor in the Market Pea Crop,*
(1938), 35–36.

13. Johns, *Times of Our Lives* in McWilliams, *Factories in the Field;* for a fictionalized
account of the role that strikers camps played in farmworker strikes of the era, an
account that apparently draws on many of the strikes discussed in this chapter, see John
Steinbeck, *In Dubious Battle* (New York: Penguin, 1986).

14. Sheriff quoted in Daniel, *Bitter Harvest,* 144–45; *Western Worker,* 1 May 1933;
nowhere else in the records of CCIH and DIH could I find evidence that similar complaints led to a demand that camps be closed—unless the offenses were repeated several

times and the operator refused to cooperate with the Commission on improvements. As the strikes of 1933 progressed, however, DIH increasingly demanded that strikers' camps be closed for infractions common in growers' camps. As the pea harvest moved to the coastal farms of San Mateo County in June, the only records of camp operator arrests and convictions are of supply camp operators in the area. Worried that the Alameda strike would rekindle in San Mateo, DIH was taking no chances. See DIR Records, Carton 85, "1933—Arrests and Convictions."

15. Jamieson, *Labor Unionism*, 89; *Oakland Tribune*, 14, 15 April 1933; *Western Worker*, 24 April 1933; Daniel, *Bitter Harvest*, 144–45.

16. On the necessarily territorial nature of class struggle, see Henri Lefebvre, *The Production of Space* (Oxford: Basil Blackwell, 1989, trans. Donald Nicholson-Smith).

17. LFC *Report*, Part IV, 501–4.

18. Jamieson, *Labor Unionism*, 92–95; Daniel, *Bitter Harvest*, 154–57.

19. See the tabulation of store prices in the Paul Taylor *Papers*, Bancroft Library, University of California, Berkeley (CR-3), "Information Presented by Strikers"; Statement of Charles Merritt, LFC *Hearings*, Conference on Housing of Migratory Agricultural Workers," December 1934, Part 62, Exhibit 9577–A, 22545; statement of Frank Palomares, ibid., 22552.

20. Daniel, *Bitter Harvest*, 157.

21. Soon after the CAWIU meeting, strike meetings were held throughout the peach picking region that stretched from Sutter and Butte counties in the north to Fresno and Tulare counties in the South. A brief strike netted workers an increase from 17½¢ to 25–27½¢ per hour. CAWIU's militant activism convinced San Jose peach growers and canners to seek arbitration. Though CAWIU had demanded 30¢ an hour, they considered the arbitrator's 25¢ compromise a victory.

22. Jamieson, *Labor Unionism*, 94; Daniel, *Bitter Harvest*, 95, 157–58.

23. Jamieson, *Labor Unionism*, 97; Daniel, *Bitter Harvest*, 161.

24. Local police monitored the organizing efforts carefully, and their reports may be found in LFC *Hearings*, Part 71, Exhibit 13389, 26668–26674; On the "Colonel's" colorful history, see LFC *Report*, Parts IV and V; accounts of the Lodi strike are available in Daniel, *Bitter Harvest*, 162–63; Jamieson, *Labor Unionism*, 98.

25. Daniel, *Bitter Harvest*, 163.

26. Paul Taylor and Clark Kerr, "Documentary History," 199947; "Notes from C. Decker Talk at International House (Berkeley) 11–27–33," Paul Taylor Papers (CR-3). "Notes in Re California Cotton Pickers Strike."

27. "Hearings Held on the Cotton Strike in the San Joaquin Valley by the Fact Finding Committee Appointed by James Rolph, Governor of the State of California," LFC *Hearings*, Part 54, Exhibit 8763, 19917; "Report of the Labor Commissioner Frank C. McDonald to Governor James Rolph, Jr., on the San Joaquin Valley Cotton Strike, September-October, 1933," LFC *Hearings*, Part 54, Exhibit 8762–B; Taylor and Kerr, "A Documentary History"; McWilliams, *Factories in the Field*, 220; "Notes on C. Decker Talk"; Daniel, *Bitter Harvest*, 180–81.

28. Interview with Clarence H. Wilson, District Attorney, Kings County, 22 December, 1933, Paul Taylor Papers (CR-3), "Field Notes."

29. *Corcoran News*, 6 October 1933, in Taylor and Kerr, "A Documentary History," 19975.

30. Taylor and Kerr, "A Documentary History," 19775; Interview with Morgan, Paul Taylor Papers (CR-3), "Field Notes"; Daniel, *Bitter Harvest,* 187.

31. "Notes from C. Decker talk"; Interview with Morgan; "Report on Cotton Strikers, Kings County," Paul Taylor Papers, "California Emergency Relief Administration"; Taylor and Kerr, "A Documentary History," 19975; Daniel, *Bitter Harvest,* 187; E. A. Brown, "Oct. 7—Headquarters in the cotton Fields," DIR Records, Carton 86, loose material; Conference on Housing Migratory Laborers, December, 1934, 22545–22547.

32. Schooling had often been haphazard for the children of migratory workers, and when schooling was available migratory children were segregated from local children. Mexican migratory children were segregated because they were Mexican; later white Dust Bowl migratory children were segregated because they were migratory. "Report on the Cotton Strikers"; Interview with Morgan; McWilliams, *Factories in the Field,* 220–21; Taylor and Kerr, "A Documentary History," 19975.

33. Interview with Clarence Wilson; Taylor and Kerr, "A Documentary History," 19776.

34. *Los Angeles Times,* 25 October 1933; quoted in Taylor and Kerr, "A Documentary History," 19976.

35. Interview with Morgan, Paul Taylor Papers, "Field Notes"; Taylor and Kerr, "A Documentary History."

36. Conference on Housing of Migratory Agricultural Laborers, December 1934, 22547–22551; as noted earlier, DIH played a quite limited role in the cotton strike, though it did comment internally on the great influx of scab workers recruited from outside the region—presumably by Palomares; E. A. Brown, "Oct. 7—Headquarters in the Cotton Fields," DIR Records, Carton 86, Loose Material; FWP, "The California Cotton Pickers' Strike—1933," Monograph 5 (1938), 47–48.

37. *Hanford Journal,* 12 October 1933; 22 October 1933; *Corcoran News,* 20 October 1933, *Tulare Advance-Register,* 19 October 1933; all in Taylor and Kerr, "A Documentary History," 19977.

38. *Bakersfield Californian,* 7 October 1933; Taylor and Kerr, "A Documentary History," 19987–19988.

39. "Hearing Held on the Cotton Strike in the San Joaquin Valley by the Fact Finding Committee," 19940.

40. Taylor and Kerr, "A Documentary History," 19984; Diane Avery, "Images of Violence in Labor Jurisprudence: The Regulation of Picketing and Boycotts, 1894-1921," *Buffalo Law Review* 37 (1988/89): 1–117; Don Mitchell, "Political Violence, Order, and the Legal Construction of Public Space: Power and the Public Forum Doctrine," unpublished paper, Department of Geography, University of Colorado.

41. *Tulare Advance-Register,* 18 October 1933, collected in Paul Taylor Papers (CR-3), "Information Presented by Strikers."

42. Interview by Taylor, quoted in Taylor and Kerr, "A Documentary History," 19990.

43. Taylor and Kerr, "A Documentary History," 19990–19991; Daniel, *Bitter Harvest,* 196–201.

44. "Hearings Held on the Cotton Strike in the San Joaquin Valley by the Fact Finding Committee," 19928; Daniel, *Bitter Harvest,* 195; Taylor and Kerr, "A Documentary History," 19988–19989; McWilliams, *Factories in the Field,* 221–22.

45. Visalia *Times-Delta,* 2 November 1933; Taylor and Kerr, "A Documentary History, 19988–19989; Daniel, *Bitter Harvest,* 201–2.

46. Daniel, *Bitter Harvest,* 202.

47. Daniel, *Bitter Harvest,* 204–12; Taylor and Kerr, "A Documentary History," 19994; "Report on the Cotton Strikers," Paul Taylor Papers (CR-3), "California Emergency Relief Administration."

48. "Report of the State Labor Commissioner: 19906–19908; "Report on Cotton Strikers"; Daniel, *Bitter Harvest,* 213.

49. Taylor and Kerr, "A Documentary History."

50. Daniel, *Bitter Harvest,* 216–17; Taylor and Kerr, "A Documentary History," 20007.

51. Stephen Daniels and Denis Cosgrove, "Introduction: Iconography and Landscape," in Denis Cosgrove and Stephen Daniels (eds.), *The Iconography of Landscape: Essays on the Symbolic Representation, Design and Use of Past Environments* (Cambridge: Cambridge University Press, 1988), 1–11, quotation from 1; Stephen Daniels, "Marxism, Culture and the Duplicity of Landscape," in Richard Peet and Nigel Thrift (eds.), *New Models in Geography, Volume II* (London: Unwin Hyman, 1989), 196–220, quotation from 206.

52. Jean Baudrillard, *America* (London: Verso, 1988), 72.

7 / Reclaiming the Landscape: Learning to Control the Spaces of Revolt

1. Leonard Commission, "Report to the Labor Board by Special Commission," United States Senate, Subcommittee of the Committee on Education and Labor (the La Follette Committee), Hearings on S. Res. 266, *Violations of Free Speech and the Rights of Labor,* 75 parts (Washington, DC: Government Printing Office, 1936–1940), Part 54, Exhibit 8766; The Leonard Commission included Simon Lubin, and many of its recommendations clearly reflected the old interests of CCIH. See Cletus Daniel, *Bitter Harvest: A History of California Farmworkers, 1870–1941* (Ithaca: Cornell University Press, 1981 and Berkeley: University of California Press, 1982), 224. "Original Inspection Only (Not Reinspection) Imperial County," and "Imperial County Labor Camp Reinspection," both in Department of Industrial Relations, Division of Immigration and Housing Records, Bancroft Library, University of California, Berkeley (hereafter DIR records), Carton 86, "Imperial County Labor Unrest."

2. Stuart Jamieson, *Labor Unionism in American Agriculture* (New York: Arno Press, 1976 reprint), 108–9; Daniel, *Bitter Harvest,* 224–28; Leonard Commission, "Report of the Labor Board," 20043; "The Imperial Valley Farm Labor Situation" (hereafter, Hutchison Report), LFC *Hearings,* Part 54, exhibit 8767–A, 20053–20063; "Campbell McCullough's Report—Labor Conditions in the Imperial Valley," LFC *Hearings,* Part 54, Exhibit 8765, 20037–20041.

3. United States Senate Subcommittee of the Committee on Education and Labor (the La Follette Committee), *Violations of Free Speech and the Rights of Labor, Report of the Committee on Education and Labor, Pursuant to S. Res. 266* (hereafter LFC *Report*). Report 1150, parts 1–4, 77th Congress (Washington, DC: Government Printing Office, 1942) and Report 398, parts 4 and 5, 78th Congress (Washington, DC: Government Printing Office, 1944). (Report 1150), Part 9, 1651; Leonard Commission, "Report to

the Labor Board," 20044; Hutchison Report, 20058–20059; McCullough Report, 20038; Daniel, *Bitter Harvest,* 227–29; Jamieson, *Labor Unionism,* 108–9.

4. Leonard Commission, "Report to the Labor Board," 20044, 20049, Hutchison Report, 20059; Daniel, *Bitter Harvest,* 229–31.

5. The Hutchison Committee consisted also of W. C. Jacobsen of the State Department of Agriculture, and Assemblyman John Phillips, a notoriously right-wing growers advocate (who later in the decade returned from a tour of Europe with great praise for the disciplined societies of Germany and Italy).

6. Hutchison Report, 20059.

7. Daniel, *Bitter Harvest,* 228.

8. Leonard Commission, "Report to the Labor Bureau," 20049.

9. Hutchison Report, 20060–20063; Leonard Commission, "Report to the Labor Board," 20052; LFC *Hearings,* "Supplement to the Report Entitled 'The Imperial Farm Labor Situations,'" Part 54, Exhibit 8767–B, 20065–20068; Donald Worster, *Rivers of Empire: Water, Aridity and the Growth of the American West* (New York: Pantheon, 1985); George Henderson, "Romancing the Sand: Constructions of Capital and Nature in Arid America," *Ecumene* 1 (1994): 236–55.

10. Interview with DIH inspectors Mott and Rugg by C. B. Hutchison, and Statement of Charles E. Weir, Claude Hutchison Papers, Bancroft Library, University of California, Berkeley, "Notes"; For a discussion of similar attitudes about fenced compounds and guards in the northern part of the state, see Philip Bancroft, "Politics, Family and the Progressive Party in California," Oral History Interview by Willa Klug Baum, Regional Cultural History Project, Bancroft Library (1962), 371–73; Jamieson, *Labor Unionism,* 109–10.

11. Mott to Brown, 19 February 1934, DIR Records, Carton 86, "Imperial Unrest, 1934"; Interview with Dr. W. F. Fox, County Health Office, Claude Hutchison Papers, "Notes."

12. Mott to Brown, 19 February 1934, DIR Records, Carton 86, "Imperial Unrest, 1934."

13. Mott to V. Brown, 20 February 1934, DIR Records, Carton 86, "Imperial Unrest, 1934"; Interview with F. J. Rugg and Notes on Talk with DIH Inspector, Hutchison Papers, "Notes"; for more on the role that DIH employees played in this strike see Wyzanski to Glassford, 27 March 1934, LFC *Hearings,* Part 55, Exhibit 8914, 20298.

14. Leonard Commission, "Report to the Labor Bureau"; Mott to E. Brown, 17 March and 24 April 1934, DIR Records, Carton 86, "Imperial Unrest, 1934"; Daniel, *Bitter Harvest,* 237–39; LFC *Hearings,* Part 55, 20136–20351; *Los Angeles Times,* 18 March 1934, collected in DIR Records, Carton 86, "Imperial Unrest, 1934."

15. Quoted in Daniel, *Bitter Harvest,* 248–49.

16. Cletus Daniel's analysis of this strike and state involvement in it is excellent; see *Bitter Harvest,* 240–49, quotation from 249; see also LFC *Hearings,* Part 55, Exhibit 8915–8918, 20298–20312.

17. Warren to V. Brown, 30 April 1934, DIR Records, Carton 86, "Alameda County Labor Unrest, 1934."

18. *San Francisco Examiner,* 8 April 1934, FWP, *Labor in the Market Pea Crop* (1938), 53. Report for April, 1934, DIR Records, Carton 65, "Timothy Reardon"; Brown Statement, "Conference on Housing of Migratory Agricultural Workers," 15 December 1934; LFC *Hearings,* Part 62, Exhibit 9577–A, 22550–22551; Monthly Report [March 1934], and

Labor Camp Report, April 1934, DIR Records, Carton 65, "Timothy Reardon"; LFC *Hearings,* Part 70, Exhibit 12464, 25723–25724; Exhibit 12466, 25725.

19. V. Brown Statement, "Conference on Housing Migratory Agricultural Workers," 22550; July Report [1934] DIR Records, Carton 65, "Edward A. Brown"; *Marysville Appeal-Democrat* 14 July 1934; *Oakland Tribune,* 14 March 1935.

20. *San Francisco News,* 5 May 1934, reprinted in LFC *Hearings,* Part 70, Exhibit 12463, 25720–25721; Warren to Lubin, 30 April 1934; Lubin to Warren, 1 May 1934, LFC *Hearings,* Part 70, Exhibit 12463, 25722; Vincent Brown Statement, "Conference on Housing Migratory Agricultural Workers," 22550.

21. LFC *Hearings,* "Selected Large-Scale Farming Operations in California," Part 62, Exhibit 9587, 22776–22777; Jamieson, *Labor Unionism,* 112.

22. Edwards to Brown, 11 November 1929, DIR Records, Carton 5, "E. A. Brown"; LFC *Hearings,* "Proceedings of a Series of Conferences on Housing Migratory Laborers," Part 62, Exhibits 9577A-D, 22541–22642; Bancroft, "Politics, Family, and the Progressive Party"; Winters to Shakey, 25 February 1933, DIR Records, Carton 85, "General Correspondence, 1933."

23. *Sacramento Valley Labor Bulletin,* "Brentwood Camp of Balfour Guthrie Warrants Real Investigation," 7 August 1931, collected in DIH Records, Carton 87, "Will J. French"; LFC *Hearings,* Testimony of C. B. Weeks, Part 49, 18017–18022.

24. LFC *Hearings,* "Proceedings of a Series of Conferences on Housing Migratory Laborers"; LFC *Hearings,* Testimony of C. B. Weeks; Jamieson, *Labor Unionism,* 112.

25. Bancroft, "Politics, Family, and the Progressive Party," 360–61.

26. Ibid., 12.

27. *San Francisco Examiner,* "200 Herded into Cattle Pen for Bay County Red Ouster," collected in DIR Records, Carton 86, "Contra Costa County—Labor Camp Unrest"; LFC *Hearings,* Testimony of C. B. Weeks; and "Radical Efforts to Precipitate Strike of Workers in Orchards and Packing Plants in Brentwood, Contra Costa County, Apricot District," Part 49, Exhibit 8283, 18155–18157; Jamieson, *Labor Unionism,* 112.

28. Garrison to Frazier, 28 June 1934, LFC *Hearings,* Part 73, Exhibit 13549, 26912–16914; *Western Worker,* 11 June 1934; "Radical Efforts to Organize," 18155–56; Daniel, *Bitter Harvest,* 252–54; Jamieson, *Labor Unionism,* 112–13. The Communist Party dissolved CAWIU as it reverted to an older policy of "boring from within" more conservative unions as part of its "Popular Front" initiative of the mid-1930s. The problem with this strategy in the California fields is that there really were no unions within which to bore. The abandonment of the union in the name of a "Popular Front" in California agriculture simply meant the abandonment of workers. While the record of CAWIU was as mixed as was that of the IWW in the fields of California, it did reinforce the legacy of radicalism that has long marked the poorest workers in the state. And it pioneered important spatial strategies for fighting against the power of agribusiness.

29. "Press Release, Beginning 1935 Harvest," LFC *Hearings,* Part 73, Exhibit 13550, 26914; unmarked newspaper clipping (mid August 1934), DIR Records, "1934 E. A. Brown."

30. LFC *Hearings,* Testimony of Sheriff J. Miller, 17999–18013; Miller to Aram and Wretman, 25 November 1936, LFC *Hearings,* Part 49, Exhibit 8264, 18137–18138; Daily Reports of J. Miller, 30 June 1935, 27 June 1935, 15 June 1935, 13 June 1935, LFC *Hearings,* Part 49, Exhibits 8272–8274, 8276, 18143–18145, 18146–18147.

31. Miller to Aram and Wretman, 25 November 1936; Employment Record Card, LFC *Hearings,* Part 49, Exhibit 8264, 18139–18140.

32. Testimony of J. Miller; Miller to Aram and Wretman, 25 November 1936.

33. Miller to Aram and Wretman, 25 November 1936; Bancroft, "Politics, Family, and the Progressive Party," 364–65.

34. "Press Release, Beginning 1935 Harvest"; Testimony of J. Miller; on the employment agencies, see Carey McWilliams, *Factories in the Field* (Santa Barbara: Peregrine Smith, 1971 ed.), 285–96.

35. Miller to Aram and Wretman, 1 December 1936, LFC *Hearings,* Part 49, Exhibit 8275, 18146; testimony of J. Miller.

36. Daily Report of J. Miller, 6 July 1936, LFC *Hearings,* Part 49, Exhibit 8277, 18147–18148.

37. LFC *Report,* Part VIII; see also the series of reports and correspondences in LFC *Hearings,* Part 73, Exhibits 13548–13631, 26911–26963; LFC *Hearings,* Employment Record Card, Part 49, Exhibit 18139–18140; Employees Record (c. 1935) and Employees Living Quarters Agreement (c. 1935), I. W. Wood Papers, Bancroft Library, University of California, Berkeley, Box 1, "Forms Used in Camps."

38. LFC *Report,* Part VIII; Daniel, *Bitter Harvest,* chapter 8.

39. Raymond Williams, *The Country and the City* (Oxford: Oxford University Press, 1973); see also Michel Foucault, "The Eye of Power," in C. Gordon (ed.), *Power/ Knowledge: Selected Interviews and Other Writings, 1972–1977* (New York: Pantheon, 1980); Matthew Hannah, "Space and Social Control in the Administration of the Oglala Lakota ('Sioux'), 1871–1879," *Journal of Historical Geography* 19 (1993): 412–32.

40. WPA, *California: Guide to the Golden State* (New York: Hastings House, 1939), 582–83; Peirce Lewis, "Axioms for Reading the Landscape: Some Guides to the American Scene," In D. W. Meinig (ed.), *The Interpretation of Ordinary Landscapes: Geographical Essays* (New York: Oxford University Press, 1979), 11–32; Bruno Latour, *Science in Action: How to Follow Scientists and Engineers through Society* (Cambridge, MA: MIT Press, 1987).

41. Julius Nathan, "California Farm Labor Problems," *Commonwealth Club Transactions* 30 (1935–36): 178–80; quotation from 179.

8 / Workers as Objects/Workers as Subjects: Re-making Landscape

1. State Rural Resettlement, California Division of Rehabilitation of the (United States) Resettlement Administration, "Statement in Support of Project to Establish Camps for Migrants in California," 22 August 1935, I. W. Wood Papers, Bancroft Library, University of California, Berkeley, Box 1, "Documents Re: Migrant Laborers and Establishment of Camps, June-Dec, 1935," a-8; quotation from a.

2. "Memoranda on Operation of Camps for Migrant in California Agriculture, 8-3-35," 14–15, I. W. Wood Papers, Box 1, "Documents Re: Migrant Laborers. . . ."

3. Paul Taylor, "Paul Schuster Taylor: California Social Scientist," Earl Warren Oral History Project, Regional Cultural History Project, Volume I: "Education, Field Research, and Family," interview by Suzanne B. Reiss, 137; "Conference on Housing of Migratory Agricultural Laborers," 12 October 1935, United States Senate, Subcommittee

of the Committee on Education and Labor (the La Follette Committee), Hearings on S. Res. 266, *Violations of Free Speech and the Rights of Labor,* 75 parts (Washington, DC: Government Printing Office, 1936–1940), Part 62, Exhibit 9577-C, 22592–22609 (hereafter LFC *Hearings*); for a history of political developments related to the camp program, see Walter Stein, *California and the Dust Bowl Migration* (Westport, CT: Greenwood Press, 1973), 150–59.

4. "Statement in Support."

5. Bertha M. Rankin to Irving Wood, 6 October 1936, Simon Lubin Society Papers, Bancroft Library, University of California, Berkeley, Carton 10, "Correspondence: Aid to Agric. Workers." Rankin owned the land upon which the Kern County (Arvin) camp was built.

6. Notes in Paul Taylor Papers (CR-3), Bancroft Library, University of California, Berkeley, "File: Documentary History of the Cotton Strike."

7. Clements to Cecil, 18 December 1936, in LFC *Hearings,* Part 53, Exhibit 8752, 19696.

8. John Steinbeck, *The Grapes of Wrath* (New York: Viking, 1939), 254–57; see Stein, *California and the Dust Bowl Migration,* chapter 5; California State Relief Administration, *Transients in California* (Sacramento: Mimeo, 1936); on squatters in early American California history and their impact on land-use patterns see, Ellen Liebman, *California Farmland: A History of Large California Landholdings* (Totowa, NJ: Rowman and Allenheld, 1983).

9. CSRA, *Transients in California,* 56, 60, 113.

10. Steinbeck, *Grapes of Wrath,* 165; "Statement in Support of Project," 8.

11. Histories of the RSA/FSA program may be found in Stein, *California and the Dust Bowl Migration;* see also Greg Hise, "From Roadside to 'Garden' Homes: Housing and Community Planning for California's Migrant Workforce, 1935–1941," unpublished paper, Department of Architecture, University of California, Berkeley (n.d.); "Statement in Support of Project."

12. Cletus Daniel, *Bitter Harvest: A History of California Farmworkers, 1870–1941* (Ithaca: Cornell University Press, 1981 and Berkeley: University of California Press, 1982), 270; Stein, *California and the Dust Bowl Migration,* 151; Carey McWilliams, *Factories in the Field* (Santa Barbara: Peregrine Smith, 1971 ed.), 303.

13. Omar Mills, "Farm Labor Programs of the Farm Security Administration," LFC *Hearings,* Part 59, Exhibit 9376, 21924–21936; unpaginated map, LFC *Hearings,* Part 59, Exhibit 9372, between, 21918–21919; Stein, *California and the Dust Bowl Migration,* chapter 6; Linda C. Majka and Theo Majka, *Farmworkers, Agribusiness, and the State* (Philadelphia: Temple University Press, 1982), chapter 7; McWilliams, *Factories in the Field,* chapter 16.

14. Statement of Frank Palomares, "Conference on Housing of Migratory Agricultural Laborers," 15 December 1934, LFC *Hearings,* Part 62, Exhibit 9577-A, 22552; "Statement in Support of Project"; Daniel, *Bitter Harvest,* 270.

15. On Collins, see Stein, *California and the Dust Bowl Migration,* 202–3; McWilliams, *Factories in the Field,* 302–3. Many of Collins's field reports and ethnographic observations are collected in the I. W. Wood Papers, Box 1. In the early 1970s, researchers at the Federal Records Center (National Archives) in California combined Collins's ethnographic reports, Steinbeck's prose, and Dorothea Lange's moving photographs (many

taken when she was employed by RSA and FSA) in an exhibition recalling the plight of agricultural workers during the Depression. The three sets of images complement each other eloquently as representations of conditions in the state at the time.

16. Tom Collins, "The Human Side in the Operation of a Migrant Camp," address at the dedication of the Marysville Camp, 12 October 1935, 2, 7, I. W. Wood Papers, Box I, "Documents Re: Migrant Labor. . . ."

17. Statement of Charles Weeks, "Conference on Housing of Migratory Agricultural Laborers," 25 October 1935, LFC *Hearings,* Part 62, Exhibit 9577–C, 302–303.

18. Weekly Report for Arvin Camp, 29 February, 1936, I. W. Wood Papers, Box 1, "Arvin Migratory Labor Camp: Weekly Reports, 1935–1936."

19. Weekly Report for Arvin Camp, 8 February 1936, I. W. Wood Papers, Box 1, "Arvin Migratory Labor Camp: Weekly Reports, 1935–1936." Collins's weekly reports are filled with stories about "Okie" behavior, culture, and religion, and they include samples of migrants' folk wisdom, songs, and jokes. Collins saw part of his role as being a preserver of these aspects of "Okie" folklife.

20. United States Senate Subcommittee of the Committee on Education and Labor (the La Follette Committee), *Violations of Free Speech and the Rights of Labor, Report of the Committee on Education and Labor, Pursuant to S. Res. 266* (hereafter LFC *Report*). Report 1150, parts 1–4, 77th Congress (Washington, DC: Government Printing Office, 1942) and Report 398, parts 4 and 5, 78th Congress (Washington, DC: Government Printing Office, 1944). Part VIII; Stein, *California and the Dust Bowl Migration,* 172–82; John Steinbeck, *Their Blood Is Strong* (San Francisco: Simon Lubin Society, 1936), 16.

21. See Stein, *California and the Dust Bowl Migration,* 172–82.

22. The *Reports* of the La Follette Committee remain the best analysis of worker and grower power in the fields of California and how it was arrayed during the 1930s.

23. Steinbeck, *Grapes of Wrath,* 326–27, 387.

24. "Statement in Support of Project"; Weekly reports of Tom Collins; Donna Haraway, *Primate Visions: Gender, Race, and Nature in the World of Modern Science* (New York: Routledge, 1989), 29–30.

25. *The Worker,* 11 February 1938; Steinbeck, *Grapes of Wrath,* 317.

26. The Associated Farmers were the focus of a great deal of interest on the part of the La Follette Committee. Their organizational structure, financing and legal and extra-legal activities are well-doumented, particularly in LFC *Report,* Part IV and Part VIII; see also, Clarke Chambers, *California Farm Organizations* (Berkeley: University of California Press, 1952); Daniel, *Bitter Harvest,* 251–54; McWilliams, *Factories in the Field,* 230–32.

27. "An Ordinance of the County of Sonoma to Prohibit Unlawful Interfering with Lawful Activities, Occupations and Businesses," LFC *Hearings,* Part 61, Exhibit 9500, 22343–22344.

28. Ibid., 22344; for more on the way the Supreme Court equated picketing with inevitable violence, see Don Mitchell, "Political Violence, Order, and the Legal Construction of Public Space: Power and the Public Forum Doctrine," unpublished paper, Department of Geography, University of Colorado.

29. *American Steel Foundries v. Tri-City Central Trades Council* 257 US 184 (1921), 205–6.

30. "Condensed Version of Employment Relations Initiative . . . ," LFC *Hearings,*

Part 61, Exhibit 9526, 22374; Gibson, Dunn, and Crutcher to Bishop, 26 August 1938, LFC *Hearings,* Part 61, Exhibit 9527, 22375–22377.

31. David Harvey, *The Limits to Capital* (Oxford: Basil Blackwell, 1982), 401.

32. *San Francisco Examiner,* "Pest No. 1 Label on M'Williams—Officials Accused of Inciting Radical Outbreaks," 9 December 1939, in LFC *Hearings,* Part 61, Exhibit 9516, 22353–22354; McWilliams, *Factories in the Field,* 305, 283, and chapters 16 and 17 generally.

33. Carey McWilliams, *California: The Great Exception* (Santa Barbara: Peregrine Smith, 1976, ed.), 160–61.

34. McWilliams, *Factories in the Field,* 325.

35. Donald Worster, *Rivers of Empire: Water, Aridity and the Growth of the American West* (New York: Pantheon, 1985), 245.

36. Quoted in McWilliams, *California: The Great Exception,* 159.

37. The Bracero Program is usefully summarized in Linda C. Majka and Theo Majka, *Farmworkers, Agribusiness and the State* (Philadephia: Temple University Press, 1982), chapter 8.

38. Steinbeck, *Grapes of Wrath,* 98, 100; Kevin Starr, *Americans and the California Dream, 1850–1915* (New York: Oxford University Press, 1973).

39. Steinbeck, *Grapes of Wrath,* 463.

Conclusion / The Lie of the Land

1. Michael Curry, "The Architectonic Impulse and the Reconceptualization of the Concrete in Contemporary Geography," in Trevor Barnes and James Duncan (eds.), *Writing Worlds: Discourse, Text and Metaphor in the Representation of Landscape* (London: Routledge, 1992), 97–117.

2. Heath Schenker, "Picturing the Central Valley," *Landscape* 32 (2) (1994): 1–11, quotation from 2; Stephen Johnson, Gerald Haslam, and Robert Dawson, *The Great Central Valley: California's Heartland* (Berkeley: University of California Press, 1993).

3. Gerald Haslam's text inverts this relationship: it focuses almost exclusively on labor history since the 1960s, with only a few oblique references to Wheatland or the upheavals of the 1930s. The point is that in neither the photographs nor the text is the dynamic history of the Valley shown to be intimately connected to the present form.

Index